One Case at a Time

ONE
CASE
AT A
TIME

Judicial Minimalism
on the
Supreme Court

Cass R. Sunstein

Harvard University Press

Cambridge, Massachusetts

London, England

First Harvard University Press paperback edition, 2001

Library of Congress Cataloging-in-Publication Data
Sunstein, Cass R.
One case at a time : judicial minimalism on the Supreme Court /
Cass R. Sunstein.
p. cm.
Includes bibliographical references and index.
ISBN 0-674-63790-9 (cloth)
ISBN 0-674-00579-1 (pbk.)
1. United States. Supreme Court—Decision making. 2. Law and
politics. 3. Minimalist theory (Linguistics) I. Title.
KF8748.S875 1999
347.73′26—dc21   98-36954

For Ellen

Contents

Preface

The most remarkable constitutional case in recent years involved the "right to die." The particular question was whether the Constitution confers a right to physician-assisted suicide. The Supreme Court appeared to say that the Constitution confers no such right; at least this was how the case was widely reported. But a careful reading shows something different. A majority of five justices merely said that there is no general right to suicide, assisted or otherwise, and it left open the possibility that under special circumstances, people might have a right to physician-assisted suicide after all. In other words, the Court left the most fundamental questions undecided. Far from being odd or anomalous, this is the current Court's usual approach. In this way, the Court is part of a long historical tradition. Anglo-American courts often take small rather than large steps, bracketing the hardest and most divisive issues.

My goal in this book is to identify and to defend a distinctive form of judicial decision-making, which I call "minimalism." Judicial minimalism has both procedural and substantive components. I devote more space to the procedural components, but the substance is also important.

Procedure and Substance

Procedure first: A minimalist court settles the case before it, but it leaves many things undecided. It is alert to the existence of reasonable disagreement in a heterogeneous society. It knows that there is much that it does not know; it is intensely aware of its own limitations. It seeks to decide cases on narrow grounds. It avoids clear rules and final resolutions. Alert to the problem of unanticipated consequences, it sees

itself as part of a system of democratic deliberation; it attempts to promote the democratic ideals of participation, deliberation, and responsiveness. It allows continued space for democratic reflection from Congress and the states. It wants to accommodate new judgments about
facts and values. To the extent that it can, it seeks to provide rulings
that can attract support from people with diverse theoretical commitments.

Judicial minimalism can be characterized as a form of "judicial restraint," but it is certainly not an ordinary form. Minimalist judges are
entirely willing to invalidate some laws. They reject "restraint" as a
general creed, because it is excessively general. Minimalists are not committed to majority rule in all contexts. Majoritarianism is itself a form
of maximalism.

Nor do minimalists embrace the contemporary enthusiasm for reliance on the original meaning of the Constitution. For good minimalists, "originalism" is unacceptable precisely because it is so broad and
ambitious. Originalists have a general theory and favor wide rules; minimalists are for this reason highly suspicious of originalism.

But judicial minimalism is hardly well treated as a form of judicial
"activism." Minimalists are protective of their own precedents and cautious about imposing their own views on the rest of society. Certainly
they disfavor broad rules that would draw a wide range of democratically enacted legislation into question. Nor is minimalism easily characterized as "liberal" or "conservative." On the contrary, minimalists
attempt, to the extent that they can, to bracket debates between liberals
and conservatives. They prefer to leave fundamental issues undecided.
This is their most distinctive characteristic.

With respect to substance: Any minimalist will operate against an
agreed-upon background. Anyone who seeks to leave things undecided
is likely to accept a wide range of things, and these constitute a "core"
of agreement about constitutional essentials. In American constitutional law at the turn of the century, a distinctive set of substantive
ideals now forms that core. All members of the constitutional culture
agree, for example, that the Constitution protects broad rights to engage in political dissent; to be free from discrimination or mistreatment
because of one's religious convictions; to be protected against torture
or physical abuse by the police; to be ruled by laws that have a degree
of clarity, and to have access to court to ensure that the laws have been

accurately applied; to be free from subordination on the basis of race and sex. Minimalism's substance can be captured in these central ideas. Constitutional debates operate with these fixed points in the background.

From these points it follows that a minimalist court is not skeptical or agnostic. On the contrary, it is committed to a set of animating ideals. One of my goals here is to elaborate, in minimalist fashion, a particular set of ideals, taken as the preconditions of a well-functioning constitutional democracy. The ideal of democracy comes with its own internal morality—the internal morality of democracy—and there is a large difference between democracy, properly understood, and whatever it is that a certain majority has chosen to do at a certain time. The most important features of democracy's internal morality are connected with the principle of political equality. This principle animates the free speech ideal; it shows why the government may not entrench itself; it shows why there is a special barrier to government efforts to interfere with political speech; and it also explains why some efforts to regulate the "speech market" may be consistent with the free speech principle. The principle of political equality also helps explain the operation of the equal protection clause. It shows why government may not impose second-class citizenship on any group—why there are no "castes" here. I connect this understanding with discrimination on the basis of race, sex, and sexual orientation, and also with the project of minimalism.

A Minimalist Supreme Court

Observers, including academic observers, tend to think that the Supreme Court should have some kind of "theory." But as a general rule, those involved in constitutional law tend to be cautious about theoretical claims. For this reason, much of academic work in constitutional law has been out of touch with the actual process of constitutional interpretation, especially in the last two decades. The judicial mind naturally gravitates away from abstractions and toward close encounters with particular cases. Even in constitutional law, judges tend to use abstractions only to the extent necessary to resolve a controversy.

The current Supreme Court embraces minimalism. Indeed, judicial minimalism has been the most striking feature of American law in the 1990s. The largest struggles on the Supreme Court have been over when to speak and when to remain silent, and opposing camps among the justices contest exactly that issue, with the minimalists generally prevailing. There are many examples. Return to the question of physician-assisted suicide. This issue is important in itself, but it is even more important because its resolution bears on the whole question of whether there is a general constitutional right to privacy (including abortion, sexual autonomy, parental rights, and a great deal more). In his opinion for the five-justice majority, Chief Justice William Rehnquist wrote the ambitious, emphatically nonminimalist opinion that he and Justice Scalia have been (unsuccessfully) urging on the Court in the abortion cases—an opinion that would limit the right of privacy, and indeed all fundamental rights under the due process clause, to those rights that are "deeply rooted" in our long-standing "traditions and practices." For better or worse, this idea would nearly bring to a halt the judicial protection of fundamental rights (aside from those specifically mentioned in the Bill of Rights).

Five justices signed the Rehnquist opinion, which seems like a large development that goes well beyond what was necessary to decide the particular case. But for those attuned to the Court's minimalist tendencies, the crucial aspects of the case lie elsewhere. Justice Sandra Day O'Connor wrote one of her characteristic separate opinions, suggesting that any new development was small and incremental. In her view, all the Court held was that there was no general right to commit suicide. She cautioned that the Court had not decided whether a competent person experiencing great suffering had a constitutional right to control the circumstances of an imminent death. That issue remained to be decided on another day. And, in a revealing and in its way hilarious opening to his own separate opinion, Justice Stephen Breyer wrote, "I believe that Justice O'Connor's views, which I share, have greater legal significance than the Court's opinion suggests. I join her separate opinion, except insofar as it joins the majority."

What this means is that a majority of five justices on the Court has signaled the possible existence of a right to physician-assisted suicide in compelling circumstances—and thus a five-justice majority has rejected the whole approach in Rehnquist's opinion (for a five-justice majority). O'Connor's opinion speaks for a group of justices who are not quite clear on how to handle fundamental rights under the due process clause and who want to leave the hardest and most contested issues for continuing democratic, and judicial, debate.

This is one of a large number of examples. In dealing with free speech and new communications technologies, discrimination on the basis of sexual orientation, affirmative action, and same-sex education, the Court has spoken narrowly and left the fundamental questions undecided. Thus the right to die case signals something large about the Supreme Court as a whole, and offers a clue to understanding the Court's minimalist character. Several of the justices, most notably O'Connor (but also Justices Breyer, Ginsburg, Stevens, and Souter), are cautious about broad rulings and ambitious pronouncements. Usually, they like to decide cases on the narrowest possible grounds. Justice O'Connor's concurrences typically limit the reach of majority decisions, suggest ways of accommodating both sides, and insist to the losers that they haven't lost everything, or for all time. By contrast, other justices, most notably Justice Antonin Scalia (but also Justice Clarence Thomas and sometimes Chief Justice William Rehnquist), think that it is important for the Court to lay down clear, bright-line rules, producing stability and clarity in the law.

One of my goals in this book is to draw some general lessons from an understanding of the U.S. Supreme Court as it enters the new century. In its enthusiasm for minimalism, the Court is not exactly unique, for American constitutional law is rooted in the common law, and the common law process of judgment typically proceeds case by case, offering broad rulings only on rare occasions, when the time seems right. But the current Court is sharply distinguishable from its predecessor courts under Chief Justices Earl Warren and Warren Burger. The Warren Court in particular was enthusiastic about broad rulings, and the Court was not reluctant to accept theoretically ambitious arguments about equality and liberty. The most vivid example is the great case abolishing segregation in the United States, Brown v. Board of Education; but consider also the requirements of the emphatically non-minimalist one person–one vote decision and the mandated Miranda warnings—simply two more illustrations of a tendency to produce broad, rule-like decisions. The Burger Court was quite different—a heterogeneous Court, with a variety of shifting coalitions—but it too showed no general preference for minimalism. I attempt to capture the character of the Supreme Court in the present era and to defend its controversial way of proceeding as admirably well suited to a number of issues on which the nation is currently in moral flux.

Minimalism and the Democratic Project

My most important goal is to explore the connection between judicial minimalism and democratic self-government. When should a constitutional court rule broadly, and when narrowly? For what conception of democracy ought the Constitution be taken to stand? How might a court best preserve both democratic government and individual rights? How should the Court understand the constitutional ideals of liberty and equality?

In asking such questions, I attempt to show how certain minimalist steps promote rather than undermine democratic processes and catalyze rather than preempt democratic deliberation. My particular areas of concern include affirmative action, discrimination on the basis of sex and sexual orientation, the right to die, and new issues of free speech raised by the explosion of communications technologies. One of my principal goals is to identify the distinctive kinds of minimalism that serve to improve political deliberation; the underlying conception of democracy thus places a high premium on both deliberation (in the sense of reflection and reason-giving) and accountability (in the sense of control by the voters).

The most tyrannical governments are neither deliberative nor accountable. Contemporary America might well be said to have a high degree of accountability but a low level of deliberation. In the notion of deliberative democracy lies the basis of a claim about how a minimalist Supreme Court, concerned about both constitutional ideals and its limited place in the American order, might promote a democratic nation's highest aspirations without preempting democratic processes.

I
ARGUMENT

1

Leaving Things Undecided

The Constitution speaks broadly and abstractly and about some of our highest aspirations. Many of the great constitutional issues involve the meaning of the basic ideas of "equality" and "liberty." When, if ever, might the government discriminate on the basis of race or sex or sexual orientation? Does the government restrict free speech by, for example, regulating expenditures on campaigns, or controlling the Internet, or requiring educational programming for children or free air time for candidates?

These are large questions. Sometimes the Supreme Court answers them. We will have occasion to discuss the substance of those answers. For the moment let us notice something equally interesting: frequently judges decide very little. They leave things open. About both liberty and equality, they make deliberate decisions about what should be left unsaid. This is a pervasive practice: doing and saying as little as is necessary in order to justify an outcome.

Consider some recent examples. When the Court ruled that the Virginia Military Institute could not exclude women, it pointedly refused to say much about the legitimacy of other single-sex institutions; it left the general question undecided.[1] When the Court struck down an affirmative action program in Richmond, Virginia, it self-consciously refused to impose a broad ban on race-conscious programs; it left that question for another day.[2] When the Court invalidated a Colorado law forbidding measures banning discrimination on the basis of sexual orientation, it said almost nothing about how the Constitution bears on other issues involving homosexuality.[3]

Let us describe the phenomenon of saying no more than necessary to justify an outcome, and leaving as much as possible undecided, as "decisional minimalism." Decisional minimalism has two attractive features. First, it is likely to reduce the burdens of judicial decision. It may be very hard, for example, to obtain a ruling on the circumstances under which single-sex education is legitimate. It may be especially hard to do this on a multimember court, consisting of diverse people who disagree on a great deal. A court that tries to agree on that question may find itself with no time for anything else. And a court that tries to agree on that question may find itself in the position of having to obtain and use a great deal of information, information that may not be available to courts (and perhaps not to anyone else).

Second, and more fundamentally, minimalism is likely to make judicial errors less frequent and (above all) less damaging. A court that leaves things open will not foreclose options in a way that may do a great deal of harm. A court may well blunder if it tries, for example, to resolve the question of affirmative action once and for all, or to issue definitive rulings about the role of the First Amendment in an area of new communications technologies. A court that decides relatively little will also reduce the risks that come from intervening in complex systems, where a single-shot intervention can have a range of unanticipated bad consequences.

There is a relationship between judicial minimalism and democratic deliberation. Of course minimalist rulings increase the space for further reflection and debate at the local, state, and national levels, simply because they do not foreclose subsequent decisions. And if the Court wants to promote more democracy and more deliberation, certain forms of minimalism will help it to do so. If, for example, the Court says that any regulation of the Internet must be clear rather than vague, and that a ban on "indecent" speech is therefore unconstitutional simply because it is vague, the Court will, in a sense, promote democratic processes by requiring Congress to legislate with specificity. Or if the Court says that any discrimination against homosexuals must be justified in some way, it will promote political deliberation by ensuring that law is not simply a product of unthinking hatred or contempt.

An understanding of minimalism helps to illuminate a range of important and time-honored ideas in constitutional law: that courts should not decide issues unnecessary to the resolution of a case; that courts should refuse to hear cases that are not "ripe" for decision; that courts should avoid deciding constitutional questions; that courts should respect their own precedents; that courts should not issue advisory opinions; that courts should follow prior holdings but not necessarily prior dicta; that courts should exercise the "passive virtues" associated with maintaining silence on great issues of the day. All of these ideas involve the *constructive use of silence*. Judges often use silence for pragmatic, strategic, or democratic reasons. Of course it is important to study what judges say; but it is equally important to examine what judges do not say, and why they do not say it. As we shall see, the question whether to leave things undecided helps unite a series of otherwise disparate debates in constitutional law.

In this chapter I spell out these ideas. My basic goal is to give a descriptive account of minimalism. In the process I offer two preliminary suggestions about a minimalist path. The first suggestion is that certain forms of minimalism can be democracy-promoting, not only in the sense that they leave issues open for democratic deliberation, but also and more fundamentally in the sense that they promote reason-giving and ensure that certain important decisions are made by democratically accountable actors. Sometimes courts say that Congress, rather than the executive branch, must make particular decisions; sometimes they are careful to ensure that good reasons actually underlie challenged enactments. In so doing, courts are minimalist in the sense that they leave open the most fundamental and difficult constitutional questions; they also attempt to promote democratic accountability and democratic deliberation. Judge-made doctrines are thus part of an effort to ensure that legitimate reasons actually underlie the exercise of public power.

My second suggestion is that a minimalist path usually—not always, but usually—makes a good deal of sense *when the Court is dealing with a constitutional issue of high complexity about which many people feel deeply and on which the nation is divided (on moral or other grounds)*. The complexity may result from a lack of information, from changing circumstances, or from (legally relevant) moral uncertainty. Minimalism makes sense first because courts may resolve those issues incorrectly, and second because courts may create serious problems even if their answers are right. Courts thus try to economize on moral disagreement by refusing to take on other people's deeply held moral commitments when it is not necessary for them to do so in order to decide a case.[4] For this reason courts should usually attempt to issue rulings that leave things undecided and that, if possible, are catalytic rather than preclusive. They should indulge a presumption in favor of minimalism.

We can link the two points with the suggestion that in such cases, courts should adopt forms of minimalism that can improve and fortify democratic processes. Many rules of constitutional law attempt to promote political accountability and political deliberation. Minimalism is not by any means democracy-promoting by its nature; but it is most interesting when it is democracy-promoting in this way.[5]

Theories

What is the relationship among the Supreme Court, the Constitution, and those whose acts are subject to constitutional attack? We can easily identify some theoretically ambitious responses.

Perhaps the simplest one is *originalist*. On this view, the Court's role is to vindicate an actual historical judgment made by those who ratified the Constitution. Justices Antonin Scalia and Clarence Thomas have been prominent enthusiasts for originalism, at least most of the time. The infamous *Dred Scott* case, saying that the Constitution forbids efforts to eliminate slavery, is a vigorous early statement of the originalist approach.[6] Originalists try to bracket questions of politics and morality and embark on a historical quest. In Chapter 9, I will discuss originalism in some detail. For the moment the central point is that originalism represents an effort to make constitutional law quite rule-like, and in that sense to settle a wide range of constitutional issues in advance. Indeed, that is a central part of the appeal of originalism.

The second response stems from the claim that majority rule is the basic presupposition of American democracy. This claim suggests that courts should uphold any plausible judgments from the democratic branches of government. On this view, courts should permit nonjudicial judgments unless those judgments are outlandish or clearly mistaken. James Bradley Thayer's famous law review article, advocating *a rule of clear mistake*, is the classic statement of this position.[7] The position can be found as well in the writings of Justice Oliver Wendell Holmes, the first Justice Harlan, Justice Felix Frankfurter, and, most recently, Chief Justice William Rehnquist. Innumerable post–New Deal Supreme Court cases, upholding social and economic regulation, fall in this category. Here too there is an effort to resolve constitutional cases by rule and in advance, via a strong presumption in favor of whatever emerges from majoritarian politics.

The third response is based on a claim that the Supreme Court should make *independent interpretive judgments* about constitutional meaning, based not on historical understandings, but instead on the Court's own account of what understanding makes best sense of the relevant provision.[8] When the Court struck down maximum-hour and minimum-wage legislation in the early part of the twentieth century, it spoke in these terms. When the Court created and vindicated a "right of privacy," it did the same thing.[9] So too when the Court struck down bans on commercial advertising and restrictions on campaign spending.[10] Ronald Dworkin—Thayer's polar opposite in the American legal culture—is the most prominent advocate of this approach to constitutional law. Dworkin thinks that the Court should be willing to invalidate legislation if good arguments from principle suggest that legislation is invalid, at least if those arguments "fit" with the existing legal materials. Thus Dworkin stresses the value that he calls "integrity," which urges principled consistency across cases. In defending rights of private property, Richard Epstein stands in the same interpretive camp.[11]

The fourth response characterizes one understanding of the Supreme Court under Chief Justice Earl Warren, a Court that continues to cast a long shadow over public debate. This response is represented by the most famous footnote in all of constitutional law: footnote 4 in the Carolene Products case.[12] On this view, the Court acts to improve the democratic character of the political process itself. It does so by protecting rights that are preconditions for a well-functioning democracy, and also by protecting groups that are at special risk because the democratic process is not democratic enough. Insofar as it stressed the need to protect political outsiders from political insiders, McCulloch v. Maryland[13] is probably the earliest statement of the basic position; there are many more recent examples in the area of voting, including Baker v. Carr, Reynolds v. Sims, and Shaw v. Hunt.[14] This conception of the judicial role, defended most prominently by John Hart Ely,[15] is based on the notion of *democracy-reinforcement.*

It is striking but true that as a whole, the current Supreme Court has not come close to making an official choice among these four approaches. The Court has not committed itself to a single theory. Even individual Supreme Court justices can be hard to classify. Justices Scalia and Thomas are outspokenly originalist, and certainly neither can fairly be accused of rampant inconsistency. But in opinions calling for broad protection of commercial advertising, Justice Thomas has interpreted the First Amendment with little reference to history, indeed his opinions look like a form of independent interpretive argument; and Justice Scalia's strong opposition to campaign finance regulation and affirmative action do not appear to result from extended historical inquiry.[16] Chief Justice Rehnquist has often endorsed the rule of clear mistake, and he is probably the most consistent proponent of this view in recent decades. But in cases involving affirmative action,[17] which he opposes on constitutional grounds, the Chief Justice speaks in quite different terms; here his method is more like a form of independent interpretive judgment.

We need not charge anyone with hypocrisy here. Perhaps different constitutional provisions are best treated differently. Thus we might say that the rule of clear mistake makes sense for the due process clause, whereas the idea of democracy-reinforcement is appropriate for the First Amendment and the equal protection clause. Indeed, the idea of democracy-reinforcement creates a great deal of space for the rule of clear mistake in those cases in which no democratic defect is at stake. Or we might think that independent judgment makes sense only for certain special cases, and that the rule of clear mistake, or originalism, is best elsewhere. Or we might adopt a presumption in favor of originalism but look elsewhere when history reveals gaps or ambiguities.

Against Theories, against Rules

To come to terms with these abstract debates, it is necessary to take a position on some large-scale controversies about the legitimate role of the Supreme Court in the constitutional order. An endorsement of one or the other precommits the Court in a wide range of subsequent cases. To be sure, each of the theories has play in the joints. Thus, for example, the original understanding can be described in different ways and at various levels of generality; history leaves many gaps, and committed originalists disagree sharply on some issues. So too, the notion of representation-reinforcement is quite open-ended. People with diverse theoretical positions can accept that notion, and those who accept it are not committed to particular decisions in disputed cases. Perhaps the most underrepresented group is consumers, and perhaps aggressive judicial review of political regulation of the economy can be justified by notions of representation-reinforcement. But there can be no doubt that any of the four approaches constrains further inquiry. And perhaps it is both necessary and desirable for Supreme Court justices to stake out some position on the general question of constitutional method.

But let us notice a remarkable fact. Not only has the Court as a whole refused to choose among the four positions or to sort out their relations, but many of the current justices have refused to do so in their individual capacities. Consider Justices Ruth Bader Ginsburg, David Souter, Sandra Day O'Connor, Stephen Breyer, and Anthony Kennedy. These justices—the analytical heart of the current Court—have adopted no unitary "theory" of constitutional interpretation. Instead of adopting theories, they decide cases. It is not even clear that any of them has rejected any of the four approaches I have described. The most that can be said is that none of them is an originalist in the sense of Justices Scalia and Thomas, and that none of them believes that any of these approaches adequately captures the whole of constitutional law.

In their different ways, each of these justices tends to be minimalist. I understand this term to refer to judges who seek to avoid broad rules and abstract theories,[18] and attempt to focus their attention only on what is necessary to resolve particular disputes. Minimalists do not like to work deductively; they do not see outcomes as reflecting rules or theories laid down in advance. They pay close attention to the particulars of individual cases. They also tend to think analogically and by close reference to actual and hypothetical problems. I believe that all of the justices named above understand themselves as minimalists in this sense, and that they have chosen to be minimalist for reasons that are, broadly speaking, of the sort I will be discussing here. In other words, these justices embrace minimalism—usually, not always—for reasons connected with their conception of the role of the Supreme Court in American government.

We might contrast minimalism with "maximalism." The term is far from perfect, for no one seeks to decide, in every case, everything that might be decided. Let us understand the term as a shorthand reference for those who seek to decide cases in a way that sets broad rules for the future and that also gives ambitious theoretical justifications for out-

comes. At the opposite pole is reasonlessness, represented by a failure
to give reasons at all. Close to reasonlessness is what might be called
"subminimalism," understood as decisions that are conclusory and
opaque, and offer little in the way of justification or guidance for the
future. We can thus imagine a rough continuum of this sort:

> reasonlessness/silence → subminimalism → minimalism →
> ambitiousness → complete rules/full theoretical grounding

Let me explain these ideas in more detail.

Narrowness and Width

As I am using the term here, the practice of minimalism involves two
principal features, narrowness and shallowness. First, minimalists try to
decide cases rather than to set down broad rules. In this way, minimalists ask that decisions be *narrow rather than wide*. They decide the
case at hand; they do not decide other cases too, except to the extent
that one decision necessarily bears on other cases, and unless they are
pretty much forced to do so.

Narrowness is a pervasive phenomenon on the current Court. Recall
the Court's decision to strike down the all-male program at the Virginia
Military Institute, a narrow decision that pointedly refused to say much
about the legitimacy of sex segregation in education, and the Court's
decision on the topic of physician-assisted suicide, a decision that, by a
bare five-to-four majority, left open the possibility that a competent
patient has a right to die when death is imminent and physical pain is
severe. Or consider the Court's 1996 decision in Romer v. Evans, invalidating a law apparently discriminating against homosexuals (see
Chapter 7); in that case the Court spoke narrowly and said nothing
about the range of possible cases involving discrimination against homosexuals, such as exclusion from the military or a ban on same-sex
marriage.

It is important to say that narrowness is relative, not absolute. A
decision that discrimination against the mentally retarded will face rational basis review, and ordinarily be upheld, is narrow compared to
imaginable alternatives; it is much narrower than a decision that discrimination on all grounds other than race will face rational basis review,
and ordinarily be upheld. But it is much broader than other imaginable

decisions, such as a decision that holds for or against the mentally re-tarded in the particular case, without announcing a standard of review at all. The consistent minimalist seeks to render decisions that are no broader than necessary to support the outcome. Of course narrowness may run into difficulty if it means that similarly situated people are being treated differently; this very danger may press the Court in the direction of breadth.

Within the current federal judiciary, there is by no means a consensus that minimalism in the form of narrow rulings is the right way for a court to proceed. Justice Scalia, for example, is no minimalist, because he favors width. In this way he is a maximalist, sharply opposing self-consciously narrow decisions. Justice Thomas is a maximalist too. In his separate opinions, he often urges the Court to provide wider judgments and clearer guidance. Both the Marshall Court and the Warren Court issued many maximalist opinions, extending far beyond the facts of the individual case. Chapter 9 takes up the question of width in detail.

Shallow Rather than Deep

The second point is that minimalists generally try to avoid issues of basic principle. They want to allow people who disagree on the deepest issues to converge. In this way they attempt to reach *incompletely theorized agreements*.[19] Such agreements come in two forms: agreements on concrete particulars amid disagreements or uncertainty about the basis for those concrete particulars, and agreements about abstractions amid disagreements or uncertainty about the particular meaning of those abstractions. Both forms are important to constitutional law.

Participants in public life often accept an abstraction when they disagree on particular outcomes. The latter strategy is dominant in constitution-making, as people converge on the principles of "freedom of speech" or "equality" despite their uncertainty or disagreements about what these principles specifically entail. Indeed, constitution-making is often possible only because of the technique of producing agreement on abstractions amid disagreements about particulars. Consider this parody of South Africa's efforts at constitution-making:[20]

    1. The Constitution is the Constitution of South Africa and constitutes constitutionalism.

2. The Constitution is applicable to the extent that it applies to all those to whom it is applicable. It furthermore binds all who are bound by it.

3. The rights in the Constitution are limited only to the extent that they are limitable, subject only to reasonable limitations imposed by national legislation.

4. The Constitution is the supreme law of the land and may only be amended when the amendment is necessary. Any amendment must be regarded as necessary, unless the national assembly, with a majority of two-thirds, decides that it is not necessary.

5. In a spirit of decency and propriety, all organs, including organs of state, must remain in their own functional areas, and not encroach on the functional areas and spheres of influence pertaining to other organs.

6. If parties referred to in 5 are no longer in existence or unable to assume the earlier mentioned powers and functions, an Independent Panel of National Unity must govern in a spirit of inter-related independence, mutual trust, the fostering of friendly relations and peace.

This is a parody, to be sure, but it signals something important about constitution-making, as participants have often found in both Eastern Europe and Africa. In Hungary and Russia, in the Czech Republic and in Georgia, constitution-making has succeeded by virtue of incompletely theorized agreements in the form of incompletely specified abstractions on such topics as liberty, property rights, welfare rights, and equality. The same is emphatically true of South Africa, where an impressive constitutional settlement was facilitated by the adoption of abstractions whose specific meaning will be discerned—it is universally understood—at a later date. In a parallel process, judges faced with constitutional disputes may not specify the appropriate legal principle, because they may think that whatever the appropriate specific legal principle, it is clear who should win and who should lose. Thus they may adopt a standard in the form of a "reasonableness" test; the standard may not say with any particularity what "reasonableness" requires in particular cases.

In pointing to shallowness rather than depth, however, I will be emphasizing something different: *the possibility of concrete judgments on particular cases, unaccompanied by abstract accounts about what accounts for those judgments.* The concrete outcomes are backed not by abstract theories but by unambitious reasoning on which people can converge from diverse foundations, or with uncertainty about appropriate foundations. Of course many philosophical debates, including those about law, operate at a high level of abstraction, but the combatants can often be brought into agreement when concrete questions are raised about appropriate law. Kantians and utilitarians might well agree, for example, that speed-limit laws of a certain kind make sense, or that the law of negligence points in proper directions, or that there is no right to kill infants.

The same is true in constitutional law. Judges who disagree or who are unsure about the foundations of constitutional rights, or about appropriate constitutional method, might well be able to agree on how particular cases should be handled. They might think that whatever they think about the foundations of the free speech principle, the state cannot ban people from engaging in acts of political protest unless there is a clear and present danger. Judges who have different accounts of what the equal protection clause is all about, or who are unsure what the equality principle ultimately means, can agree on a wide range of specific cases. They might agree, for example, that government cannot segregate schools on the basis of race or exclude women from professions. Indeed, people with widely varying views on the most basic issues do agree that discrimination on the basis of race is generally banned (at least outside of the contested area of affirmative action). People who disagree on a great deal may agree that torture is unconstitutional, or that people deserve compensation for physical invasions of their property. Agreements on particulars and on unambitious opinions are the ordinary stuff of constitutional law; it is rare for judges to retreat to first principles.

Incompletely theorized agreements are by no means unaccompanied by reasons. On the contrary, judicial decisions infrequently take on foundational questions, and they are nonetheless exercises in reason-giving. There is a big difference between a refusal to give an ambitious argument for an outcome and a refusal to give any reasons at all. Sometimes ambition is simply unnecessary and low-level explanations, commanding agreement from diverse people, are entirely sufficient.

Incompletely theorized agreements on particular outcomes are an important means by which diverse citizens are able to constitute themselves as a society. Such agreements permit people to live together in a productive way; they also show a form of mutual respect. This is especially so when people hold fast or insistently to their more abstract beliefs (consider theological commitments, or commitments about freedom or equality). These beliefs operate as "fixed points," and sometimes they cannot be productively debated. Often debates become tractable only when they become more concrete. A kind of *conceptual descent* can produce agreement or in any case progress. Of course it is true that sometimes people hold more tenaciously to their commitments to particular cases than they hold to their theories; sometimes it is the particular judgments that operate as "fixed points" for analysis. All I am suggesting is that when theoretical disagreements are intense and hard to mediate, courts often make progress by trying to put those disagreements to one side, and by converging on an outcome and a relatively modest rationale on its behalf.

In this way minimalists try to make decisions *shallow rather than deep*. They avoid foundational issues if and to the extent that they can. By so doing the Supreme Court can use constitutional law both to model and promote a crucial goal of a liberal political system: to make it possible for people to agree when agreement is necessary, and to make it unnecessary for people to agree when agreement is impossible. Judicial minimalism is well suited to this goal.

Extreme Cases and Real-World Analogues

Reasons are by their nature abstractions. Any reason is by its nature more abstract than the case for which it is designed. Any reason, if it is binding, will extend beyond that case. From this point we can imagine the most extreme or limiting situation: all judgments are unaccompanied by reasons, and no judgment has stare decisis effects, that is, no judgment has any effect on subsequent cases. In such a system, the costs of reaching the decision ("decision costs") should be quite low. In such a system, mistakes may be numerous and serious (producing high "error costs"), as courts leap from one view to another; but at least an erroneous decision in one case cannot possibly produce errors in subsequent cases.

An extreme system of this sort would undoubtedly seem a kind of bizarre nightmare world, the stuff of Kafka, Orwell, science fiction, Mao's China. It is useful to identify it if only to show why it would make little sense; reason-giving is a valuable check on mistakes and on illicit judgments, and it helps ensure consistency over time. But the idea of reason-free decisions—of outcomes unaccompanied by grounds—is not as unfamiliar to American life and law as it might seem. There are important contexts in which a decision or an agreement is unaccompanied by any rationale at all.[21] Those who grade exams (especially if there are a lot of them) may not offer reasons; parents sometimes respond to a child's question, "Why?" with a single word: "Because." Something of this kind is typically a jury's practice in giving a verdict. It is also the Supreme Court's usual practice in refusing to hear a case by denying certiorari. Denials are reasonless. They are entirely rule-free and untheorized. There is of course a difference between not giving a reason and not having a reason; one might have a reason but fail to give it.

Why might anyone want an outcome to be unaccompanied by a reason? For one thing, an approach of this kind does not foreclose other decisions in other cases. Thus a mistaken ground for decision will not produce later mistakes. If people are sometimes better at knowing *what* is right than knowing *why* it is right, this is an advantage. Such decisions also take relatively less time to produce, since it can be far easier to come up with a decision than to come up with an explanation. This is one reason for the Court's failure to explain its failure to grant certiorari. An unexplained denial has a practical advantage too, since judges with divergent rationales can converge on the outcome without converging on an account. These ideas also help account for the practices of producing unpublished opinions and of affirming lower courts' decisions without opinions. These practices are controversial but pervasive and growing; they should be expected to grow further over time with the increasing press of judicial business.

Somewhere between minimalist decisions and reasonless decisions are those that offer a rationale that is too shallow and hence not, on reflection, adequate to justify the outcome. Reasons are given, but they are insufficient. Of course dissenting opinions always make this claim, but sometimes opinions seem so conclusory that the accusation of sub-minimalism has force. As we will see, this is the accusation of Justice Scalia about the Court's important opinion in Romer v. Evans, involving discrimination on the basis of sexual orientation; as we shall see in Chapter 7, the accusation has some merit. Opinions of this sort violate norms associated with legal craft. If an opinion is supposed to do anything, it is supposed to explain the outcome of the case. But if outcomes unaccompanied by any reasons have their social uses, outcomes accompanied by subminimalist reasons might also have their social uses. As we shall see, this is a possible response to Justice Scalia in connection with *Romer.*

Like narrowness, shallowness is a matter of degree; it is relative rather than absolute. The clear and present danger test is shallow compared with a judgment that the First Amendment is rooted in a conception of autonomy. But it is deep compared with a judgment that whatever the appropriate test, a political protest by members of the Ku Klux Klan is protected by the First Amendment.

Shallow and Narrow, Deep and Wide

There are many possible interactions along the dimensions of depth and width. Consider Table 1.1. The distinctions operate along a continuum, but for purposes of simplicity categorical distinctions will be helpful.[22] A denial of certiorari is as narrow as can be—it does not affect any other case—and it is also entirely untheorized and hence as shallow as possible (cell 1). The Supreme Court's decision involving sexual orientation in Romer v. Evans also belongs in cell 1; it can be understood as very narrow, since it does not purport to touch other possible cases, and also as shallow, since its rationale need not be taken to extend much further than its holding (see Chapter 7). Of course subsequent cases may extend *Romer* and make it come to stand for a much broader and deeper principle; this is a question about the path of the law. The Supreme Court's 1994 decision in United States v. Lopez—the first case since the New Deal in which the Court struck down a statute as beyond Congress's power under the commerce clause—was emphatically both narrow and shallow. In that case, the Court concluded that Congress could not ban the possession of guns near schools; it justified its decision by reference to a set of factors, not by a broadly applicable rule,

Table 1.1

	Narrow	Wide
Shallow	(1) Supreme Court denial of certiorari (unexplained refusal to hear a case); Romer v. Evans (invalidating Colorado constitutional amendment banning laws prohibiting discrimination on basis of sexual orientation); United States v. Lopez (invalidating national law regulating guns near schools); Denver Area Educational Telecommunications Consortium v. FCC (complex ruling on free speech and cable television)	(2) Brandenburg v. Ohio (clear and present danger test); Roe v. Wade (protecting right to abortion)
Deep	(3) 44 Liquormart, Inc. v. Rhode Island (plurality opinion) (striking down a law regulating commercial advertising); United States v. Virginia (striking down sex discrimination at Virginia Military Institute)	(4) Reynolds v. Sims (one person–one vote); Dred Scott v. Sanford (protecting institution of slavery); Brown v. Bd. of Education (invalidating school segregation); Dworkin's Hercules

and it gave no deep account of federalism. The same can be said of the *Denver Area Educational Telecommunications Consortium* case, where the Court, emphatic about the complexity of new telecommunications technologies, left many issues open and gave no deep account of the underlying First Amendment principles (see Chapter 8).

We can also imagine decisions that are both deep and wide (cell 4). Reynolds v. Sims, announcing the famous one person–one vote rule, was very broad and also fairly deeply theorized. The one person–one vote idea applied to many cases and depended on an account of what political representation is all about—a conception of what it means for people to be political equals. Similarly, the *Dred Scott* case, protecting the institution of slavery, generated a very broad ruling that rested on an exceptionally ambitious account of the Constitution's posture toward slavery and African Americans.

An extreme case of depth and width comes from a thought experiment offered by Ronald Dworkin. For purposes of understanding legal reasoning, Dworkin has described an idealized judge, Hercules, who seeks to ensure that past decisions are put in their "best constructive light."[23] This is Dworkin's notion of law as integrity. That notion raises many questions; for present purposes what is important is that Hercules is ambitious along both dimensions. Hercules attempts to make theoretically deep judgments and also to see how the decision in the case at hand squares with multiple other decisions, actual and hypothetical. Real-world judges rarely seek both width and depth, but it is certainly possible to understand the claim that this is an appropriate aspiration for law.

Some judgments are shallow but wide (cell 2). In Brandenburg v. Ohio,[24] the Court issued a highly speech-protective decision, adopting a form of the clear and present danger test that is very wide in the sense that it is used in a great range of cases. But the Court did not give a deep theoretical grounding for the test. It did not, for example, try to root its test in a conception of democratic deliberation, or explore the link between the interest in autonomy and the right to free expression. The same things can be said about Roe v. Wade. That decision was wide in the sense that it settled a range of issues relating to the abortion question. But it did not give a deep account of the foundations of the relevant right. Of course any claim that a decision is wide, narrow, shallow, or deep depends on the standard of comparison. *Roe* is broad in its coverage of the abortion issue; it is narrow in the sense that by its terms, it need not be taken to speak to the issue of sexual autonomy in general or the right to die.

It is hardest to imagine cases in cell 3: those that are deeply reasoned but also narrow. The reason is that a deep account will in all likelihood have applications to cases other than the one before the Court. Ambitious reasoning typically produces width. If a court says that the equal protection clause is rooted in a principle involving the (constitutionally relevant) immorality of using skin color as a basis for public decisions, its decisions will be wide as well as deep, or more precisely wide because it is deep. But we can find some examples of cell 3 cases. In United States v. Virginia, the Court was careful to limit its decision to VMI, a "unique" institution. But the Court also ventured some ambitious remarks about the nature of the equality guarantee in the context of gender. The Court adopted a fairly deep and also quite contentious account of the goal of the equal protection clause in this context. In some commercial speech cases, most notably *44 Liquormart,* the Court has spoken with some ambition about the relationship between autonomy and free speech, but without ruling broadly about the nature of government's power over advertising.

We are now in a position to identify some complexities in the idea of minimalism. Suppose, for example, that the Court is asked to strike down a law regulating sexually explicit speech on the Internet on First Amendment grounds. Suppose that the Court says that the law is impermissibly vague—and in that way brackets the question whether sexually explicit speech on the Internet should receive the same kind of protection as sexually explicit speech in the print media. The Court says, in other words: "We do not say exactly what speech is protected when it is found on the Internet. But this law is so unacceptably vague that it is unconstitutional whatever the standard." In an important sense this is a minimalist decision (and precisely the kind of democracy-forcing minimalism that I will be urging in Chapter 3). It is minimalist in the sense that it leaves certain key questions open. But it is non-minimalist in some crucial ways, for a vagueness doctrine may also be both broad (if the vagueness constraint applies to many contexts) and deep (if the doctrine depends on an ambitious account of, for example, the rule of law). It may itself be generative of many other outcomes. We can easily imagine opinions that are minimalist in some ways but maximalist in others. A simple conclusion follows: decisions are not usually minimalist or not; they are minimalist *along certain dimensions.*

Of Stare Decisis, Readers, and Clear, Democracy-Reinforcing Backgrounds

The effect of width and depth is not merely a function of what the Court says. It will depend a great deal on the applicable theory of stare decisis. If precedents receive little respect, a wide and deep opinion will not control the future. The familiar distinction between holdings (the crucial part of any outcome, one that controls the future) and dicta (mere statements that have no authority over the future) has everything to do with the debate over minimalism. A legal system that treats previous statements as important for current decisions will tend toward maximalism, since it will increase the width and depth of each case. But a legal system that insists that many statements are mere "dicta" will drive prior cases in the direction of minimalism, whatever courts say in the initial cases.

Courts that attempt to be maximalist may be quite surprised by the conduct of subsequent courts, which characterize prior language as "dicta." Thus if subsequent courts have a great deal of discretion to recharacterize holdings, they can in effect turn prior decisions into minimalist ones, however they may have originally been written and conceived. But if subsequent courts perceive themselves as bound to take precedents as they were written, minimalism must be a creation of the court that decides the case at hand. Thus we can imagine the various possibilities shown in Table 1.2.[25]

The strongest rule-like constraints emerge from cell 2. Here opinions say a great deal, and what they say is binding on the future. The great transformative opinions of the New Deal era are key examples. Cell 3 is of course the most rule-free. Here courts say little, and what they say is minimally binding. Administrative adjudication sometimes seems to have this character.

Cells 1 and 4 are the most interesting. Cell 1 probably captures the ordinary picture of Anglo-American common law. Courts decide cases, and do not issue wide rules, but their decisions are given enormous weight in subsequent proceedings. Cell 4 is akin perhaps to some caricatures of the Warren Court. Judicial decisions that fall in this cell set out broad and deep pronouncements that have little weight in subsequent cases. This approach might seem irresponsible, but so long as the law is not applied retroactively, it can have certain advantages in promoting planning while at the same time allowing change if prior decisions seem to go wrong. We can now see, on the two relevant dimensions, a continuum rather than a sharp division.

A legal system will of course move in the direction of minimalism if previous (maximalist) decisions are abandoned when they seem plainly wrong. But it will also move in that direction if subsequent courts have a great deal of flexibility to disregard justificatory language as "dicta" or to recharacterize previous holdings. A Supreme Court that is reluctant to overrule past decisions can accomplish much of the same thing

Table 1.2

	Minimal opinions	Nonminimal opinions
Strong stare decisis	(1) Common law (conventional picture)	(2) Great New Deal opinions, e.g., United States v. Darby; Erie RR Co. v. Tompkins
Weak stare decisis	(3) Administrative adjudication	(4) Warren Court caricature

through creative reinterpretation. And a Court's power to recharacterize past decisions may make minimalist decisions into something very different. There are many examples; consider Reed v. Reed,[26] the first case invalidating a law on grounds of sex discrimination. Reed v. Reed was minimalist when written—both shallow and narrow—but it has come to stand for a broad principle to the effect that laws may not be justified by reference to outmoded gender stereotypes. Stare decisis adds a temporal dimension to minimalism.

Courts deciding particular cases have limited authority over the subsequent reach of their opinion. They cannot establish the rules that will govern the reception of their decisions. A court that is determined to be maximalist may fill its opinion with broad pronouncements, but those pronouncements may subsequently appear as "dicta" and be disregarded by future courts. The converse phenomenon is also familiar. A court may write a self-consciously minimalist opinion, and be wary of extending its reach, but subsequent courts may take the case to stand for a broad principle that covers many other cases as well.

A strong theory of stare decisis, especially in statutory cases, can be understood as an effort to create good incentives for those in the democratic process. If courts will not alter their interpretation of statutes, even when the interpretation may have been wrong, Congress will have an especially clear background against which to work, knowing that if mistakes are to be fixed, Congress itself must supply the corrective. Courts will not do its work for it. Thus a strong theory of stare decisis is part of a range of devices designed to create appropriate incentives for democracy by providing a clear background for Congress. Consider the "plain meaning" rule in statutory interpretation, a refusal to consider legislative history, the unwillingness to "imply" private rights of action, the refusal to impose constraints on jury awards of punitive damages. All of these devices can be understood as democracy-promoting, at least in their aspiration, insofar as they provide a clear background for Congress and inform legislators and others that correctives must come legislatively because they will not come judicially.

Here there is an argument for width as a judicial virtue. It is a virtue because it promotes rule of law values, by limiting judicial discretion and improving predictability. But it is also a democratic virtue, because it creates a reliable backdrop for use by citizens and representatives. The relative murkiness of narrow rulings is, on this view, an obstacle to a well-functioning democratic process, because legislators will not know how courts will act, and because there is an incentive to let judges do the relevant work. This idea unites a good deal of Justice Scalia's writing; it provides a strong connection between his opinions and the ideal of deliberative democracy. The traditional response is that the prescription is too simple. For example, Congress's agenda may be too loaded to support the view that congressional inaction, as against clear backgrounds, reflects considered judgments by Congress, and more particularized judgments from judges can lead to results that Congress would reach if it could consider every issue, or at least give rationality and fairness the benefit of the doubt (see Chapter 9 for detailed discussion).

There is a related point. The public reception of a judicial opinion may matter as much as the applicable theory of stare decisis. Often judicial decisions are written as small steps, but they are taken as large signals. Public officials may take an opinion as settling a range of issues or as signaling a major change in course despite the Court's determined effort to proceed narrowly. In recent years, this has happened with Supreme Court decisions involving legislative power and affirmative action. Alternatively, public officials may take an opinion to be narrow, or distinguishable, despite the Court's effort at breadth. A full understanding of the topic of minimalism would have to extend far outside the judicial domain, to the public reaction to Supreme Court decisions. We can find (and will explore) cases in which the public takes a decision to be more or less minimalist than the judges intended.

One final suggestion. There is a large difference between, on the one hand, forming a broad and deep judgment and, on the other hand, making that judgment public. Thus far I have treated the two actions as if they were the same. But we can readily imagine a situation in which a judge, or a majority on a multimember court, has decided (whether tentatively or not) in favor of a rule or a deep justification for an outcome, but nonetheless refuses to state the rule or justification in public. Judges might be publicly silent for a variety of reasons. They may be silent because they are not sure that they are right or because they fear a public reaction and seek to lay the ground for more width or depth. Consider, for example, the area of discrimination on the basis of sexual orientation, where reasonable judges may proceed in this way. We can also imagine contrasting cases in which the judges are uncertain in their own minds on these things, or in which no majority can be obtained in favor of a rule or a deep justification. These latter cases are what I mean to emphasize here, though the former are also important. Obviously these points raise questions about democracy. Let us turn, then, to the democratic uses of minimalism, and in particular to that form of minimalism that attempts to promote democratic goals.

2

Democracy-Promoting Minimalism

Mr. James' philosophy took shape as a deliberate protest against the monisms that reduced everything to parts of one embracing whole. . . . His was the task of preserving . . . respect for the humble particular against the pretentious rational formula.   —John Dewey[1]

We address specifically and only an educational opportunity recognized . . . as unique, an opportunity available only at Virginia's premier military institute, the State's sole single-sex public university or college.   —United States v. Virginia

[A]ware as we are of the changes taking place in the law, the technology, and the industrial structure, relating to telecommunications, we believe it unwise and unnecessary definitely to pick one analogy or one specific set of words now. . . . [W]e are wary of the notion that a partial analogy in one context, for which we have developed doctrines, can compel a full range of decisions in such a new and changing area.
                —Denver Area Educational Telecommunications Consortium v. FCC
                                                    (plurality opinion of Justice Breyer)

There is a close connection between minimalism and democracy. To make progress on that subject, it is important to say a little more about what is meant by both democracy and minimalism. To do so, it will be necessary to venture in some nonminimalist directions.

As I have suggested, the American constitutional system aspires not to simple majoritarianism, and not to aggregation of private "preferences," but to a system of deliberative democracy. In that system, representatives are to be accountable to the public. Electoral control is an important part of the system. Constitutional doctrines can help to promote electoral control by helping to ensure that politically accountable actors make important decisions; some forms of minimalism have exactly this goal. But in a deliberative democracy, a premium is also placed on the exchange of reasons by people with different information and diverse perspectives. In a heterogeneous society, deliberation is to be welcomed precisely because of social pluralism. In the absence of pluralism, deliberation would not be pointless; but it would have much less of a point. And in a pluralistic society, disagreement can be a productive force, helping to isolate factual disagreements and showing how differences with respect to governing values might be clarified.

Thus democracy is no mere statistical affair. It embodies a commitment to political (not economic) equality and also to reason-giving in the public domain. For the deliberative democrat, political outcomes cannot be supported by self-interest or force. "Naked preferences," in the form of legislation supported by power but not reasons, are forbidden. Existing judgments and desires must be made to survive a process of reflection and debate; they are not to be taken as sacrosanct or automatically translated into law.

There are also constraints on the kinds of reasons that count as valid. Legislation cannot be supported on purely religious grounds; legislation rooted only in religious convictions could not count as valid for citizens who reject those grounds as justificatory.[2] Nor can legislation be justified on grounds that deny the fundamental equality of human beings, or that reflect contempt for fellow citizens, or that attempt to humiliate them. These ideas are part of a liberal conception of political legitimacy; they embody an ideal of reciprocity, in which citizens are aware of and responsive to one another's interests and claims. The relevant reasons should be offered publicly, not secretly, and should be subject to processes of democratic deliberation.

Maximalism, Minimalism, and Democracy

The ideals of deliberative democracy are themselves contentious, and a minimalist court might stay away from those ideals for that very reason. Such a court might attempt to make decisions without taking a stand on the right conception of democracy. Moreover, those committed to deliberative democracy could support that commitment in more or less minimalist ways. With their eye on democratic ideals, some courts could be quite maximalist. They might, for example, endorse ambitious understandings of the First Amendment and the equal protection clause, rooted in the notion of deliberative democracy, and use those understandings to push political processes in particular directions. They might use "rationality review" to ensure that all decisions are supported by reasons, and by reasons of the right kind. Ideas of this sort have had an occasional influence on American law. And if judges can converge on theoretically ambitious positions that are both correct (by the relevant criteria, whatever they may be) and possible to implement, it is hard to find a basis for reasonable complaint. At least if the Constitution, rightly interpreted, authorizes them to do so, why shouldn't judges insist on the correct understandings of both liberty and equality?

Thus we can imagine a deeply theorized approach to judicial review, one that would be rooted in principles of deliberative democracy (or in some other suitable account of constitutional goals). Democracy-promoting maximalism is an easily imaginable project. But judges know that they may be prone to error, and for this reason they are usually cautious about foreclosing outcomes of political processes that do not accord with an ambitious and possibly incorrect understanding of democratic ideals. Cautious judges can promote democratic deliberation with more minimalist strategies, designed to bracket some of the deeper questions but also to ensure both accountability and reflection. Many minimalist decisions attempt to ensure more in the way of democracy and more in the way of deliberation. Some such decisions reflect the justices' awareness of their limited place in the constitutional structure, by, for example, economizing on moral disagreement, refusing to rule off-limits certain deeply held moral commitments when it is not necessary to do this to resolve a case.

It is therefore important to distinguish among *democracy-promoting, democracy-foreclosing,* and *democracy-permitting* outcomes. Democracy-promoting outcomes attempt to require deliberative judgments by democratically accountable bodies. Democracy-foreclosing outcomes rule some practices off-limits to politics. Democracy-permitting outcomes simply validate what democratic processes have produced.

To avoid foreclosure and allow democratically accountable bodies to function, a court might decline to hear a case at all or rule narrowly rather than broadly. Democracy-permitting outcomes may well be desirable when considerations of democracy do not themselves call for a broad ruling. This is one reason why courts should and do act cautiously when they are in the midst of a "political thicket." Courts know that they may be wrong, and they know too that even if they are right, a broad, early ruling may have unfortunate systemic effects. It may prevent the kind of evolution, adaptation, and argumentative give-and-take that tend to accompany lasting social reform.

In contrast, some decisions are democracy-promoting because they try to trigger or improve processes of democratic deliberation. Minimalist courts can provide spurs and prods to promote democratic deliberation itself. Thus, for example,

1. A court might strike down vague laws precisely because they ensure that executive branch officials, rather than elected representatives, will determine the content of the law.[3]
2. A court might use the nondelegation doctrine to require legislative rather than executive judgments on certain issues.[4]
3. A court might interpret ambiguous statutes so as to keep them away from the terrain of constitutional doubt, on the theory that constitutionally troublesome judgments, to be upheld, ought to be made by politically accountable bodies, and not by bureaucrats and administrators.[5] This "clear statement" idea is the post–New Deal version of the nondelegation doctrine; it shows that the doctrine is not really dead but is used in a more modest and targeted way to ensure that certain decisions are made by Congress rather than by the executive branch.
4. A court might invoke the doctrine of desuetude, which forbids the use of old laws lacking current public support, to require more in the way of accountability and deliberation (see Chapter 7).
5. A court might require discrimination to be justified by reference to actual rather than hypothetical purposes, thus leaving open the question of whether justifications would be adequate if actually offered and found persuasive in politics (see Chapter 5).
6. A court might attempt to ensure that all decisions are supported by public-regarding justifications rather than by power and self-interest; it might in this way both model and police the system of public reason.[6]

All of these ideas call for approaches that are at least comparatively narrow and that leave open many of the largest questions. Thus maximalists who are deliberative democrats can be contrasted with minimalists who proceed from the same foundation but prefer to use clear statement principles, void-for-vagueness doctrines, and the like. This is the form of minimalism that I shall be defending here. Sometimes it is not necessary to choose deliberative democracy over some other conception of democracy. But when a choice is necessary, democracy-promoting forms of minimalism, designed to promote both accountability and reason-giving, are appropriate and salutary judicial functions; they promote constitutional ideals without risking excessive judicial intervention into political domains.

Minimalism and Judicial Restraint

Minimalism can interact in diverse ways with judicial validation or invalidation of statutes. Minimalism does not mean judicial "restraint," if this term is understood to mean judicial unwillingness to invalidate legislation. To get hold of the relation between minimalism and democracy, the diverse possibilities should be kept in mind. Consider Table 2.1.[7]

From the table it is clear that the largest scope for democratic judgment emerges from cell 1: rule-bound decisions that broadly validate possible practices. Thus the cases immediately after the New Deal basically authorized the national government to proceed as it wished under the commerce clause, and to do so without fear of constraint from the due process clause. Justice Scalia would like similarly to uphold punitive damage awards and discrimination against homosexuals. Cell 1 decisions also have the advantage of giving a clear signal to other branches and of putting pressure on them to make corrections if corrections are necessary. Of course from the standpoint of deliberative democracy, cell 1 outcomes may be nothing to celebrate, since the measures that are upheld may be problematic from the standpoint of deliberative democracy itself. The best defense of cell 1 involves the incentives it creates: a "clear background" against which legislatures and relevant interests can work. Thus cell 1 has been especially appealing to Justice Scalia, largely on democracy-reinforcing grounds. Often this argument is attractive in the abstract, but whether cell 1 outcomes can be justified as democracy-reinforcing depends on some contextual factors: Is there a structural obstacle to democratic deliberation in the context at hand? Does the legislature's failure to respond reflect interest-group pressures, myopia, or blockages of certain kinds? Is there

Table 2.1

	Validation	Invalidation
Maximalist	(1) Post–New Deal cases allowing Congress broad authority under commerce clause; Ferguson v. Scrupa and other post–New Deal cases refusing to use economic due process (democracy-promoting rationale: clear background against which legislature and citizens can work); Justice Scalia voting to uphold punitive damages and discrimination on the basis of sexual orientation	(2) Miranda v. Arizona; Loving v. Virginia, striking down laws forbidding racial intermarriage not only on equal protection but also on substantive due process grounds; Roe v. Wade; Justice Scalia on affirmative action; New York Times v. Sullivan; Justice Thomas on commercial advertising
Minimalist	(3) Early punitive damages cases, upholding particular punitive damage awards but leaving room for future invalidation; Denver Area Educational Telecommunications Consortium v. FCC; Rostker v. Goldberg; Korematsu v. United States	(4) Romer v. Evans; United States v. Lopez; Kent v. Dulles; Hampton v. Mow Sun Wong; Cleburne v. Cleburne Living Center; United States v. Virginia

a constitutional commitment that broad validation overlooks? (I take up these issues in detail in Chapter 9.)

Cases that fall in cell 3—upholding practices in a narrow way—leave things open, but not in a way that increases democratic space compared with cell 1. This is because cell 1 cases uphold a wide range of practices, whereas cell 3 cases retain room for future invalidation. In Rostker v. Goldberg, the Court upheld an exclusion of women from compulsory registration for the draft, but left open the possibility that much other sex discrimination would be invalidated; in Korematsu v. United States, the Court upheld the uprooting of Japanese Americans during World War II, but left open the possibility that other forms of discrimination would be invalidated. From the standpoint of closing off democratic processes, maximalists are simultaneously the best and the worst—the worst because cell 2 creates the greatest foreclosure of political deliberation. Thus among current justices, Justice Scalia, who would like to invalidate almost all affirmative action programs, can be seen as the most generous to majoritarian processes in some settings and as the least generous in others. Justice Thomas is in the same category; hence he would rule broadly that commercial speech receives the same protection as political speech, even in a case in which that question need not be decided.

This is pervasively true of consistent maximalists; Justice Hugo Black[8] is in this way Justice Scalia's great jurisprudential ancestor. For both Scalia and Black, things are very clear in the sense that law is rule-bound and predictable, but often democratic processes find themselves broadly foreclosed. Rule-bound foreclosures may of course be justified; perhaps Miranda v. Arizona made sense in light of the extreme difficulty of proceeding case by case to see whether confessions were actually involuntary. But foreclosures may also cause trouble. Hence, for example, in Loving v. Virginia the Court ruled not only that the ban on racial intermarriage violated the equal protection clause but also—in an unnecessary, contentious, and confusing alternative ground—that it violated substantive due process by invading a fundamental "right to marry." The existence of a "right to marry" raises many questions about laws forbidding marriage between people who are related or of the same sex. The Court did not need to raise those questions to decide *Loving*.

Cell 2 seems to be the least democratic; here the Court is broadly invalidating political judgments. But there are complex relationships between maximalist invalidations and democracy. If an invalidation is justified on democratic grounds, it might qualify as democratic even though it is an invalidation. A wide ruling in favor of freedom of political dissent can fairly be counted as democratic. An invalidation that is not justified in this way may also spur democratic debate. The decisions in Roe v. Wade and *Dred Scott* helped promote more discussion of the underlying issues, though in a sense the discussion was futile unless something could happen (new appointments, a constitutional amendment) to convince the Court to move. I will be urging that cell 2 should be avoided unless there is a good argument for invalidation on democratic grounds, or unless the Court has considerable confidence in its judgment.

Cell 4 is the most intriguing of all, at least when it simultaneously involves invalidation and an effort to spur democratic processes. It is to cell 4 cases that I will be devoting special attention. In such cases, courts attempt to promote what I have suggested are the two goals of a deliberative democracy: political accountability and reason-giving. The goal of accountability is fostered by ensuring that officials with the requisite political legitimacy make relevant decisions. Hence the non-delegation and void-for-vagueness doctrines ensure legislative rather than executive lawmaking; hence certain public law doctrines try to ensure that Congress, rather than the bureaucracy, has focused on certain issues. Attempts to ensure against continued rule by old judgments "frozen" by political processes belong in the same category. Reason-giving, a central part of political deliberation, is associated with the control of factional power and self-interested representation, the constitutional framers' dual concerns.

Much of administrative law consists of an effort to ensure reason-giving by regulatory agencies, partly because of a fear that they lack sufficient political accountability and may be subject to factional influences. The standard judicial decision, in this context, tests the agency's reasoning against the agency's outcome; if the reasoning fails, the agency's decision is "remanded" for further proceedings. The agency is entitled to do what it did before, but it must generate a convincing explanation, one that shows that something other than interest-group power or legally illegitimate factors underlay that decision. Sympathetically conceived, administrative law consists largely of an effort at democracy-promoting minimalism. In constitutional law, democracy-promoting minimalism can be understood in similar terms. Many judge-made doctrines are an effort to ensure reason-giving, and are in the process an effort to ensure that legitimate rather than illegitimate reasons are at work.

Consider, as a key example, the controversial (and emphatically minimalist) 1995 decision in United States v. Lopez,[9] invalidating a statute as beyond congressional power under the commerce clause, the first such invalidation since the New Deal. *Lopez* depended on a set of factors, not on any rule; it left the law quite unsettled. The decision may well have much of its importance as a signaling device, one that operates as a kind of reminder or remand to Congress. After *Lopez*, it is necessary for Congress to focus on the fact that the Constitution is one of enumerated rather than plenary powers, and *Lopez* is likely to play a continuing role in deliberations outside of the Court about whether there is really a need for national action. Indeed, in the aftermath of *Lopez* Congress has given renewed attention to the question whether the national government really should intervene into areas traditionally reserved to the states.

Minimalism in Action: Problems and Prospects

> Because we cannot be confident that for purposes of judging speech restrictions it will continue to make sense to distinguish cable from other technologies, and because we know that changes in these regulated technologies will enormously alter the structure of regulation itself, we should be shy about saying the final word today about what will be accepted as reasonable tomorrow.
> —Denver Area Educational Telecommunications Consortium v. FCC
> (Justice Souter, concurring)

> The plurality opinion . . . is adrift. . . . [I]t applies no standard, and by this omission loses sight of existing First Amendment doctrine.
> —Denver Area Educational Telecommunications Consortium v. FCC
> (Justice O'Connor, concurring in part and dissenting in part)

Let us now consider some prominent examples of democracy-promoting minimalism in law.

1. *Communists and the State Department.* In Kent v. Dulles,[10] the Supreme Court was confronted with the denial of a passport to someone who had long been a believer in communism. The relevant statute said that the "Secretary of State may grant and issue passports under such rules as the President shall designate and prescribe for and on behalf of the United States. . . ." Several opinions would have been simple to write. The Court could have invalidated the statute as an open-ended and hence unconstitutional delegation of authority to the executive. It could have said that the denial of the passport violated the right to travel or the right to free speech. It could have said that the statute was valid and plainly authorized the Secretary's decision.

The Court did none of these things. The Court said that the statute, however open-ended its language, would not be construed so as to enable the Secretary to limit the right to travel. The Court did not say that if Congress had expressly decided to enable the Secretary to do this,

Congress would be found to have acted unconstitutionally. Instead it said more modestly that the executive could have this authority only as a result of a clear statement from Congress. Any limitation on travel by believers in communism would have to be explicitly authorized by the institution charged by the Constitution with making national law.

2. *Means, ends, and Griswold.* It will be recalled that in Griswold v. Connecticut,[11] the Supreme Court posited a broad "right to privacy." Indeed, *Griswold* was the birth of this controversial constitutional right. The dissenters thought that this was a matter of implausible constitutional creativity—of creating a constitutional right out of the blue.

Rejecting both the majority and the dissents, Justice White wrote in narrow terms. He was willing to agree that a prohibition on premarital or extramarital activity would be legitimate. But he doubted that the ban on the use of contraceptives within marriage "in any way reinforces the state's ban on illicit sexual relationships." Thus he concluded that the real problem in the case lay in the absence of a close relationship between the state's justification and the particular prohibition at issue. More specifically, he doubted the plausibility of "the premise that married people will comply with the ban in regard to their marital relationship, notwithstanding total nonenforcement in this context and apparent nonenforceability, but will not comply with criminal statutes prohibiting extramarital affairs and the anti-use statute in respect to illicit sexual relationships, a premise whose validity has not been demonstrated and whose intrinsic validity is not very evident."[12]

In so saying Justice White suggested that the weakness of the connection between means and ends showed that the statute in fact rested on something other than the state's asserted justification—in all likelihood, on the belief that nonprocreative sex was immoral even within marriage. That belief helped support the enactment of the statute and probably helped ensure against its repeal. But the belief no longer reflected anything like the considered judgment of the Connecticut citizenry and hence would not support criminal prosecutions. In essence, Justice White's opinion reflects both a refusal to speak about a broad right to privacy and a decision to focus more narrowly on the absence of a plausible connection between the state's justification and the state's enactment. Justice White's opinion was both narrow and shallow.

3. *Affirmative action.* Justice Lewis Powell's famous and highly minimalist opinion in the *Bakke* case[13] has special importance in view of the

continuing broad-gauged constitutional attack on affirmative action in education. In that case, four justices thought that color-blindness was legally required by the relevant statute, whereas four other justices thought that affirmative action programs should be upheld, under both the Constitution and the statute, as efforts to undo the continuing effects of past discrimination. Thus eight justices sought a kind of width.

Justice Powell rejected both positions. His opinion rested on a close analysis of the relationship between the particular affirmative action program at issue and the justifications invoked on its behalf. In his view, the most important justification involved the medical school's need to ensure a racially diverse student body, not because racial diversity was an end in itself, but because racial diversity could promote the educational mission of the school. In Justice Powell's view, this justification was both legitimate and weighty. The problem was that the University of California program could not be said to have been necessary to promote that interest. A system that treated race as a "plus," rather than a rigid, two-track admissions system, would be adequate to serve the university's goals, and it would also be constitutionally acceptable. Thus Justice Powell rejected the view that all affirmative action programs would be illegitimate (essentially the view of the dissenters) and also the view that all such programs should be upheld as a response to past discrimination (not far from the view of four concurring justices).

For Justice Powell, the legitimacy of an affirmative action program would turn not on whether it was an affirmative action program, and hence not on any clear rule, but on a close investigation of the particular program and in particular its function in promoting legitimate social goals. In this way Justice Powell's opinion was narrow; it left many questions open. (It was not at the same time shallow, since it offered a number of relatively abstract judgments about the legitimacy of various grounds for affirmative action programs.) Justice Powell emphasized in particular the fact that the university admissions program had not been supported by any democratically elected body, and was the creation of a university administration, an institution that lacked electoral legitimacy. In this way Justice Powell's opinion was democracy-promoting.

4. *Democracy, alienage, and bureaucracy.* In Hampton v. Mow Sun Wong,[14] the Court was presented with a constitutional challenge to a Civil Service Commission regulation barring most aliens from civil service positions. The plantiffs urged that the bar violated the equal pro-

tection clause. The government responded that it had an especially important interest in reserving positions in the federal civil service for American citizens.

The Supreme Court rejected both positions. It left open the possibility that "there may be overriding national interests which justify selective federal legislation that would be unacceptable for an individual state." But it noticed that the ban had been issued by the Civil Service Commission, not by the President or the Congress. The ban therefore faced a kind of legitimacy deficit. This was so especially because the Civil Service Commission had relied on the interests in providing an incentive to become nationalized and in allowing the President an expendable token for treaty negotiation. These interests were far afield from the ordinary mission and competence of the Commission.

The Court said that if a class of people is going to be deprived of federal employment, it must be because of a decision from politically accountable actors acting within their ordinary competence, and not by members of a bureaucracy invoking considerations with which it is not familiar. In so saying, the Court did not deny the possibility that the President or Congress could exclude aliens from the civil service. That question was left open. Thus the Court's decision was exceedingly narrow. Because the Court did not give much of a theoretical account for its judgment, the decision was shallow as well.

As exercises in democracy-promoting minimalism, these various cases have a great deal in common. They involve narrow judgments that leave the largest questions for another day. They also involve judgments on which diverse people may—certainly need not, but may—converge. They are highly particularistic. And they all have democracy-reinforcing functions. This is most conspicuously true for Kent v. Dulles and Hampton v. Mow Sun Wong, for in both cases the Court's judgment was expressly founded on the idea that publicly accountable bodies should make the decision that was challenged in the case. But democratic considerations underlie Justice White's *Griswold* concurrence as well. We do not need to venture far from the text of the White opinion to see that the poor match between means and ends suggested that an unarticulated end, one that no longer matched public convictions, actually underlay the enactment under review. The fact that no democratically accountable body had in the recent past offered a reflective endorsement of Connecticut's ban on the use of contraceptions linked the *Griswold* case closely with Kent v. Dulles and Hampton v. Mow Sun Wong. To the extent that Justice White was speaking in terms of a form of desuetude (see Chapters 5 and 7), his opinion is centrally concerned with the absence of sufficient democratic support for the relevant statute.

Justice Powell's opinion was not so far from these points. He emphasized in particular the fact that the program in *Bakke* had received no democratic endorsement. And the narrowness of his opinion left the democratic process large room to maneuver, adapt, and generate further information and perspectives. Thus Justice Powell's opinion can be understood as an effort to promote both democracy and deliberation.

Dred Scott, Brown, and *Roe*

It will be useful to compare these cases with three of the most important cases in American constitutional law. Not surprisingly, all of them reject minimalism. One of them, Dred Scott v. Sanford,[15] may well be the most vilified decision in the Court's history; another, Brown v. Board of Education, may well be the most celebrated; and the third, Roe v. Wade, is one of the most sharply contested. In saying a few words about the three cases here, I do not, of course, mean to offer full evaluations of the Court's opinions. My goal is to draw attention to the sheer ambition of the three decisions and to see how that ambition should be evaluated.

In *Dred Scott,* the Court decided several crucial issues about the relationship between the Constitution and slavery. Most important, the Court struck down the Missouri Compromise, which abolished slavery in the territories, and also ruled that freed slaves could not qualify as citizens for purposes of the diversity of citizenship clause of Article III. Of course the Court's decision was a disaster, helping to fuel the Civil War. But let us put the substance to one side and focus on institutional issues. One of the notable features of the case was that instead of deciding only those issues that were necessary for disposition, the Court decided every issue that it was possible to decide. There was no need for the Court to have been so ambitious. If the Court had wanted to do so, it could have avoided the controversial issues entirely. After concluding that it lacked jurisdiction under Article III, the Court might have refused to discuss Congress's power to abolish slavery in the territories. Or the Court could have rested content—as it had initially voted to do—with a narrow judgment saying that Missouri law controlled the question of Scott's legal status. In that event, the large issues in the case would have been left alone, and the *Dred Scott* case would have been a relatively unimportant episode in American law.

Notably, the Court itself rejected its initial choice of minimalism because it wanted to take the slavery issue out of politics and resolve it once and for all time.[16] This attempted course was a catastrophe, partly because of the moral judgment itself, partly because of the futility of the Court's attempt as a matter of institutional role. It is hazardous to draw firm inferences from single cases. But the Court's abysmal failure in this regard is certainly a cautionary note. It is a cautionary note because it shows the possible unreliability of moral judgments from the Court, and also because it shows that judicial efforts to resolve questions of political morality now and for all time may well be futile.

In Roe v. Wade, the Court was asked for the first time to decide whether a constitutional right of "privacy" protected the decision to have an abortion. An inspection of the pleadings reveals a potentially important aspect of the case: Roe herself alleged that she had been raped. Of course Roe is known for its elaborate trimester system and for the complex body of rules and standards contained in that system. But a minimalist would have said more simply that the state may not forbid a woman from having an abortion in a rape case, or that a state may not ban all abortions in all circumstances.[17] Such a decision would have left the ultimate constitutional status of the abortion right in considerable doubt. It would have left the details undecided, to be filled in, at least in the first instance, by lower courts and democratic judgments.

How should this imaginary alternative be evaluated? Until we have done a lot of work on the underlying substance, we cannot be confident that the minimalist approach would have been better. Perhaps the *Roe* outcome was correct as a matter of substantive constitutional theory; perhaps an inquiry into decision costs and error costs would support the *Roe* opinion. But at least it seems reasonable to think that the democratic process would have done much better with the abortion issue if the Court had proceeded more cautiously and in a humbler and more interactive way.

Brown appears to be the strongest example against the claim that I mean to defend here: that minimalism is usually the appropriate course for moral or political issues on which the nation is sharply divided. And it is reasonable to think that *Brown* requires the thesis to be qualified, perhaps for the most compelling cases where the underlying judgment of (constitutionally relevant) political morality is insistent. As I have indicated, the choice between minimalism and the alternatives depends on an array of contextual considerations, and it would be extravagant to say that minimalism is always better.

But before taking *Brown* as an exception to the general thesis, let us notice two important features of the *Brown* litigation. That decision did not come like a thunderbolt from the sky. Along this dimension, it was entirely different from *Dred Scott* and *Roe*. The *Brown* outcome had been presaged by a long series of cases testing the proposition that "separate" was "equal," and testing that proposition in such a way as to lead nearly inevitably to the suggestion that "separate" could not be "equal." In short, *Brown* was the culmination of a series of (more minimalist) cases, not the first of its kind.

There is a further point. *Brown* itself was not self-implementing; it said nothing about remedy. *Brown II*,[18] the remedy case, had a minimalist dimension insofar as it allowed a large room for discussion and dialogue via the "all deliberate speed" formula. *Brown II* made clear that immediate implementation would not be required. In this way it had something in common with Kent v. Dulles and Hampton v. Mow Sun Wong. It left certain crucial matters undecided. It allowed those matters to be taken up by other officials in other forums. And indeed the process of desegregation ultimately involved the legislative and executive branches, not just the Court, especially in the aftermath of the Civil Rights Act of 1964. It was not until the enactment of that act, and the involvement of the Department of Justice, that significant desegregation actually occurred.[19]

There are of course reasons to question this degree of flexibility, on both strategic and moral grounds. I do not mean to answer these questions here. *Brown II* ended up placing courts in charge of complex implementation questions, and thus required managerial judgments for which courts are ill suited. But it is at least relevant to the evaluation of *Brown* that the Court did not impose its principle all at once, and that it allowed room for other branches to discuss the principle and to adapt themselves to it. The *Brown* decision was far less maximalist than it might seem; it can even be taken as a form of democracy-promoting minimalism.

Democracy, Humility, and the Passive Virtues

Insofar as the minimalist judge seeks to promote democratic goals while recognizing social pluralism, the minimalist project is easily linked with the idea of "passive virtues," as discussed by Alexander Bickel.[20] These virtues are exercised when a court refuses to assume jurisdiction. Sometimes judges do not want to decide cases or issues at all, and even the minimal amount necessary to resolve a conflict seems to require courts to say too much. A denial of certiorari might well be based on this understanding. Perhaps it is premature for the Court to participate in a certain controversy. Perhaps the Court wants to receive more information, is so divided that it could not resolve the case in any event, or is attuned to strategic considerations stemming from the likelihood of adverse public reactions. For all these reasons it may be prudent to wait. In the past, a judgment of this kind has been made in important cases involving racial intermarriage, affirmative action, and homosexuality, as the Court has refused to hear cases, not because they were unimportant, but because it seemed untimely to do so. Thus those who emphasize passive virtues focus on the need for judicial prudence.

Of course a denial of certiorari reduces decision costs for the Court. It may reduce error costs as well, if the Court is not in a good position to produce a judgment in which it has confidence, or if the Court thinks that additional discussion, in lower courts and nonjudicial arenas, is likely to be more productive. To be sure, a denial of certiorari may create undesirable uncertainty and also allow the perpetuation of constitutionally unacceptable injustice. Thus the denial of certiorari can be analyzed as a form of minimalism and evaluated by reference to the criteria that I will explore below.

The basic principles of justiciability are designed to limit the occasions for judicial interference with political processes. These principles—involving mootness, ripeness, reviewability, and standing—say that judges can intervene only at certain times and at the behest of certain people. In this way the principles are obviously an effort to minimize the judicial presence in American public life. It may be tempting to see these principles as firm, rule-bound law, allowing no room for discretionary judgments. But realistically speaking, justiciability doctrines are used prudentially and strategically and in response to considerations of the sort I am discussing here. For example, a judgment that a complex issue is not now ripe for decision may minimize the risk of error and increase the scope for continuing democratic deliberation on the problem at hand. It should not be surprising to find some pressure to find otherwise borderline cases "not ripe" or "moot" precisely because of the costs associated with deciding the substantive question. In cases involving homosexuality and racial intermarriage, the Court has occasionally proceeded in this way, thinking that judicial intervention is premature.

A judgment of mootness will certainly minimize short-term decision costs; it may reduce error costs as well; and it will increase the scope for democratic deliberation about the issue at hand. My suggestion is that the notion of the "passive virtues" can be analyzed in a more productive way if we see that notion as part of judicial minimalism and as an effort to increase space for democratic choice and to reduce the costs of decision and the costs of error.

These points do not mean that courts should use the passive virtues so as to perpetuate injustice. In cases involving homosexuality and racial intermarriage, it would be reasonable to say that the Court has allowed injustice to continue for too long. This is a debate over issues of substance, and any particular decision to exercise the passive virtues depends on substance as well as institutional considerations. All I mean to suggest is that the arguments that call for minimalism also call, in some contexts, for a refusal to hear a case at all.

One final point. Those who favor passive virtues, narrow decisions, and incompletely theorized agreements tend to be humble about their own capacities. They are not by any means skeptics; but with respect to questions of both substance and method, they are not too sure that they are right. They know that their own attempts at theory may fail. They know that both law and life may outrun seemingly good rules and seemingly plausible theories. They know that outcomes often turn on information that they lack. It is for this reason that many judges have not settled on any general approach to constitutional law. It is for this reason too that many judges have not generated an "account" of the First Amendment, the equal protection clause, the takings clause, and other provisions that form the staple of the Court's constitutional work.

To be sure, and importantly, cases cannot be decided without some understanding of the purpose or point of the legal provisions at issue. Reasons are by their very nature abstractions, and cases that depend on reasons will necessarily rest on an account of some kind. But some justices attempt to decide cases in the hope and with the knowledge that several different conceptions of the point can allow convergence on a particular outcome. Their attempt stems from their knowledge that some of their own convictions may not be right, and from their effort to accommodate reasonable disagreement. This point returns us to a central point: judicial minimalism is rooted in a conception of liberty amid pluralism, a conception that is central to the democratic idea.

Beyond Rules and Standards

There is a flourishing literature on the choice between legal rules and legal standards.[21] In the familiar formulation, a rule says that no one may drive over 65 miles per hour; a standard says that no one may drive at an excessive speed. A rule therefore operates as a full or nearly full before-the-fact specification of legal outcomes.[22] By contrast, a standard leaves a great deal of work to be done at the moment of application. Costs must be incurred in order to create a rule, and after a rule is in place the decision may be relatively mechanical. With a standard, the costs are incurred in the context of specification.

This is an illuminating distinction, and often courts do choose between rules and standards. Hence there is a large internal debate on the Court on exactly that choice, with Justices Scalia and Thomas most prominently favoring rules, and Justice O'Connor often arguing for standards. In a prior generation the same debate can be found, with Justice Frankfurter arguing for standards, and Justice Black favoring rules. But if we attend to democratic considerations, and in particular to judicial minimalism, we can see that the distinction captures only part of what is at stake and only part of the realistic alternatives. It is better to distinguish between minimalism and maximalism, and better yet to specify the ways in which the alternatives fall in either camp.

A standard is a good way to keep things open for the future; but that can be done in many other ways too. Things can be left undecided, for example, with a rule that is quite firm and thus has a narrow scope. A narrow rule (all people born on September 21, 1954, must obey a 55-mile-per-hour speed limit) does not resolve many cases. A rule unsupported by reasons that apply elsewhere (the University of California at Davis may not discriminate against people over the age of fifty) may have narrow coverage. And the goal of leaving things undecided may be accomplished not via a standard or narrow rules but by a refusal to hear a case at all. So too with a decision accompanied by reasons that are both narrow and shallow. Those reasons may take rule-like form, but their domain may be limited. A court might rule that the 55-mile-per-hour speed limit applies to people trying to get to an important meeting on the job, without saying whether it also applies to police officers, ambulances, or people who are trying to get medical attention at the nearest hospital.

In short, there are many devices for avoiding width and depth. It would be possible to bring the considerations that underlie the rules–standards debate—the need for predictability, the value of flexibility, limits in information, maintaining space for the future, or, more simply, the need to minimize both error costs and decision costs—to bear on a wide range of issues not ordinarily understood in these terms. This is in fact one of my principal goals here.

Analogies and Incompletely Theorized Agreements

Analogical reasoning is part and parcel of the project of minimalism. It is of course a hallmark of legal reasoning to proceed by reference to actual and hypothetical cases. In constitutional and common law, a usual question is: how does this case compare to those cases that have come before? Thus constitutional law has crucial analogical dimensions. Indeed, most of the important constraints on judicial discretion come not from constitutional text or history, but from the process of grappling with previous decisions.

Most important, analogical reasoning reduces the need for theory-building, and for generating law from the ground up, by creating a shared and relatively fixed background from which diverse judges can work. Thus judges who disagree on a great deal can work together far more easily if they think analogically and by reference to agreed-upon fixed points. The process of case analysis also allows (even if it does not require) judges to proceed narrowly if they see fit. It does this because the line between holdings and dicta, and the power to recharacterize holdings, gives subsequent courts a good deal of authority to say that earlier cases, properly understood, have left many things undecided. And the process of case analysis can allow greater flexibility than the process of rule-following, and in that way can take on the minimalist's concerns about the burdens of decision, the risks of error, and the need for latitude over time and changing conditions.

But the most important point has a democratic dimension: people can often reach agreement on an analogy when they disagree about the most complex theoretical issues.[23] Thus analogical reasoning is a good way of obtaining the virtues of incompletely theorized agreements. From diverse perspectives people may be able to agree, for example, that discrimination on the basis of sex is like discrimination on the basis of race, or that a ban on a speech by a member of the Communist Party is like a ban on a speech by a right-wing extremist. Legal doctrine is often possible only because it is analogical in character. The fact that precedents provide the backdrop removes certain arguments from the legal repertoire and in that way much simplifies analysis. The search for relevant similarities, and low-level principles on which diverse people can converge, often makes legal doctrine possible. Of course intense disagreements may remain.

Even rule-interpretation has a large element of case analysis. Rules are frequently understood by reference to the prototypical or exemplary cases that they call to mind. When the case at hand is very different from the prototypical or exemplary case, the project of rule-interpretation can become very difficult, and the central issue may well involve analogical reasoning. Consider a recent problem. Congress has imposed a thirty-year mandatory minimum sentence on anyone who "uses" a firearm "in relation to" a drug offense. In Smith v. United States,[24] the Court was asked to decide whether someone who sold a firearm for drugs had run afoul of this statute. The Court responded affirmatively, in part because of its judgment that the use of a firearm as an object of barter raised all of the problems created by the use of a firearm as a weapon. In other words, the Court said that the use of the gun by Smith was relevantly similar to the use of the gun in the core or paradigm cases.

Another issue arose in Bailey v. United States.[25] Suppose that a drug transaction occurs and that in its midst a federal agent finds a gun, one that is owned by the defendant, not on his person but accessible to him, and thus usable when and if needed to facilitate a drug crime. A lower court held that in such a case the gun was being used in relation to a drug-trafficking crime. Thinking analogously, the Supreme Court disagreed. The Court concluded that the statute required a demonstration of "active employment" of the firearm. It supported its conclusion partly by reference to text and history, but partly by reference to an extended set of examples reasoning from the obvious, defining cases of "use," and drawing lines based on analogy and disanalogy from those cases. In this way the Court's discussion of examples suggested that the statutory rule would be given meaning by a process not very different from that used by common law courts.

We may draw a general lesson. Rules are often understood by reference to defining cases. Often the case in dispute is obviously akin to the core or defining cases, and hence the interpretation of rules is often very easy. When rule-interpretation becomes difficult, it is usually because there is a distinction between the defining cases and the application at issue; the existence of a plausible distinction calls the application of the rule into doubt. The lesson extends well beyond law. Human reasoning often works by reference to prototypical cases, as human beings, lacking comprehensive rationality, approach new situations by comparing them with those that come most readily to mind.[26]

Why does case analysis have such a large hold on the judicial mind? Much of the answer lies in the minimalism of this way of thinking.[27] Judges who rely on cases can reduce the burden of decisions; at least for the individual judge, reliance on past cases may well be better on this count than attempts to build law from the ground up. Case analysis can be far less time consuming than efforts to uncover the deep foundations of some area of law. When rule interpretation is done by analogy, courts convert rules into something less wide, a phenomenon that carries with it significant advantages (see Chapter 9 for details).

Emphasis on cases can reduce the number of mistakes as well. Rules laid down in advance may, of course, misfire. The process of a case-by-case decision maintains a degree of flexibility for the future; past cases might well be distinguished if they seem to go wrong as applied to new circumstances. Of course it cannot be said in the abstract that from the standpoint of reducing decision and error costs, reliance on cases and analogical thinking is better than the alternatives. A conclusion of this sort would be quite implausible. We need to know something about how certain cases, and not others, become treated as prototypical or as the foundations for analogical thinking. When a court strikes down an affirmative action program or a law forbidding same-sex marriage, do we have a rerun of Brown v. Board of Education or instead Lochner v. New York? We also need to know something about the alternatives and about the capacities of various social institutions. These claims bring us directly to the topic of the next chapter.

3

Decisions and Mistakes

Why would courts attempt a minimalist path? When should they move in the direction of width or depth? In this chapter I offer some general observations. As we have seen, minimalism is associated with democratic goals. It also can minimize the burdens of decisions and the costs of mistakes. It can do so while playing a healthy role in a pluralistic society in which people often disagree about fundamental issues. But there is no context-free case for minimalism. When planning is important, or when judges have confidence in a wide or deep ruling, nonminimalist approaches may well be best. The appropriate areas for minimalism involve issues of high factual or ethical complexity that are producing democratic disagreement and debate; here minimalism is likely to be the best route.

Minimalist Virtues

As a first approximation, we might try to systematize the inquiry, and disputes over width and depth, in the following way: good judges try to minimize the sum of decision costs and error costs. In other words, they try to decrease the burden of decisions and the number and seriousness of mistakes. Note that we can find such notions useful without thinking that it is necessary or helpful to understand the idea of "costs" in a fully economistic manner, as if the various consequences of decisions can be monetized, or aligned along a single metric. The costs of decision are qualitatively different from the costs of error, and the ingredients in both decision costs and error costs are qualitatively distinct from one another. It is valuable to think about minimizing the sum of decision costs and error costs, but we should not proceed as if these costs are qualitatively indistinguishable, or as if there is some metric along which they can be assessed. Consider, for example, the risk that a certain rule in constitutional law will produce excessive restrictions on political speech, a risk that may be less well understood if we see it as a "cost" like all other costs.

A clue to understanding minimalism is to recognize that in deciding constitutional cases, judges often lack relevant information, and their rulings might well have unintended consequences. Their interest in shallow and narrow rulings is a product of their understanding of their own cognitive (and motivational) limitations. They know that they do not know. Thus judges might be drawn to minimalism because of bounded rationality, a large theme in psychology and economics with important implications for law.

Decisions and Decision Costs

Everyone knows that it is sometimes hard, or costly, to decide. In all contexts human beings face decision costs, and they adopt a range of devices to reduce them.[1] They may adopt rules or presumptions, or take small steps rather than large ones. Indeed, small steps are often a response to the high costs of resolving large problems.

In the legal setting, decision costs are faced by both litigants and courts. If, for example, judges in a case involving the "right to die" attempted to generate a rule that would cover all imaginable situations in which that right might be exercised, the case would take a very long time to decide. This might be so because of a sheer lack of information. It might be so because of the pressures imposed on a multimember court consisting of people who are unsure or in disagreement about a range of subjects. Such a court may have a great deal of difficulty in reaching closure on broad rules. Undoubtedly the narrowness of many decisions is a product of this fact. Romer v. Evans, invalidating a law discriminating on the basis of sexual orientation while failing to mention Bowers v. Hardwick and otherwise leaving things undecided, is a recent example; the opinion may well be a product of the difficulty of getting consensus from six diverse justices (see Chapter 7).

Quite apart from the pressures of inadequate information and disagreement, minimalism might make special sense in view of the pervasive possibility of changed circumstances. Perhaps things will be quite different in the near future; perhaps relevant facts and values will change, and thus a rule that is well suited to present conditions may become anachronistic. Of course the point is relevant to the creation of rules in everyday life. A solution that seems, at time A, to make a good deal of sense may misfire at time B, and judges who want to generate decent rules will have to spend time pondering this possibility. As we shall see, these ideas support minimalism in applying free speech principles to emerging communications technologies, where things are changing very rapidly.

All of these points suggest that minimalism may be desirable because of the high costs of decision. But an inquiry into decision costs will not always support minimalism. Sometimes the total costs of decision are far lower with clear rules. Once rules are in place, work is much simpler for those in the future. A court that economizes on decision costs for itself may in the process "export" decision costs to other people, including litigants and judges in subsequent cases who must give content to the law. Such costs may also be faced by those who are trying to plan their affairs and who must try to figure out what the law will ultimately be. It is imaginable that a narrow decision in the first case—involving, let us continue to suppose, free speech and the Internet, or the right to die—would lead to very high aggregate decision costs, since litigants and district courts would have to struggle with that issue in subsequent cases. Part of the case for width is that when law is uncertain, decision costs can proliferate, as people invest in activities designed to find out the content of law and also to press law's content in certain directions. High decision costs are especially pernicious when planning is important; it is for this reason that stare decisis and broad rules are extremely valuable in cases involving the need to plan. Thus, for example, if companies do not know whether they might face no, low, or high punitive damages, they will have to invest a large amount of resources in speculating about how to proceed.

One group of people will predictably do well when decision costs are high: lawyers. But high decision costs can be a disaster from the standpoint of society as a whole. It is for this reason that the ban on advisory opinions is relaxed in cases when uncertainty impedes necessary planning.[2]

Errors and Error Costs   *(analogy to paper w/ Chuck)*

We can understand error costs to include the costs of mistaken judgments, as these affect the social and legal system as a whole. The costs of errors are a function of both their number and their magnitude. High error costs can come from a large number of small mistakes or a small number of large mistakes. If it is wrong, a wide ruling may have especially high error costs, because it will affect many subsequent cases.

This concern often provides a good reason for minimalism. It is possible, for example, that any decision involving the application of the First Amendment to new communications technologies, including the Internet, should be narrow, because a broad decision, rendered at this time, would be so likely to go wrong. On this view, a narrow judgment is best because a broad one would be so likely mistaken as applied to cases not before the court. A slower and more evolutionary approach, involving the accretion of case-by-case judgments, could produce fewer mistakes on balance, since each decision would be appropriately informed by an understanding of particular facts. Thus lack of information is a crucial argument for decisional minimalism. Changed circumstances argue in the same direction; imagine the difficulties of designing good rules for a changing telecommunications market. The common law process, so central to American constitutional law, prizes minimalism partly for this reason; analogical reasoning, as distinct from rule-bound judgment, is a crucial part of the process.

Those who favor a theoretically ambitious judiciary often emphasize the need to ensure that individual rights are respected and that our society is just. Why—it is asked—should people whose rights are being violated have to wait? On what account should judges allow injustice to continue? Isn't this a form of weakness or cowardice? It would be harder to answer these questions if judges were in a position to make accurate decisions about what justice requires. But if judges make mistakes, and if error costs will be higher if judges favor width and depth, minimalism may be justified as a way of increasing rather than decreasing justice, and of increasing rather than decreasing the recognition of rights, properly understood.

It is not, however, clear that minimalism is the best way to reduce total error costs. Perhaps a wide rule, even if overinclusive and underinclusive, would be better than a narrow judgment, because lower courts and subsequent cases would generate an even higher rate of error. Perhaps a wide rule would be easily adaptable by private actors, and thus allow adjustments over circumstances, as in the basic rules of contract and tort. Perhaps a refusal to issue clear rules now would seem "wise" or "prudent," but would leave subsequent judgments to district courts whose decisions cannot be entirely trusted. Perhaps a maximalist Court can later change the rules if they turn out to be wrong; through this route it might be able to reduce the error costs of width and depth.

In this light it would be foolish to suggest either that minimalism is generally a good strategy or that minimalism is generally a blunder. Everything depends on contextual considerations. The only point that is clear even in the abstract is that sometimes the minimalist approach is the best way to minimize the sum of error costs and decision costs.

Reasonable (and Unreasonable) Pluralism

In a heterogeneous society, reasonable people disagree on a large number of topics. The phenomenon of "reasonable pluralism" is a defining characteristic of free societies.[3] Sometimes it is a source of great benefits; sometimes it is a source of serious problems, even violence. By bracketing the largest disputes, a minimalist court attempts to achieve a great goal of such a society: making agreement possible when agreement is necessary, and making agreement unnecessary when agreement is impossible. This goal is associated both with promoting social stability and with achieving a form of mutual respect.

We might compare the minimalist project to the basic idea of political liberalism. In John Rawls's formulation, political liberalism is intended to ensure that diverse people, operating from their own foundational accounts, can converge on a range of basic principles, thus making it possible to achieve an "overlapping consensus" on those principles.[4] Judicial minimalism has a great deal in common with political liberalism insofar as both are efforts to achieve both social stability and a degree of reciprocity, together with mutual respect, under conditions that threaten to endanger these important values. Incompletely theorized judgments allow people to live together amid intense disagreements. They also reflect that form of respect that is embodied in a reluctance to challenge the basic commitments of one's fellow citizens when it is not necessary to do so. Political liberalism has similar goals.

On the other hand, to do most of their work judicial minimalists need not take a stand for or against political liberalism. That form of liberalism, constituted as it is by a set of contentious abstractions, is less modest than minimalism as I understand it here. Often social life goes on among people who have no idea where they stand on political liberalism or who even disagree about its value and point. In the legal realm, the debates over political liberalism can usually be put to one side; for the most part judges are not obliged to choose between, for example, political and perfectionalist liberalism in the context of deciding cases. Hence judges' interest in accommodating pluralism leads them to seek incompletely theorized agreements on particular cases— agreements that may well leave open the deep disputes in political theory, including disputes between political liberals and their adversaries. Judicial minimalists know of course that some commitments are unreasonable; but in light of their awareness of their own limitations, they know that their judgments about who is reasonable may themselves go awry. Hence their desire to accommodate pluralism leads them in the direction of shallowness.

One of the goals of political liberalism, as Rawls understands it, is to put to one side many of the great debates in philosophy and to allow participants in political life to leave philosophy "as it is."[5] Minimalism has the same relation to the particular debate over political liberalism as political liberalism has to the great debates in philosophy. It attempts to leave that particular debate just "as it is." Of course some controversies may push judges in the direction of greater ambition. The basic point is that minimalism helps a society to deal with reasonable pluralism.

Cognitive Limitations, Bounded Rationality, and Unintended Consequences

In cognitive psychology, and increasingly in political science, economics, and law, attention has been given to the fact that people are boundedly rational—and sometimes aware of that fact. Information-processing can be extremely difficult. People use heuristics to simplify their tasks. But people also tend to be overconfident about their own knowledge and capacities. This overconfidence can lead them into trouble.

In particular, people often have difficulty in anticipating unintended bad consequences. A German psychologist, Dietrich Dorner, has conducted illuminating experiments designed to see whether people can engage in successful social engineering.[6] The experiments are run via computer. Participants are asked to solve problems faced by the inhabitants of some region of the world. The problems may involve poverty, poor medical care, inadequate fertilization of crops, sick cattle, insufficient water, or excessive hunting and fishing. Through the magic of the computer, many policy initiatives are available (improved care of cattle, childhood immunization, drilling more wells), and participants can choose among them. Once particular initiatives are chosen, the computer projects, over short periods and then over decades, what is likely to happen in the region.

In these experiments, success is entirely possible; some initiatives will actually lead to effective and enduring improvements. But most of the participants—even the most educated and professional ones—produce calamities. They do so because they do not see the complex, systemwide effects of particular interventions. For example, they may understand the importance of increasing the number of cattle, but once they do that, they create a serious risk of overgrazing, and they fail to anticipate that problem. They may understand the value of drilling more wells to provide water, but they do not anticipate the energy and environmental effects of the drilling, which then endangers the food supply. Only the rare participant is able to see a number of steps down the road—to understand the multiple effects of one-shot interventions in the system.

This is pervasively troublesome for government, which is generally faced with the task of intervening into systems in which everything is connected to everything else, and in which a one-shot intervention will affect a number of parts not likely to be on the official's viewscreen. Judges face these problems too. A right to physician-assisted suicide may seem attractive in principle, but a judicial declaration of such a right is in the nature of an intervention into a complex system of physician-patient-family interactions. The result of the intervention may be to decrease patient autonomy, with terrible consequences for the terminally ill (see Chapter 5). This is simply an illustration of the problems that judges face whenever they are asked to strike down a statute on constitutional grounds.

The best decision-makers take steps to counteract the difficulty posed by bounded rationality, including lack of knowledge of unanticipated adverse effects. Minimalism is a promising response, quite outside of the judiciary.[7] Within the judiciary, minimalism is a sensible reaction to the limitations that judges know they face, not least in predicting the consequences of their decisions. Indeed, minimalism and analogical reasoning[8] are closely allied on this count. Case-based decision-making is a perfectly ordinary response to limitations in cognitive capacity. More generally, shallow and narrow decisions have virtues insofar as they are responsive to judges' knowledge of their own limitations in processing information, including the information that would enable them to see and to evaluate the consequences of what they do.

Democracy

The final and perhaps most important point involves the relationship between minimalism and democracy. We have seen that one of the major advantages of minimalism is that it grants a certain latitude to other branches. It allows the democratic process a great deal of room in which to adapt to coming developments, to produce mutually advantageous compromises, and to add new information and perspectives to legal issues.

Return to a key example and assume that the Supreme Court is asked to decide that a certain attempt to regulate the Internet violates the First Amendment. The claim raises complex issues of value and fact, and the Court needs to have information on both values and facts before it lays down a broad rule. A narrow decision, pointing to a range of factors in a particular case, is a way of allowing breathing space for participants in the democratic process.[9] Or the Court might (if it can) strike down a law as unconstitutionally vague and in the process refuse to decide exactly how much regulation would be acceptable under a sufficiently clear law. Or suppose that the Court is asked to say that the equal protection clause requires states to recognize same-sex marriages. The Court might want to leave that issue undecided not only or not mostly because it (1) cannot reach a consensus or (2) lacks relevant information, but also because it is (3) not sure about the (legally relevant) moral commitments, (4) thinks that people may have a right to decide this issue democratically, or (5) believes that a judicial ruling could face intense political opposition in a way that would be counterproductive to the very moral and political claims that it is being asked to endorse.

If the Court may deny certiorari partly in order to take account of considerations of this kind, surely it can use minimalism for the same purpose. Minimalism is connected with democracy because it allows democratic processes room to maneuver. Judges should allow such room because they know that their judgments might be wrong and because they know that their judgments may be counterproductive even if right. This argument helps explain some prominent (and in my view convincing) objections to Roe v. Wade as originally written. In the Court's first confrontation with the abortion issue, it laid down a set of rules for legislatures to follow whenever that issue arose. The Court decided far too many issues too quickly. The Court should have allowed the democratic processes of the states more time to adapt and to deliberate, and to generate solutions that might be sensible but that might not occur to a set of judges. In this way the democratic argument for minimalism invokes the need for social adaptation over time and humility in the face of limited judicial capacities and competence.

Problems with Minimalism, Democratic and Otherwise

> Reviewing speech restrictions under fairly strict categorical rules
> keeps the starch in the standards for those moments when the daily
> politics cries loudest for limiting what may be said.
> —Denver Area Educational Telecommunications Consortium v. FCC
> (Justice Souter, concurring)

What might be said against minimalist judgments? A great deal, in law as in ordinary life. Minimalism is an appropriate course only in certain contexts. It is hardly a sensible approach for all officials, or even all judges, all of the time. It may even compromise democratic goals. I deal with the questions of width and depth in Chapters 9 and 10; for the moment a few general points will suffice.

As we have seen, the minimalist claims to reduce costs of decision and costs of error. And the minimalist especially invokes the need to allow room for democratic deliberation in the period between the case at hand and future cases, secure in the knowledge that new facts and perspectives may come to light. But we have found reasons to doubt all of these points. Decision costs may be low for the judge in the case at hand, but a narrow, shallow judgment in case A will lead to dramatically increased decision costs for judges in cases B through Z. Thus the minimalist judge may be shifting costs from her own court to others. The result may be to deprive participants in democratic processes of a clear background against which to work. The resulting problems may not be readily apparent to those deciding the single case, but they may be serious. Surely this is true, for example, in the contexts of homosexual rights and punitive damages, where the absence of clear standards for assessing the constitutional issue has produced enormous complexity in subsequent cases. Thus denials of certiorari may in the end greatly increase the strain on the legal system as a whole.

Nor is there any assurance that a narrow judgment in case A will produce lower aggregate costs from errors. (Recall that the term "costs" is not being used in any monetary or technical sense.) Perhaps the court in case A will be able to generate a rule, or a decent and relatively elaborate account of its judgment, and perhaps a minimalist judgment in case A will produce a range of mistakes in cases B through Z, as lower court judges struggle to make sense of case A. And if the rule in case A is a pretty good one, and if we lack confidence in the capacity of other institutions to produce a better one, we will get more rather than fewer errors through the minimalist route. This is a justification for the rule-bound approaches of Miranda v. Arizona (attempting to lay down clear rules governing confessions), United States v. Miller (attempting to lay down clear rules for obscenity), and Roe v. Wade (attempting to lay down clear rules governing abortion).

As we have also seen, an especially important problem comes from the need for planning. Minimalism might be threatening to the rule of law insofar as it does not ensure that decisions are announced in advance. With respect to many things, it is more important for people to know what the law is than for the the law to have any particular content.

What about democracy? If the concern is not the process but the substance—getting democracy's content right—it is possible that judicial minimalism will be all wrong. As I have suggested, democracy has its own internal morality, and from the standpoint of democracy, a set of nonminimalist judgments on the content of that morality would surely be best if those judgments are correct. A well-functioning system of free expression probably depends on a set of free speech principles that are wide whether or not deep. In any case there are problems with a situation in which participants in democratic processes stumble their way toward the (just) rule that courts could have adopted long ago. Thus enthusiastic democrats might well urge nonminimalist rulings as a way of ensuring adherence to the preconditions of democracy itself. Constitutions can themselves be understood as an effort to set out those preconditions.

Nor are things clear if we turn our attention to issues of process. Perhaps the relevant issue is one ill suited to democratic choice, either because the interest at stake ought to be judged off-limits to politics or because there is a problem in existing processes of democratic deliberation that prevents them from functioning well. Well-organized interest groups might be able to frustrate deliberative processes, perhaps by taking advantage of collective action problems faced by their adversaries. Perhaps this is so for constitutional issues relating to punitive damages, commercial advertising, and homosexual rights, where powerful private groups may be producing unreasonable legislation or blocking desirable change.

There are further problems. The absence of clear rules will deprive participants in democratic processes of a clear background against which to work. And clear rules—in the form of maximalist validations— may have a democracy-forcing feature. If the Court rules that punitive damages are always constitutional, or that the Constitution allows government to do as it wishes with respect to homosexuality, there may be greater pressure on Congress and the states to respond to the relevant problems. Maximalist validations may have the desirable function of pushing issues, and concerned groups, away from courts and toward democratic arenas. Thus maximalist invalidation is sometimes justified on democratic grounds, and the same is true for maximalist validation.

From these points it is clear that we cannot, in the abstract, decide whether and how much minimalism is appropriate. This is not a sensible question. The choice between minimalism and the alternatives depends partly on pragmatic considerations and partly on judgments about the capacities of various institutional actors. Of course we might reject minimalism, and favor rules, because we are convinced that the proposed rules are good enough, that they will reduce costs of decision, and that the alternatives will produce considerable error. Of course we could be confident in rejecting minimalism if the Supreme Court were excellent at developing both rules and theories, and if lower courts and other officials were very poor at both. If democratic processes are not deliberative and fail at compiling and using information, courts should feel less cautious about intruding into them. And of course minimalism would be the right course if the Court were generally error-prone and other institutions, deciding what the Court leaves undecided, would do much better. But none of these general conclusions can claim much support. More particular questions have to be asked about the settings in which leaving things open is an option.

When Minimalism? When Maximalism?

Despite these qualifications, some generalizations will be helpful. As a practical matter, minimalism may be the only possible route for a multimember tribunal, which may be incapable of bridging its many disagreements, and which may be able to converge only on a minimal ruling. If this is so, minimalism will be not so much desirable as inevitable. But it is worthwhile to attempt a broad and deep solution (1) when judges have considerable confidence in the merits of that solution, (2) when the solution can reduce costly uncertainty for future courts and litigants, (3) when advance planning is important, and (4) when a maximalist approach will promote democratic goals either by creating the preconditions for democracy or by imposing good incentives on elected officials, incentives to which they are likely to be responsive. Minimalism becomes more attractive (1) when judges are proceeding in the midst of (constitutionally relevant) factual or moral uncertainty and rapidly changing circumstances, (2) when any solution seems likely to be confounded by future cases, (3) when the need for advance planning does not seem insistent, and (4) when the preconditions for democratic self-government are not at stake and democratic goals are not likely to be promoted by a rule-bound judgment. It follows that the case for minimalism is not separable from an assessment of the underlying substantive controversies. If judges are convinced that same-sex schools always violate the Constitution, there may be little problem with a judicial judgment to this effect.

Consider in this regard Justice Breyer's remarkable opinion in the

Denver Area case. One of the issues on which the Court divided was whether Congress could grant cable operators "permission" to exclude indecent programming from the airwaves. Justice Thomas would have resolved this issue via a simple rule: since the relevant First Amendment rights are those of the operators, of course Congress could do this; Congress was merely giving operators permission that they would have had without government regulation. Justice Kennedy also urged a simple rule: strict judicial scrutiny should apply to any content-based law; the relevant law was content-based; and therefore it should be invalidated. The issue was tricky and both of these approaches were unsatisfactory. Even if Justice Thomas is right in his premise, it does not follow that a content-based permission is constitutionally acceptable: if Congress had granted cable operators the authority to exclude programming critical of the Congress, it would be acting unconstitutionally. Justice Kennedy overstates his argument: some content-based laws are permissible. Justice Breyer instead emphasized a set of factors. This regulation was based on content but not on viewpoint. It was designed to protect children, an important interest. It was reminiscent of a regulation upheld in a previous case,[10] and thus supported by an analogy. The regulation was permissive rather than mandatory. In any case it was relevant, even if not decisive, that without a regulatory system, programmers would have no guaranteed access to the operators' airwaves.[11]

Thus Justice Breyer avoided any rule and proceeded, in a democracy-permitting, minimalist way, via a somewhat unruly set of factors. Was this a mistake? The answer depends largely on whether the Court could have confidence in a more rule-bound opinion; such an opinion would conceivably have lower aggregate decision costs (because it would leave less uncertainty for future judges) and much lower error costs (because future judges would make mistakes and the rule-bound opinion would be by hypothesis pretty good), while at the same time promoting planning, as Justice Kennedy emphasized. But Justice Breyer's position was quite reasonable. This is not an area where an absence of a clear rule seriously interferes with private ordering; it is not as if the fundamental rules of contract and property are unclear. Some uncertainty about constitutional requirements is hardly devastating to cable operators and to lawmakers grappling with novel issues. In any case regulation of "indecent" programming in the new electronic media raises issues for which old analogies may (or may not) be treacherous. Technologies are changing very rapidly in a way that may bear on less restrictive alternatives (such as parental screening) and on the harms of such programming (giving more information on how much and how children are being affected). It is certainly sensible to think that the Court should at this early stage be cautious about possible rules and wait for later cases.

But let me venture a more general hypothesis. The case for minimalism is especially strong when the area involves a highly contentious question now receiving sustained democratic attention. In such areas, courts should be aware that even if they rely on their own deepest convictions, they may make mistakes; *Dred Scott* and *Lochner* are only the most famous illustrations. A mistake of this kind is hardly innocuous; its consequences may be disastrous and hard to correct. Even if the question is not one of constitutional morality, it may involve informational deficits that should prompt the Court to proceed minimally and to leave many issues open.

Of course the Court's resolution may be right, in the sense that the Court identifies the just result. But even if it is right, things may go badly wrong. The Court may not produce appropriate social reform even if it seeks to do so. There may be unintended adverse consequences (as we will see is possible in the context of the right to physician-assisted suicide). The Court's decision may activate opposing forces and demobilize the political actors that it favors. It may produce an intense social backlash, in the process delegitimating itself as well as the goal it seeks to promote. More modestly, it may prevent social deliberation, give and take, learning, compromise, and moral evolution over time. A cautious course—refusal to hear cases, invalidation on narrow grounds, democracy-spurring rulings—will not impair this process and should improve it.

Nothing I have said generates a full-scale argument on behalf of minimalism. If advance planning is important, or if the judges have confidence in a wide ruling or a theoretically ambitious argument, then minimalism is a mistake. The rules of contract and property are wide partly because of the need for planning. Brown v. Board of Education was wide because the Court was entitled to have confidence in a flat ban on segregation. United States v. Virginia was deep because by 1996 the Court had a good understanding of what underlies the prohibition on sex discrimination. By contrast, many of the most difficult issues in constitutional law cannot sensibly be resolved by rule. As we shall see, these points argue in favor of democracy-promoting minimalism; and they bear directly on the Court's role in cases involving affirmative action, homosexuality, gender, free speech, and the right to die. The whole topic cannot, however, be understood without a sense of minimalism's substance, and it is to that topic that I now turn.

4

Minimalism's Substance

Like everyone else, judges often use silence constructively. But every silence operates against a backdrop of actual decisions, ones that are being taken for granted and accepted by many or even all of those involved. Shallowness and narrowness work against a shared background, one that is along certain dimensions wide and possibly deep. If, for example, judges decide not to say whether same-sex education always violates the Constitution, they are simultaneously agreeing on a whole host of substantive matters: the institution of judicial review, the ban on legislation motivated solely by prejudice, the prohibition on racial classifications, the presumption in favor of most social and economic legislation, and so forth.

It is therefore important to distinguish between minimalist procedure and minimalist substance. In its procedural form—the major topic thus far—minimalism is designed to leave things open, to decide cases as narrowly as possible. The most enthusiastic minimalists try to bracket particular substantive contests; but some substantive issues are always being taken for granted. This is so even if those issues need not be taken for granted in principle, even if they have not been taken for granted in the past, and even if they may not be taken for granted in the future. And while procedural minimalists try to leave many fundamental issues undecided, different substantive commitments can produce different kinds of minimalism. An incompletely theorized agreement might be possible on any particular set of commitments; as we have seen, a strong free speech principle can command support from various different positions. But it is also easy to imagine minimalists of many different substantive stripes. A conservative minimalist might try to preserve what is essential to conservatism, but leave many important issues undecided, on the ground, for example, that for certain purposes the internal disputes among conservatives need not be resolved, or that it is unnecessary and unwise to decide particular contests between conservatives and their antagonists. A minimalist who is also a deliberative democrat would attempt to promote the "core" of that commitment.

We could even imagine liberal minimalism, socialist minimalism, Ku Klux Klan minimalism, libertarian minimalism, Aristotelian minimalism, communist minimalism, Nazi minimalism, and so forth. These various kinds of minimalists could try to produce narrow rather than wide decisions, and those who accept these ways of thinking might try to avoid a lot of theoretical depth. (On the current Court, Justice Sandra Day O'Connor might be understood as a relatively conservative minimalist, whereas Justice Ruth Bader Ginsburg is a somewhat more liberal one, though these terms are crude.) Of course some of these minimalisms would overlap a great deal while others would barely overlap at all. And it is easy to find, in history and in contemporary political orders (not to mention science fiction), many different forms of substantive minimalisms, embedding, in constitutional doctrine or political life, a set of agreed-upon (minimal) commitments, together with open areas ranging from violence to sharp contestation to peaceful indecision, whether judicial, political, or both.

Substantive minimalism, like its procedural cousin, is relative, not absolute. Justices Hugo Black and Antonin Scalia are substantive maximalists in the sense that Justice Black had, and Justice Scalia has, an elaborate understanding of the nature of the Constitution's substantive commitments. Justices Ginsburg and O'Connor are more minimalist in the sense that their understanding of the Constitution's undisputable minimal content is both narrower and less deeply theorized. But Justices Ginsburg and O'Connor have a far less minimalist understanding of the Constitution's core content than do judges in many emerging constitutional democracies, where the core is ill defined.

American law contains only relative minimalists, and no absolute ones. The most enthusiastic procedural minimalists in American law are committed to what many people around the world would consider a robust set of substantive commitments. In constitutional law, America's substantive minimalism is relatively wide, in the sense that it extends over a number of areas. There are also areas of depth; for example, the commitment to the ideal of the rule of law is fairly deeply theorized.

But along the dimension of depth, most substantive commitments have a minimalist feature too, for they are generally shallow, attracting support from a wide range of foundations.

What is especially noteworthy is that American constitutional law now embeds a distinctive set of underlying commitments. Of course there are many agreed-on constitutional commitments that do not directly involve rights (the composition of the House and Senate, the mechanisms for enacting law, the mode of electing the President). Many structural issues, involving separation of powers and federalism, contain a substantive core. Everyone agrees that Congress may not abolish the states, or give judicial power to its own staff, or transform the Secretary of State into an officer independent of the President. There is a large project, parallel to that attempted here, in tracing the minimalist and nonminimalist dimensions of the law of government structure; many of the debates described here appear there in other guises. It may even be possible to draw relevant distinctions. Perhaps structural issues require a greater degree of certainty, in general, than issues of individual rights—though minimalism has its role in both areas.

My major topic here, however, is not structure but individual rights, and in that setting it is not hard to describe minimalism's substance. In fact there appear to be ten basic commitments. The commitments are widely shared and judicially enforceable. They draw support from people with many different approaches to constitutional interpretation. They are supported by conservatives as well as by liberals, by people generally critical of an aggressive judicial role as well as by people hospitable to such a role. The substantive commitments of constitutional minimalism therefore belong in the same basic family as philosophical efforts to describe a well-functioning liberal polity's substantive "core."[1] Of course the precise identity of the core would require an extended statement, containing a range of qualifications. The core consists of incompletely specified abstractions, or of strong presumptions, rebuttable in unusual circumstances. But the statement to follow, brief though it is, captures most of the territory.

The Core

In outlining these commitments, my goal is descriptive, not evaluative. What is striking, and in its way inspiring, is the extent to which these minimal commitments, shared as they now are, also rank among the essential safeguards of a free people.

1. *Protection against unauthorized imprisonment.* The due process clause gives you the right not to be imprisoned unless the government can show that you have violated the law, and unless the government has given you a hearing to test the question whether you have in fact done what the government accuses you of doing. Any law, to qualify as such, must have gone through the democratic channels, and any hearing, to qualify as such, must be before an independent arbiter. In these crucial ways, Americans are protected against unauthorized punishment. Exceptions exist, but they are narrow.

2. *Protection of political dissent.* The core political right, in a free society, is the right to engage in political dissent. This means that government cannot punish people who have spoken against it. Constitutional doctrines have been developed to ensure that the government is not attempting to do something of this kind; these doctrines command widespread agreement and provide the uncontested backdrop against which harder First Amendment disputes arise. There are many disputes about the content of the free speech principle, but even people who disagree on a great deal agree that that principle provides great protection for political dissent. It follows that the government must generally show, at a minimum, a clear and present danger before it seeks to regulate speech that contains a protest or urges a point of view.

3. *The right to vote.* The Constitution provides no general right to vote. But the Fifteenth Amendment prevents states from denying the vote to African Americans; the Nineteenth Amendment does the same for women; and the equal protection clause has come to be understood to prevent states from discriminating with respect to the franchise. Thus the Supreme Court has both invalidated the poll tax and required a regime of one person–one vote; these decisions are well entrenched. With modest qualifications, the right to vote is a central part of minimalism's substance.

4. *Religious liberty.* The Constitution protects the "free exercise of religion," and it also prevents the government from "establishing" a religion. Taken together, these principles mean, at a minimum, that the government cannot favor or disfavor people because of their religious beliefs. It cannot restrict licenses or welfare benefits to Christians. It cannot deny food stamps to Jews or Buddhists. Religious beliefs cannot

be targeted as such. Religious practices can be restricted only pursuant to general, nondiscriminatory law.

5. *Protection against physical invasion of property.* Everyone agrees that under the Fifth and Fourteenth Amendments, the government must compensate people for physical invasions of their property. The precise extent of property rights is much disputed, so much so that we often lose sight of this simple and crucial point. The right against physical invasion of property obviously has an economic justification: people are unlikely to invest or to innovate if their property exists at the sufferance of the state. But the right has a political or democratic foundation as well. A right to continued ownership of property is an especially important way of ensuring a degree of independence from government. If your holdings can be taken at the state's whim, you are unlikely to be in a position to oppose the state. This idea was a central part of the framers' commitment to private property; if it is heard less often now, it is because the basic idea—government may not invade your property because you don't like government—is part of the Constitution's undisputed minimal content.

6. *Protection against police abuse of person or property.* A principal goal of a liberal constitution is to ensure that the police do not abuse their authority. This is especially important in light of the massive force that police officers have at their disposal, including the power to shoot people or to lock them up. Thus the Fourth Amendment, it is agreed, prevents the police from invading your home unless there is a special reason for government suspicion. It follows that unless there is such a reason, police officers cannot seize your person or your property against your will. These are substantial protections of liberty under law. Those who believe that the Supreme Court has given far too much protection to criminal defendants do not dispute these basic propositions.

7. *The rule of law.* The rule of law is a highly contested ideal. But it is easy to describe its minimal content.

a. *Clear, general, publicly accessible rules of criminal law laid down in advance.* The rule of law requires rules of criminal law that have a degree of *clarity*, in the sense that people need not guess about their meaning, and also *generality*, in the sense that they apply to classes rather than particular people or groups. The "rule of lenity" provides that in the face of ambiguity, criminal statutes will be construed favorably to the criminal defendant. This principle is an outgrowth of the requirement that laws be clear so as to provide notice. The ban on bills of attainder—measures singling out particular people for punishment—is a traditional requirement of generality.

Laws should be publicly accessible as well as clear and general. It follows that there is a ban on "secret law." Of course vague laws—banning, for example, "excessive" or "unreasonable" behavior—are unacceptable in the criminal context; they are akin to secret law in the sense that people are unlikely to know what they entail.

b. *Prospectivity; no retroactivity.* In a system of rules, retroactive lawmaking is disfavored, and it is banned altogether in the context of criminal prohibitions. The ban on ex post facto laws is the clearest prohibition on retroactivity. More modestly, American law includes an interpretive principle to the effect that civil laws will ordinarily apply prospectively. If the legislature wants to apply a law retroactively, it must do so unambiguously, and if it does so unambiguously, there is at least an issue under the due process clause.

c. *Official conformity to law; relationship between law on the books and law in the world.* If the law does not operate on the books as it does in the world, the rule of law is compromised. If there is little or no resemblance between enacted law and real law, the rule of law cannot exist. In many legal systems, of course, there is a split between what the law says and what the law is, and the split can be severe. The frequency of the phenomenon should not deflect attention from the fact that this is a failure of the rule of law; and it is universally agreed that officials in America cannot go beyond their statutory authority.

d. *Hearing rights and availability of review by independent adjudicative officials.* The rule of law requires a right to a hearing in which people can contest the government's claim that their conduct meets legal requirements for either the imposition of harm or the denial of benefits. Someone who is alleged to have committed a crime, or to have forfeited rights to Social Security benefits or a driver's license, is generally entitled to some forum in which he can claim that the legal standards have not in fact been violated. Ordinarily the purpose of the hearing is to ensure that the facts have been accurately found. There should also be some form of review by independent officials, usually judges entitled to a degree of independence from political pressures.

8. *No torture, murder, or physical abuse by the government.* A minimal requirement of the U.S. Constitution is that officials may not murder

people, torture them, or otherwise engage in physical abuse. Thus the Constitution embodies a ban on *official terrorism*. This principle is located in two main sources: the cruel and unusual punishment clause and the due process clause. Of course government can inflict pain on people by locking them up and in certain other ways, and it can even impose capital punishment under the appropriate circumstances; but torture is banned (there are disputes about the appropriate definition of that incompletely specified term), and any killing must be accompanied by legal authorization and a right to a hearing. Disputes about many large questions should not deflect attention from the existence of broad agreement on what stands on the constitutionally impermissible side of the line.

9. *Protection against slavery or subordination on the basis of race or sex.* What is the minimal content of the Constitution's equality principle? At a minimum, slavery is banned, and the equal protection clause means that the government cannot use law to subordinate people because of their race or gender. Government may not segregate people on grounds of race, or impose burdens selectively on people of a certain race, or deny African Americans benefits reserved to whites, or prevent women, because they are women, from receiving either employment or education. There are many disputes about the precise meaning of the equality guarantee. But those disputes operate in the midst of striking agreement about the minimal content of that guarantee.

10. *Substantive protection of the human body against government invasion.* The last few decades have produced a great deal of dispute about the content of any right to "privacy" and any free-floating right to "liberty." Does the Constitution protect a right to engage in consensual sexual behavior or to decide whether to live or die? These questions are contested; the varying answers are no part of minimalism. But constitutional minimalism has come to include at least a degree of protection of the human body against government invasion. It is generally agreed that under ordinary circumstances, the government may not sterilize you, or prevent you from having a child, or force you not to have an operation. Those who disagree with Roe v. Wade almost always accept these propositions.

These ten principles represent a remarkable achievement. They capture a widespread legal consensus in America; they also overlap a great deal with philosophical accounts of what justice requires. These accounts themselves span a wide range. Diverse forms of political thinking converge on such principles. And the principles can be supported not only by the secular liberal tradition, but by both religious and conservative thought as well, whether or not these stand as part of the liberal political tradition.

In the midst of our many substantive disagreements, we often miss the extent to which we share substantive commitments that have been violated by many countries in the twentieth century, including America itself—and indeed that are being violated by many countries right now, including, at times, America itself.

Extending, Reducing, and Elaborating the Core

If these principles operate as judicial minimalism's substantive core, does it follow that they have been recognized since the nation's founding, or that they will necessarily serve as all or part of the core in (for example) 2050? This is a question about the relationship between procedural and substantive minimalism. The answer, in brief, is: No and no. During the founding period, some of these principles did not exist; others were entirely unspecified; and there was no agreement of the sort I have described here on their minimal content. For example, there was no general or uncontested right to engage in political dissent, and the right against subordination on the basis of race and sex is a post–World War II creation, one that could not be said to be part of minimalism's substantive core until quite recently. As a part of judicial minimalism, the ban on racial segregation is a product of the 1950s and 1960s, and the ban on sex discrimination is more recent still.

It is inevitable that these commitments will be newly characterized and that other rights will be seen to be part of the core fifty years hence—and it is possible too that some of the rights just described will not be taken to be part of the core. Rights both enter and leave the core. In the early part of the twentieth century, for example, protection of rights of property and contract was far more expansive than it is now, and reasonable people might well have said that some of these rights were barely contested. Thus the core of constitutional minimalism contained both more and less in 1800 than in 1850, and it was different in 1900 from what it was in 1950, and there are significant differences between the core of 1999 and the core of a half-century before. Perhaps the Court will allow some part of the core to be reduced when public necessities appear to require it. Nor does it make any sense to say that an expansion or contraction is by itself a good thing; everything depends on the substance of the rights at issue.

How has this process of change occurred? Did the Court have to reject minimalist methods? These questions return us directly to minimalism in its procedural form. Those who are uncertain about procedural minimalism might well urge that constitutional rights have taken their impressive modern form only through some wide and deep rulings. But this is false, or at least much too simple. Convergence on these principles has occurred not through maximalism but through a process of case-by-case development, via close encounters with the facts of particular disputes. The principles did not emerge all at once. The broad right to political dissent, for example, was created largely through disputes in the middle of the century, producing a consensus on its behalf only in the 1960s. The current content of the right to protection of property is a twentieth-century phenomenon. The right to be free from subordination on the basis of sex is the most recent of all, emerging from a set of cases, many argued by Ruth Bader Ginsburg, yielding a general principle only in the last decade.

Disagreement

How do we, and how should we, handle the problem of disagreement about the Constitution's meaning? This question will receive considerable attention in subsequent chapters. At this stage two points are important. Much of constitutional law consists of reasoning with close reference to some part of the core; this is why analogical thinking lies at the heart of constitutional adjudication. A university engages in affirmative action or discriminates against homosexuals; has it violated the Constitution? That question will be answered partly by deciding whether these practices are similar to or different from the cases on which there is general agreement. Of course the process of analogical reasoning does not involve going "directly" from one case to another; it requires the identification of some principle by which cases might be united or distinguished. But the identification of that principle does not precede analogical thinking. The principle could not have been found without that way of proceeding, and it owes its "proof," or its convincing character, to how it accounts for the relevant judges' thinking about the cases that are being compared.[2] Analogical reasoning is frequently both shallow and narrow; it is an important part of minimalism in constitutional law.

There is also the normative question how to evaluate proposed changes in minimalism's substance. At any given point in time constitutional law will, of course, consist of a set of widely shared propositions together with a group of more contentious ones. Many existing rights extend beyond the minimalist list, and they command substantial current agreement, though not consensus, in the current legal culture. It should already be clear that I will be arguing here on behalf of a particular understanding and extension of the existing core, an understanding and extension founded on the ideal of deliberative democracy.[3] This is a book about constitutional law, not political philosophy, and I will not attempt to specify the foundations of that ideal, nor will I describe its content in much detail. In keeping with the minimalist spirit, I have suggested that one of the purposes of a well-functioning system of constitutional law is to support the internal morality of democracy. That morality calls for political equality, participation, reason-giving (or deliberation), and accountability (in the sense of responsiveness to the multiple voices of the public). Each of these notions can attract support from many points of view. Each of these notions can be specified in many different ways, minimalist and maximalist. Certainly we can connect these notions to the protections described above. Many of these basic rights fit securely within democracy's internal morality.

In its minimal form, the commitment to political equality bans exclusions, de jure or de facto, from the electoral process. This commitment is central to an appropriate understanding of free speech rights and rights in the electoral process. The commitment to political equality is also violated by measures that reflect an attempt to humiliate or to express contempt for fellow citizens. The commitment to reason-giving is a barrier against measures that are motivated by interest-group power, and that cannot be founded on public-regarding justifications. The minimal requirement of the equal protection clause is that legislation be justified in public terms. The requirement is mostly symbolic, but it is not only that, and in any case the symbol is extremely important, as a recognition of the nature, the limits, and the point of majority rule.

The commitment to accountability operates as an obstacle to the exercise of public power by people with insufficient connection to the electorate (including judges). This commitment calls for considerable concern about vague or open-ended statutes, on the ground that those statutes have not reflected sufficiently concrete judgments by people who are subject to voters. We will see that a minimalist court might bring the commitments of deliberative democracy to bear on a wide range of disputes. Thus a set of ideals that can command support from different starting points also has a degree of "bite" in disputed cases, helping to organize a form of democracy-forcing minimalism.

Outside of the area of deliberative democracy, however, I will argue that courts should play a cautious role—because they may make mistakes, and because when democracy is working well, there is far less reason to suppose that the political process should be disrupted. But to say this is to get ahead of the story; the argument is best made by reference to details.

Minimalism's Future

In any legal system, some form of procedural minimalism is likely to have a secure future. Courts know that there is much that they do not know, even when they do not know what they do not know. But some occasions and contexts pose special problems for minimalism, and hence courts can be pressed in the direction of width and depth. As we have seen, the case for width is strong when advance planning is valuable and when constraints on official discretion are important. The law of property and contract is an example. The case for depth gains strength when incompletely theorized agreements risk inconsistency or error, and when judges have reason for confidence in more ambitious rulings. Hence some cases become more rule-bound and more deeply theorized over time (consider the law of sex discrimination); other areas become less so with new facts and values (consider the law governing "takings" of private property—law that is, at this writing, highly ad hoc and from the theoretical point of view quite unambitious).

What about substance? There can be no doubt that the minimal commitments of constitutional law—the commitments to which all participants in the legal culture subscribe—will shift over time. Thus it is easy to imagine a legal culture in a Western nation in, say, 2100, that would include firm protection against destitution, or a right to education and employment, or a ban on high taxes, or protection of both commercial speech and freedom of contract, or safeguards against discrimination on the basis of disability and sexual orientation. Some or all of these might become part of minimalism's substance. There are many imaginable constitutional worlds. At various points in twentieth-century America, there have been tentative movements toward assimilating each of these rights to the minimalist core. Any good minimalist is well aware, however, of the hazards of prediction, and any judgment about the likely shape of a minimalist constitution is likely to run afoul of unexpected developments. Let us turn, then, to some details.

II

APPLICATIONS

5

No Right to Die?

The basic source of constitutional rights of "privacy" is the due process clause. Under current law, that clause is the basis for the right to use contraceptives, the right to have an abortion, and any rights of sexual autonomy.

The minimal content of the due process clause is, however, something very different: a right to a hearing before the government takes your life, your liberty, or your property. It is generally agreed that if the government wants to take your property or to confine you, it must afford you notice and a right to be heard. At the relevant hearing, you are entitled to contest the government's claims about the facts and also to argue that government officials have not adhered to the law. Much more controversially, due process has come to have "substantive" content—that is, the due process clause not only requires hearings, but also forbids the government from imposing certain burdens on people, even if it gives them a hearing before doing so.

It is tempting to say that this "substantive" due process is so controversial that it has no minimal content. Since this right is so closely identified with Roe v. Wade, it is not simple to say what its uncontroversial content is, if any. But even *Roe*'s critics tend to accept some minimal content to the idea of substantive due process; they usually agree that substantive due process now includes a right, under normal circumstances, not to be sterilized against one's will, or to be forced to have an abortion, or (perhaps) a right to use contraceptives at least within marriage. As we shall see, the great difficulty of specifying the minimal content of substantive due process is a major source of the problem in identifying the reach of that clause in contested cases.

New Dilemmas

All over the country, people with terminal illnesses are seeking to end their lives with the aid of a physician. Many such people suffer from hopeless conditions of increasing debilitation, sometimes accompanied by periods of excruciating pain.

It was inevitable that circumstances of this kind would raise constitutional questions. In 1996, two court of appeals decisions turned the "right to die"—more precisely, the right to physician-assisted suicide— into a key arena for the struggle to define the scope of fundamental rights under the due process clause. In Quill v. Vacco,[1] the Court of Appeals for the Second Circuit rejected the due process claim but held, somewhat astonishingly, that New York had acted "irrationally" and hence in violation of the equal protection clause because it prohibited physician-assisted suicide while simultaneously permitting the withdrawal of life-saving equipment. In Compassion in Dying v. Washington,[2] the Court of Appeals for the Ninth Circuit held straightforwardly that a prohibition on the right to physician-assisted suicide violates the due process clause. In Washington v. Glucksberg and its companion case, the Supreme Court of the United States reversed both of these decisions.[3] But it did so in a ruling that is far narrower and more complex than it seems.

In this chapter, I argue that the Supreme Court was right not to invalidate laws forbidding physician-assisted suicide. In good minimalist fashion, the Court left open the question whether people facing physical pain and imminent death may have such a right. The Court was right not to decide that question. When and if it is forced to do so, it should conclude that the state has sufficient reason to override the individual interest even in such extreme cases.

My basic claim is not primarily about substance, or about the appropriate nature of rights, but about institutional role: the Court should be wary of recognizing rights of this kind amid complex issues of fact and value, at least if very reasonable people can decide those issues either way, and if the Court cannot identify malfunctions in the system of deliberative democracy that justify a more aggressive judicial role. The issues presented by a right to physician-assisted suicide are especially well suited to a federal system, where appropriate experiments may be made, and where the experiments are likely to provide valuable information about underlying risks. It is particularly important that the issue of physician-assisted suicide is facing not neglect or indifference but intense discussion in many states. It is far too early for courts to preempt those processes of discussion, certainly if we consider the fact that there is no systematic barrier to a fair hearing from any affected group. Despite appearances, the Court's current doctrines reflect this point. Thus a general theme of this chapter is that many cases involving "fundamental rights"—including the key privacy cases and the key equal protection cases—are best seen not as flat declarations that the state interest was inadequate to justify the state's intrusion, but more narrowly as democracy-forcing outcomes, designed to overcome problems of discrimination and desuetude.

To present the argument in more specific and somewhat more technical terms, it does not seem especially controversial to say that the state needs a strong justification if it seeks to intrude on the decision of a competent adult to terminate his life under a medically hopeless and physically difficult situation. Five justices of the Court appear to have left this possibility open—though four justices, led by Chief Justice Rehnquist, would have foreclosed it. But it is extremely difficult to describe the standard for "fundamental rights"[4] that emerges from previous cases and to tell whether the right to physician-assisted suicide qualifies as "fundamental" under those cases. We might want to read current law to say that there is a presumptive right *against government intrusion into a decision whether to terminate one's life under hopeless conditions* or, alternatively and more broadly, a presumptive right *against nontrivial government-imposed intrusions into the physical space of one's own body*. In some cases the right to physician-assisted suicide certainly meets the former standard, and while it does not quite meet the latter—it is a right "to" invasion, not a right "from" invasion—that right should probably be taken as close enough to the established right in principle to qualify, under medically hopeless conditions, as "fundamental" for constitutional purposes. But—and this is the central point—the state has an array of strong justifications for intruding on that right. These justifications involve the risk of abuse by doctors and others and the danger that a right to physician-assisted suicide would, in practice, decrease rather than increase patient autonomy.

The state may believe, for example, that recognition of the right would allow people who are suffering from depression and distorted judgment to terminate their lives when their judgments cannot readily be trusted; that a right to physician-assisted suicide would ultimately lead to some number of unconsented-to deaths; that a right to physician-assisted suicide would discourage people from dealing more productively with their distress and with the fact of death; that the line between medically hopeless conditions and possible recovery can be thin in practice and that any right to physician-assisted suicide will produce some deaths that ought not to occur; that at least some doctors, carrying a great deal of authority and faced with multiple demands on their time, will present death as an option in such a way that some patients will have a hard time refusing; that some well-meaning families will impose irresistible pressures on terminal patients to "choose" death; or that any such right would have harmful effects on the performance and norms of the medical profession and perhaps of the citizenry in general. On some of these counts, the right to remove life-sustaining equipment is quite different from the right to physician-assisted suicide, because the latter creates far more serious risks of abuse. At least relevant in this regard is the fact that numerous doctors—aware of the underlying risks—appear to oppose a right to physician-assisted suicide. In these circumstances, the Supreme Court should decline to require a national solution.

There is a more general point in the background: freedom may not require respect for individual choices. In some circumstances, giving people a new choice may actually reduce their freedom, as when the new choice actually increases the authority of others, or when the new choice is accompanied by social norms that diminish liberty. In some cases, the ambiguous relation between choices and freedom weakens the argument that the due process clause requires respect for choice. When new choices can diminish freedom, there is special reason for the Supreme Court to be cautious about accepting abstract arguments about freedom as a basis for recognizing a constitutional right to choose.

This is not meant as a conclusive argument against physician-assisted suicide as a matter of public policy. Many of the individual cases present exceedingly powerful arguments for respecting the patient's wishes. A reader of those cases and the relevant literature may well conclude that in the end states should allow physician-assisted suicide—because strong autonomy interests favor the right, social and familial interests also support the right, the risks that trouble opponents of the right are not as severe as they appear, and those risks can be handled through procedural safeguards short of denying the right. It may be predicted that eventually some states and nations will indeed come to recognize a right to physician-assisted suicide under appropriate conditions, accompanied by procedural safeguards. What I am principally suggesting is that these claims do not support recognition of such a judgment as a matter of constitutional law.

Initial Clarifications

The "right to die" might be asserted in many diverse circumstances. Of course the term might refer to the interest in withdrawing life-sustaining equipment. The interest in doing so appears to have been recognized as having presumptive constitutional status in Cruzan v. Missouri,[5] in the sense that the state must come forward with a strong justification for intruding on that interest. In any case, many states allow citizens to decline medical treatment.

The distinction between the right to withdraw life-sustaining equipment and the right to physician-assisted suicide is problematic in many ways, but here I am speaking of cases that involve "active euthanasia" and not only the withdrawal of treatment. Consider the following possibilities, designed to give a sense of the range of factual contexts in which the right might be claimed. (1) A competent patient seeks death under conditions that are both medically hopeless, in the sense that the best medical judgment is that there is a fixed and relatively short time to live, and physically difficult and debilitating, in the sense that the patient will experience at least some intense pain.[6] (2) A competent patient might be seeking death under conditions that are medically hopeless but do not involve much physical pain. (3) A competent patient with a disease that will produce a long period of deterioration and a long span of life—Alzheimer's disease is the most familiar example—seeks to terminate her life at some stage before the deterioration becomes serious. (4) A patient may be unconscious or otherwise incompetent and also in a medically hopeless state; his family or guardian might seek death, with or without evidence that this would be the patient's desire. These might be called cases of nonvoluntary euthanasia, as distinguished from voluntary and involuntary euthanasia.

(5) A competent patient may be facing a severe medical problem. Though his condition is not utterly hopeless, he may seek death because he is generally depressed or no longer considers life worth living. (6) A patient may be facing a period of sustained medical difficulty; it is hard to know whether or not some improvement is eventually possible. His condition is therefore considerably better than in (5), but he seeks death because he no longer considers life worth living. (7) Any of the above conditions might involve a person who seeks death not with the assistance of a physician but with the assistance of a friend or family member.

These various situations present quite different issues. In case (4), there is a question about whether we have sufficient reason to believe the third party's judgment about the patient's desires. In case (5), the problem is not so different from that of ordinary suicide: the patient has some decent life prospects but nonetheless seeks to terminate his life. In some of the highly publicized recent cases, many involving Dr. Jack Kevorkian, it has been feared that doctors have brought about death simply because the patient is suffering from intense depression. Case (6) is close to case (5), with even more features of ordinary suicide. In case (7), we may fear that medical judgments are playing an insufficiently large role in the outcome, that the case is in that sense very close to ordinary suicide, or that there is too large a risk of abuse because of the absence of professional norms and professional involvement.

For present purposes, let us accept the following propositions. First, it can sometimes be hard to know, in the real world, whether a particular case qualifies as (1), (2), (3), (4), (5), or (6). The difficulty of making such distinctions bears on the desirability of a constitutional ruling: if apparent category (1) cases actually fall in category (6), perhaps a flat ban on physician-assisted suicide, accompanied by the good-faith exercise of prosecutorial discretion (through which prosecutors ensure against arrests and indictments in the most excusable cases), makes a good deal of sense. Second, the state has a legitimate reason to make sure that any third party representation about the patient's wishes is actually reliable. When the patient has not consented, we have involuntary euthanasia, and it is safe to assume that the state has an especially strong interest in ensuring against involuntary deaths.

Third, and perhaps most importantly and more controversially, let us assume that there is no constitutional barrier to laws forbidding ordinary suicide and ordinary assisted suicide, and hence that in categories (5) and (6) there is no constitutional problem. Let us accept this conclusion partly because of existing precedent and partly as a matter of principle. Any state has extremely strong interests in encouraging a general commitment to the continuation of life and in protecting people from engaging in behavior that may be myopic or a product of short-term depression or distortions in judgment. Some of the strongest cases for public interference with private judgments involve myopia (a focus on the short term), cognitive mistakes (a failure to process information accurately), motivational error (as in wishful thinking, a belief that X is true because of a desire that X be true), or similar distortions.[7]

It is easy to imagine cases in which people facing severe temporary (or not so temporary) distress are inclined to seek a way out, and there is extremely good reason for social norms—and laws both expressing and fortifying social norms—discouraging such people from terminating their lives. Suicide may seem the only solution to the experience of intolerable suffering, perhaps occasioned by some disastrous or life-transforming event (death of a loved one, involuntary separation, divorce, discovery of a serious or fatal illness); but the suffering may be far more short-term and far more remediable than it seems. People can be remarkably resilient, no matter how intense short-term distress may seem; what once appeared a reason to die may seem, a few months later, part of the path to recovery.

In these circumstances, the norms directed against suicide and assisted suicide have a salutary function in encouraging people to deal with even the most severe problems in an ultimately more constructive fashion. Part of the salutary function of the relevant norms and laws is to block serious thought of suicide in cases where it appears to be the only or the simplest solution. This "blocking" operates against two classes of people: those who might be tempted to commit suicide and those who might be tempted to help other people to commit suicide. In fact, it is possible that in many cases those who are "assisting" suicide are actually urging or at least legitimating it. A decent society seeks to inculcate a strong norm in favor of preserving life even when things seem extremely bad. It does so especially in view of the fact that suicide appears to be remarkably contagious. It is well established that highly publicized suicides can create bandwagon or cascade effects.[8] These are not points in favor of a judicial insistence that suicide should be banned; they merely suggest that the Court should not invoke the abstract idea of "free choice" as a basis for invalidating democratically enacted laws.

Of course we can also imagine cases in which a suicide may be warranted and in which assistance in suicide is morally acceptable and perhaps morally responsible, even in category (5). But actual criminal prosecutions are quite unusual; the principal effect of these laws is to reflect and fortify norms. Even if there are some such prosecutions, the relevant laws are generally acceptable on constitutional grounds, in the sense that they are acceptable in the vast bulk of the cases to which they apply. That proposition is sufficient for my purposes here. I will deal, then, principally with cases falling in categories (1) and (2), for these are the most insistent ones for a constitutional "right to die."

An additional point by way of clarification: medical practice will operate in the shadow of the law and will be influenced by the law without, however, simply tracking the law. Thus a legal system lacking an actual or formally recognized "right to die" may well make space (even quasi-official space) for physician judgments about whether to prolong life or hasten death in some quiet, not widely advertised way, usually made in close consultation with the patient and family members. For example, a doctor may administer painkillers that will make death come sooner; allow a patient not to take life-sustaining medicines or even food and water; or avoid "extraordinary" measures. The line between these steps and physician-assisted suicide seems thin and it is undoubtedly breached in practice. In fact, patients often exercise an informal "right to die" no matter what the law may say.

Of course the technical illegality is important; no one should feel entirely comfortable in committing an unlawful act. But the fact that social practice can outrun law is important for courts to keep in mind; it suggests that informal practice may already be creating a right where it is especially insistent, even if the law is otherwise. The content of law depends not merely on the statute books but also on prosecutorial practice, and it is safe to say that in many cases prosecutors do not and will not devote their limited resources to the most benign cases of voluntary active euthanasia. The availability of informal practice and informally agreed-upon "rights" should relieve some of the pressure for a constitutional guarantee,[9] at least if it appears that those rights will be recognized in some or many cases in category (1) and (2) contexts. With these notes let us now turn to the constitutional issue.

A Fundamental Right?

Under the Court's cases, the first question is whether the right to die, understood as a right to physician-assisted suicide in category (1) and (2) cases, qualifies as a "fundamental right" or "liberty interest," such that a state must show an especially strong reason for interfering with it. My ultimate suggestion is that the Court would have done best to assume, without holding, that the relevant right so qualifies. The best reading of the outcome in the Supreme Court in Washington v. Glucksberg is that the Court did precisely this. Although Chief Justice Rehnquist's opinion for a five-justice majority attempted to resolve the question in a decisive way, by saying that no fundamental right exists, Justice O'Connor, a member of that majority, bracketed the issue in her separate opinion. Justice O'Connor saw "no need to reach" the "narrower question whether a mentally competent person who is experiencing great suffering has a constitutionally cognizable interest in controlling the circumstances of his or her imminent death."[10] Justices Stevens, Souter, Ginsburg, and Breyer also refused to foreclose the possibility of a successful constitutional claim in such circumstances. Thus a majority of the Court proceeded in minimalist fashion and left that question undecided.

For purposes of ruling on the right to die, the discussion to follow is in a sense gratuitous. If the state has an adequate justification for intruding on a fundamental right, it is unnecessary, to resolve a case, to decide whether the right at issue is fundamental. In Washington v. Glucksberg, the Court should have put to one side the extraordinary complexities and proceeded directly to the issue of justification; indeed five justices appeared to do precisely that. But the underlying issue is important, difficult, and of great intrinsic interest, and if the Court is ultimately to answer the question, I suggest that it should conclude that the right to physician-assisted suicide is, in the most pressing cases, presumptively protected either (a) because there is a presumptive right to choose whether to live or die under medically hopeless conditions or (b) because the cases establish a presumptive right to prevent physical invasions of one's own body, and the right to physician-assisted suicide is close enough to this established right to qualify as presumptively protected as well.

The source of the doctrinal difficulty is that the Court has not—to say the least—given clear criteria for deciding when a right qualifies as a liberty interest. The cases leave a great deal of ambiguity and the doctrine lacks much coherence. Consider a number of relevant decisions (see Table 5.1).[11]

One feature of these cases is their (sub)minimalism; indeed, this is part of the problem, for highly particularistic rulings may be inconsistent and add up to no identifiable set of propositions for future use. Is it possible to make sense of this set of results? There are two common ways of reading the cases. One reading is that the Court has issued a firm "no more!" and is unwilling to recognize additional fundamental rights unless it finds specific and extremely strong recognition in Anglo-American traditions. This is the argument that Chief Justice Rehnquist appeared to accept for a majority of the Supreme Court in Washington v. Glucksberg. The other reading is that the cases should be taken to establish a presumptive right to noninterference with decisions that are "highly personal and intimate," especially if those decisions involve the use of one's body. Justice Souter's separate opinion in *Glucksberg* moved in this general direction, though in a highly qualified way.

Unfortunately, neither of these (nonminimalist) readings holds out much promise; both are far too crude. As we will see, the "no-more-except-for-tradition" reading does not fit the cases very well, and it also lacks much appeal in principle. But the terms "personal" and "intimate" are far too broad; they create too many ambiguities and lead in too many unhelpful directions.

Tradition

On occasion influential justices and the Court as a whole have said that fundamental rights, under the due process clause, qualify as such largely because of their origins in Anglo-American traditions, understood at a level of considerable specificity.[12] This was a theme of Chief Justice Rehnquist's opinion for the Court in *Glucksberg*, though Justice O'Connor's separate and narrower opinion draws its status into doubt. A central goal of due process traditionalism is to make the law wider

Table 5.1

	Qualifies as fundamental liberty interest	Does not qualify as fundamental liberty interest
Use of contraceptives	Griswold v. Connecticut; Eisenstadt v. Baird	
Access to contraceptives	Carey v. Reproductive Serv.	
Abortion	Roe v. Wade	
Heterosexual sodomy	?? (Bowers v. Hardwick)	?? (Bowers v. Hardwick)
To prevent compulsory sterilization	Skinner v. Oklahoma (equal protection fundamental right)	
Homosexual sodomy		Bowers v. Hardwick
Avoidance of life-saving medical treatment and artificially delivered food and water	Cruzan v. Director, Missouri Dep't of Health	
Avoidance of administration of antipsychotic drugs	Washington v. Harper	
Paternal visits to child conceived out of wedlock		Michael H. v. Gerald D.
Live with family members	Moore v. City of East Cleveland	
Live with friends		Village of Belle Terre v. Boraas
Marriage	Loving v. Virginia; Zablocki v. Redhail (equal protection fundamental right)	Califano v. Jobst

and more rule-bound and also theoretically deeper; this goal is the source of the appeal, and the defects, of due process traditionalism.

Let us for the moment assume that due process traditionalism is right. If the right to physician-assisted suicide must emerge from such traditions, the case is relatively simple: there is no such right. The right to physician-assisted suicide is not something that Anglo-American law traditionally protects. Of course suicide and assisted suicide have been banned by tradition. Perhaps we could say that Anglo-American practice with respect to suicide is complex, not simple, because enforcement has often been lacking and because physician-assisted suicide is a novel phenomenon; perhaps we could say that tradition yields no clear judgment that suicide is to be banned in the distinctive circumstances we are describing. But even if this is true, and hence the tradition does not speak with clarity, it would be implausible to suggest that our tradition affirmatively supports a right to terminate one's life with the help of a doctor. From the standpoint of Anglo-American traditions, a ban on the use of contraceptives within marriage may well count as anomalous; so too with a ban on the right of a grandparent to live with her grandchild; but the same cannot be said about the right to physician-assisted suicide.

If the right to die must be rooted in tradition, then, the Court was right to say that it cannot qualify as a fundamental interest. But there are severe problems with defining fundamental interests solely by reference to tradition, specifically described. The first problem is that many of the Court's cases cannot be understood in purely traditionalist terms, and hence the traditionalist understanding of the privacy cases fits poorly with existing law. Roe v. Wade is the clearest example; there is no clear tradition establishing a right to abortion. But this is not true only of abortion. From the standpoint of tradition, a large number of the Court's cases make little sense. The cases establishing a right to contraceptives outside of marriage do not vindicate a long-standing tradition. Nor is there any general right to marry within Anglo-American traditions; hence Loving v. Virginia, striking down a ban on interracial marriage under the due process clause, and Zablocki v. Redhail, recognizing a fundamental right to marry, fit poorly with due process traditionalism. Traditions, taken at a level of specificity and as brute facts, do not support the right to physician-assisted suicide; but they also explain few of the key cases, and hence traditionalism does not make sense of existing law.

Should the Court consider its own decisions doubtful and use traditionalism in the future notwithstanding its inconsistency with past decisions? This course has considerable support within the Court; it is suggested by the Court's opinion in Washington v. Glucksberg, the plurality opinion in Michael H. v. Gerald D., and Bowers v. Hardwick. And such a course might be deemed reasonable if traditionalism was extremely appealing in principle and if the alternatives were unacceptable. Perhaps a firm "no more!" would make sense despite its failure to fit with existing law; the Court's own cavalier treatment of its precedent implies a judgment of this sort. But if we assume that at least some kind of substantive due process is legitimate,[13] as all of the justices appear to assume, we will find large problems with using traditions, narrowly and specifically conceived, as the sole source of rights under the due process clause. To be sure, such a use of tradition does help to discipline judicial discretion, and that is an important gain, as a source of width. The minimalism of the existing substantive due process cases is a genuine problem insofar as it allows judges so much room to maneuver. And if traditions were extremely reliable as sources of rights, and if judges thinking more independently about the appropriate content of rights were systematically unreliable, due process traditionalism might be justified on balance. That is, due process traditionalism might be justified as a way of minimizing the costs of decision and aggregate judicial errors even if it were quite imperfect as a source of rights.

But this is not a very plausible view, for there is no reason to think that traditions, understood at a level of great specificity, are systematically reliable or so close to systematically reliable as to exclude a somewhat more reflective and critical judicial role. Anglo-American traditions include a great deal of good but also significant confusion and injustice (consider, for example, bans on racial intermarriage); it is sensible for courts to engage in at least a degree of critical scrutiny of intrusions on liberty even if those intrusions do not offend tradition. Nor is there sufficient reason to think that judges will inevitably do very badly if they think critically about rights.

Of course judges should be very cautious about rejecting judgments made by elected officials; of course judges should avoid hubris in examining the past. Certainly it is plausible to think that judges should generally proceed incrementally and in good common law fashion from previous decisions. It also makes sense to say that substantive due process should be used sparingly, because of its uncertain textual basis and because of the unreliability of judicial judgments about which rights should qualify as fundamental. Understandings of this kind provide important constraints on judicial power under the due process clause. But at the very least it is appropriate for courts to ask whether the interest said to qualify as a fundamental right is, in principle, at all different from rights that have been sanctified by tradition. If, for example, there were no relevant difference, in principle, between a traditionally unrecognized right to physician-assisted suicide and (let us suppose) a traditionally recognized right to resist treatment, courts should not say that the latter is constitutionally protected and the former is not.

Dignity, Bodily Integrity, Intimacy

If tradition is not decisive, what is the source of fundamental rights for purposes of substantive due process? Even the most enthusiastic minimalists will insist on some kind of answer. Terms such as "intimate" and "personal" provide little help. They tend to be conclusions masquerading as analytic devices. In any case, some of the cases deny protection to interests that seem highly intimate and highly personal; consider both *Hardwick* and Village of Belle Terre v. Boraas. Thus the Court's cases refuse to accept the view that intimate and personal decisions deserve constitutional protection as such.

Putting previous cases to one side, we can see that some decisions that seem intimate and personal are not strong candidates for constitutional protection; consider the decision to work longer than the maximum-hour laws allow in order to provide for one's family, the decision to take medicines or drugs of a certain sort, the decision to marry one's cousin or aunt, or for that matter the decision to commit suicide. There is good reason to think that the Constitution does not protect these decisions, however intimate and personal they appear. Thus a reference to "intimacy" or "control of one's body" seems unhelpful. Many people, and at least one lower court, have placed emphasis on the interest in promoting death "with dignity." There is indeed a strong political argument for a right to physician-assisted suicide grounded in this concern. But it is unclear what the notion adds to the due process argument.

Life and Death Decisions

As we shall see, the relevant cases seem to depend not simply on deciding that an interest has considerable importance, but also on at least implicit problems of procedural due process or equal protection, problems that suggest an underlying defect in democratic processes themselves. And it is extremely difficult to produce any verbal formula that is satisfactory, consistent with current law, and adequate to resolve the issue of physician-assisted suicide. For this reason, the best and appropriately minimalist route is for the Court simply to assume that the right qualifies as fundamental and to proceed from there to the question of justification. We have seen that though Chief Justice Rehnquist rejected this route, five justices appeared to leave it open as a possibility.

But if the Court had wanted to be more ambitious, it could have ventured a plausible alternative, and it may well be asked to do this in the future. The Court might say very narrowly that *Cruzan* should be read to recognize a presumptive right *to make a choice about whether to live or die when one is in pain and suffering a medically hopeless condition.* Such a right would recognize that this choice is as central to individual self-determination as any in previous cases and indeed as any that one can imagine; it might be buttressed with the suggestion that it is for the individual, not the state, to decide when and how life has value. If conditions are medically hopeless, moreover, it is harder to say that a state prohibition helps counteract individual irrationality. The existence of such a right would be important not only for people who are now dying but also for people not facing such conditions, who would be able to rest secure that if their condition becomes unbearable, they will have the power to end it. Thus the Court might put to one side the issues raised by "dignity" and "intimacy" and rely instead on the narrower interest in self-determination—under the extremely unusual circumstances of imminent death—as the source of constitutional doctrine. The Court might conclude that whatever may fall in that category, the right to die when one is facing a terminal illness certainly does so. Such a right would also recognize that it is hard, in principle, to distinguish between withdrawal of life-saving equipment and category (1) and (2) cases (if we put to one side the risks of abuse discussed below; those risks go not to the question whether there is a right in the first instance, but to the separate issue whether government has an adequate justification for intruding on the right).

A narrow right of this kind would avoid many of the problems created by a general right to suicide. Recall that so general a right coexists most uneasily with tradition; that from the standpoint of both precedent and principle, it is not clear that when the conditions are not narrowly defined, the right should qualify as such in light of the role of short-term pressures in many imaginable cases; and that such a right can clearly be countered by strong government justification. A large advantage of defining the presumptive right in this way is that it would avoid the various puzzles created by any broader reading of the privacy cases. But there are difficulties with such a definition. The term "medically hopeless" is vague, the notion of "self-determination" leaves many open questions, and the line between terminal and nonterminal illnesses can be indistinct in practice. Thus it is better to avoid this question if it is possible to do so.

Bodily Invasion

Suppose that the Court eventually seeks to introduce somewhat more order to the cases. It could find a principle of some appeal, and considerable consistency with the cases, if it said that there is a presumptive right against *government imposition of nontrivial physical invasions of a person's body*. A government imposition may arise because the law authorizes invasions by government officials or because law forbids people from fending off physical invasions by private persons. This basic idea—intended as a statement of a sufficient, if not necessary, condition for a fundamental interest—explains the notion that people have a presumptive right to resist the involuntary administration of drugs. It accounts for the widespread intuition that there would be serious constitutional issues if the government undertook medical experiments on people against their will or required them to have operations for what it considers their own good. It helps account for *Cruzan* as well, though the Court did not announce a general right against physical invasions of a person's body.

Less obviously, the standard helps explain both Roe v. Wade and the cases involving governmental efforts to prevent people from diminishing risks of pregnancy, at least if we understand such cases in a certain way. In these cases, the government is preventing people from taking steps to prevent a physical invasion of their bodies via pregnancy. The key point, then, is that a pregnancy is (a kind of) a physical invasion, and if the government wants to prevent people from fending off that invasion, it needs a special justification.[14] A particular advantage of the standard is that it helps explain why the Court has struck down laws involving contraception and abortion without saying that there is a right to engage in sexual activity as such; the Court has been careful to say that the Constitution does not prohibit laws forbidding fornication and adultery, and it has restricted its holdings to efforts to control fornication and adultery by creating a risk of pregnancy. The suggested standard thus distinguishes Bowers v. Hardwick, the Georgia sodomy case, on the ground that there is no prohibition on the regulation of sexual conduct if pregnancy and childbirth are not at risk. In any event, the standard seems to provide a sufficient if not necessary condition for constitutional concern; there do not appear to be any cases that fail to find a constitutionally protected interest in cases in which the standard is met.

Of course this standard does not answer all imaginable questions— it is both incompletely specified and incompletely theorized—and this fact argues against its judicial adoption in a case that does not require the Court to attempt to make sense of its privacy doctrine, which, as I have stressed, consists of a number of incompletely theorized judgments not easily reconciled with one another. The notion of "physical invasion" is vague. We can start with core or defining cases in which government official or private actors are authorized literally to invade bodily space—Cruzan and Washington v. Harper are examples—but hard questions can easily be imagined. (What about a ban on human cloning?) Some of the modern due process cases finding fundamental rights do not meet the standard; the right to marry and the right to live with one's grandchild are examples. Moreover, I have not explained what is special about the physical invasion of one's own body. The best answer might begin with an understanding of the time-honored nature of that right in Anglo-American law; tradition affords a special place to the individual's right to prevent invasion of his body. Certainly the right to self-defense can be understood in these terms. Even if tradition is not decisive, for reasons suggested above, it plainly matters under existing law, and it tends to support the right described here. Tradition aside, a right to protection of one's body against unwanted external intrusion can be defended in principle: from childhood on, such a right provides the most primitive and basic sense of personal security and independence. In this way, the right to prevent physical invasions can be seen as the most central and defining case of a series of familiar rights, including the right to private property itself.

How does this standard bear on the right to physician-assisted suicide? Understood narrowly, the standard seems not to create any such right. In such cases, the state is attempting to *prevent* a physical invasion. It is not itself undertaking a physical invasion, or making it impossible for people to stop a physical invasion from other private parties. Instead, the government is attempting to forbid people from allowing their bodies to be physically invaded. Thus the suggested standard seems to create a right to withdraw life-saving equipment without creating a right to physician-assisted suicide. With this point we come to some serious conceptual issues, involving perhaps intractable distinctions between actions and omissions. Does it make sense to say that people have a constitutional right to resist physical invasions without also saying that they have a constitutional right to bring about physical invasions? In other words, we might say that the former implies the latter, so that people have *a presumptive right to decide whether or not their bodies will be physically invaded.* A strong commitment to autonomy might well lead in this direction. But this idea seems far too broad as a matter of both settled law and basic principle. It would draw into question, for example, much of the activity of the Food and Drug Administration, which is precisely in the business of deciding what sorts of things may be ingested. Much criminal law also forbids people from allowing certain invasions of their body; consider laws forbidding use of addictive substances. The broader standard also appears to imply a very broad right to sexual autonomy, extending far beyond existing doctrine. We may conclude that the right to *prevent* physical invasions has some appeal but has the disadvantage of leaving open many questions, while the right to *decide whether to allow* physical invasions lacks both consistency with precedent and much appeal on the merits.

Summary and Alternatives

From these points, we can see that several alternatives were available to the Court in Washington v. Glucksberg, and are available to the Court in future confrontations with an asserted right to physician-assisted suicide.

First: The Court might say quite narrowly that there is, under narrowly defined circumstances, a presumptive right to decide whether one will continue to live. The question then would be whether the state has sufficient justification to override that right.

Second: The Court might hold that its decisions essentially involve a right to prevent physical invasions and do not extend to other kinds of decisional autonomy, even when the body is directly involved. But this approach has the disadvantage of failing to account for some key cases; it also remains to explain why so sharp a distinction should be drawn between removing life-sustaining equipment and administering a drug that hastens death. As we shall see, a distinction of this kind is reasonable if we focus on the potential for abuse; but at the level of presumptive rights, it is much harder to defend. In any case, it seems odd to say that this vexed and controversial distinction can support the momentous difference between rational basis review and something like the "compelling interest" standard.

Third: Still more ambitiously, the Court might come to say that the cases recognize a presumptive right to protection against physical invasion of one's body. It might add that it is not easy, in principle, to distinguish between the right to prevent bodily intrusions and the right to physician-assisted suicide, because that latter right is so obviously central to a person's most fundamental and apparently self-regarding judgments about the ultimate direction of his life, and because it is hard to explain why a person should have a constitutionally protected interest in withdrawing life-saving equipment without also having such an interest in terminating his life through "more active" means. On this view, the state must therefore meet a severe burden if it seeks to intrude on those judgments.

Fourth and simplest: The Court might say, quite explicitly, that it need not decide whether the right to physician-assisted suicide qualifies as fundamental for constitutional purposes, and proceed from that point to assess the state's justifications. As noted, Chief Justice

Rehnquist did attempt to decide the question, and resolved it nega-
tively; but five justices appeared to take this basic route.

Because of the difficulties associated with the three alternatives, probably it was best for the majority of the justices, and will be best in the
future, to take the fourth route, to assume that the right to physician-
assisted suicide qualifies as fundamental, and to proceed from there with
the issue of justification.

State Justifications

Suppose that the right to physician-assisted suicide does or is assumed
to qualify as a liberty interest for constitutional purposes. From this
point it should not be concluded, in mechanical fashion, that any state
intrusion is unacceptable. It would be more sensible to say, as the Court
did in Adarand Constructors, Inc. v. Pena, that "strict scrutiny" need
not be "fatal in fact."[15] On this view, the state must produce a strong
demonstration that the interference is reasonable, without necessarily
persuading the Court to agree with the enacting legislature. Does the
state have a sufficient reason to interfere with that interest? There are
several possible grounds. I outline them here, not to endorse them as
a matter of policy, but to suggest what reasonable people might say on
behalf of the ban on physician-assisted suicide.

1. *Depression and distorted judgment.* People who are in intense pain
or emotional distress, and who face a bleak future, may well be unlikely
to think well. They may be deeply depressed or myopic; short-term
distress may overwhelm their judgment. We could easily imagine that
people who are or appear to be terminally ill might well, much of the
time, be facing the equivalent of duress. In these circumstances, a right
to die might be denied as a way of protecting people against their own
distorted judgment. As I have suggested, the ban on suicide itself is
best justified in these terms. It is intended to signal the gravity of the
act and the importance of self-preservation, with an understanding that
people might, under the stress of extremely difficult times, be tempted
to end their lives.

When people's prospects are uncertain—when they face at best a
possible future—this argument has considerable force. It appears
weaker if we are dealing with genuine category (1) cases—in which,
say, a patient faces six months of deterioration and almost certain death

thereafter. Thus we might conclude that the argument from distorted judgment does not justify state interference in such cases. But in practice, those cases can be hard to separate from other, quite different cases, and the difficulty of separating them argues in favor of a general prohibition. In any case, it is relevant that current medical technology allows a wide range of means by which to reduce or eliminate intense pain.

There is a related issue. Sometimes physician-assisted suicide may seem the easiest way to deal with extreme and understandable distress, but in many of these cases, there are more productive alternatives, which may lead patients to deal better with their fears. People who face medically difficult circumstances and a bleak prognosis may (like anyone else facing a difficult life event) seek the simplest solution, even though a more difficult, even arduous approach may enable them to find some degree of resolution. There are cases in which physician-assisted suicide appears to have impeded this process; it seems to have encouraged people to respond to their distress through death rather than through seeking assistance from professionals or loved ones.

On this view, a prohibition on physician-assisted suicide is not so different from the general ban on suicide. It is part of an effort to see death as a part of life—to encourage distressed people and their families to come to terms with their fears, including the fear of death, in a way that can be productive, and to ensure that distressed, sick, or dying people are not treated, and do not treat themselves, as objects to be eliminated from the scene.

2. *Protecting the patient against external pressure from family and friends.* A ban on physician-assisted suicide may seem to intrude on the autonomy of the patient; this is in fact the strongest argument against the ban. Ironically, however, the ban may have the opposite effect and in that way increase patient autonomy. A vulnerable person, with perhaps a short time to live, might well be subject to various psychological pressures from family, certainly if (as is likely) family members are feeling great distress and also if (as is possible) nontrivial sums of money are at stake. The closing stages of life can, in short, create conflicts of interest between patient and family members. The patient may wish to live as long as possible; family members may believe that this is a situation of great tragedy, difficulty, and expense, and that it will be much better when it is over. Of course we can imagine situations in which

the patient freely agrees with the family on this point. But it is also possible to foresee situations in which the patient, having been granted a "right to die," bows to the family's wishes and hence very much regrets the fact that he has that right. Perhaps this is an acceptable situation. But since it is after all the patient's life that is on the line, we can imagine reasonable people thinking that the right to die should be rejected because it actually threatens to decrease patient autonomy in too many cases.

3. *Protecting the patient against pressure from physicians.* Suppose that a patient is confronted with a list of options from a doctor, one of which includes physician-assisted suicide. In some such cases the patient—whether or not confused—might feel actual or implicit pressure to accept the option of death. This is not because this option is, all things considered, the patient's preferred one, but because the physician explicitly or implicitly favors it and because, under the circumstances, the physician has assumed the role of an authority figure. Once a right is granted, real-world physicians may (consciously or unconsciously) favor death for any number of reasons, including financial pressures and the need to allocate scarce time to other, more promising cases.

Here too we have a case in which autonomy is supported rather than undermined by the ban. It is relevant that in the Netherlands, the only nation to legalize physician-assisted suicide, there are many allegations that patient consent is not always the precondition for medical decisions. It is reasonable to think that the right has increased the autonomy of doctors rather than of patients.

4. *Nonvoluntary euthanasia.* Many critics of the "right to die" believe that there is an easy slippage from voluntary to nonvoluntary euthanasia. Their argument has two forms.[16] Some people believe that the safeguards designed to ensure a trustworthy expression of the patient's will cannot be held in place—that in a number of cases, those safeguards will, as an empirical matter, prove inadequate, and the patient will be killed despite his wishes. Other people do not stress this empirical possibility but urge instead that if doctors are in a position to honor the suicide requests of (autonomous) patients, the doctors will also, inevitably, be making some evaluation of whether those patients' lives will be worth living. Once doctors are in the business of making that evaluation, they will, in practice, be making judgments about the competence of patients and the value of their lives, and ultimately terminate

lives partly or mostly on the basis of their own judgments rather than on those of their patients.

With this point we can see a possible problem with right-to-die litigation, one that points to the distorting lens of adjudication. The particular cases brought to a court's attention will certainly be the most compelling ones. They will involve competent patients facing intense pain and horrible life prospects. A focus on the particular cases will make the right seem particularly insistent, and this will be a fully reasonable reaction to those cases. But a decision on their behalf will undoubtedly affect other people not before the court, and those cases will be much more difficult. The point suggests that very poignant and compelling particular cases should not be allowed to stand for the whole of the problem.

The experience in the Netherlands is complex, but it is taken by some observers to signal a warning on this front.[17] Thus a comprehensive survey suggested that of 130,000 people who died each year, 49,000 raised issues of whether to withdraw life-saving equipment or hasten death, and about 400 cases amounted to assisted suicide. There were 9,000 annual requests for euthanasia; of these voluntary euthanasia— "any action that intentionally ends the life of someone else, on the request of that person"—was allowed in 2,300 cases, or about one-quarter. In 8,100 cases, doctors intended to hasten death via pain-killing drugs. Some people believe that abuse is extensive in the form of deaths that have not received adequate consent. Thus of the 8,100 cases involving pain-killing drugs designed to hasten death, 5,508 involved no explicit request on the patient's part. One observer suggests that "the Dutch euthanasia experience lends weighty support to the slippery slope argument. . . . Within a decade, the so-called strict safeguards against the slide have proved signally ineffectual; non-voluntary euthanasia is now widely practiced and increasingly condoned in the Netherlands."[18] Others disagree.[19] The existence of considerable uncertainty on the question suggests that there is at least a significant possibility of abuse.

5. *Systemic effects, expressive values, and the role of the physician.* Some people undoubtedly support the prohibition on suicide and assisted suicide because of the *expressive value* of the prohibition. The expressive value consists in the message that a law sends or the statement that a law makes. A ban on suicide may be supported as an intrinsic good

insofar as it reflects social attitudes about the sanctity of life. Perhaps it is inadequate to defend a law intruding so deeply on patient autonomy on purely expressive grounds. But less controversially, it might be suggested that the ban has expressive value insofar as it has salutary effects on social norms—helping to create a culture in which life is seen with a degree of reverence, and in which the termination of life, by self or others, is taken to be a tragic event.

This point has special importance insofar as a prohibition on suicide and assisted suicide, even in the most compelling cases, helps express and fortify norms in favor of dealing with difficult conditions in more constructive ways. A right to physician-assisted suicide might be taken to compromise the general social norm against suicide and assisted suicide, even if, as a technical matter, it applies only in a restricted and compelling context. We have seen that acts of suicide can be contagious. The state may want to disallow physician-assisted suicides for fear that a few highly publicized cases may spur a wide range of additional cases, with harmful effects on norms against suicide in general.

In any case, it is possible that a right to physician-assisted suicide would have adverse effects on the norms and role of physicians. Physicians are now faced with an entrenched norm in favor of the preservation of life. A right to physician-assisted suicide might have harmful effects on that norm. It is possible, for example, that such a right would make doctors more willing to hasten death whether or not this is actually the patient's choice. It may encourage physicians to make cost-benefit judgments that disserve many patients' interests. The ban on physician-assisted suicide is, on this view, intended to serve an expressive function, fortifying social norms associated with the proper role of the physician.

Constitutional Options

We have now seen that the state can invoke powerful justifications to oppose the right to physician-assisted suicide. In light of these considerations, how should the Court resolve the question whether there is a constitutionally guaranteed right to die? I believe that the Court was right to proceed in minimalist fashion and also not to accept the constitutional challenge, partly for institutional reasons connected with the limited place of the Supreme Court in American government: when the issue is very close in light of the underlying issues of fact and value, and when there is no democratic defect in the underlying political process, the Court should not strike down reasonable legislative judgments. I consider three sets of possibilities: substantive due process, equal protection, and (following the lead of Judge Guido Calabresi) the form of procedural due process known as "desuetude."

Substantive Due Process

Narrowly vindicating the right. Some people believe that there is a fundamental liberty interest in deciding whether to live or die, at least under narrow circumstances, and that the various state justifications are not sufficient to overcome that interest. As we have seen, a majority of the Court has left this possibility open. This view might be supported with the plausible suggestion that the various risks can be counteracted through less restrictive alternatives. A state concerned about those risks might take steps to make sure that the patient really wants to die by requiring a certain burden of proof, ensuring that the circumstances meet certain constraints, imposing procedural safeguards of various kinds, and using the criminal law against doctors who are pressuring patients and not simply following their wishes. This approach would be reminiscent of Roe v. Wade in the sense that it would follow the familiar two-step process of finding a fundamental right and declaring that the state does not have a "compelling" interest that it is unable to support with less restrictive means.

Should the Supreme Court eventually take this route? An affirmative answer would not be entirely indefensible. At least if we have a category (1) or category (2) case—the patient's wishes are clear, the condition is genuinely hopeless, and the patient is facing physically difficult circumstances—reasonable people might believe that the state's interests do not seem overriding. Perhaps the basic risks could be adequately handled through procedural safeguards (as indeed I believe is true as a matter of policy). Indeed, it is possible to think that such a route would be stronger than that in several of the privacy cases, including Roe v. Wade itself. Here the individual interest may be at least as insistent and the countervailing interests might seem far weaker, insofar as the individual in question has extremely poor life prospects. There is no direct argument, as there is in the abortion context, about preventing harm to third parties.

But this would not, all things considered, be a good resolution. The privacy cases are actually far narrower than this two-step process suggests, and the Court should seek to narrow those cases by taking account of their distinctive features. Those features very much involve problems with democratic deliberation. First, equal protection considerations—themselves calling up democratic concerns connected with political inequality—were present in many of these cases as well. Roe v. Wade was in important part a case of gender equality, as then-Judge Ginsburg suggested in 1982[20] and as the Court has since explicitly acknowledged,[21] and if that decision is to be made acceptable, it must be partly because of the connection between sex equality and the abortion right. In this way Roe v. Wade can be seen as a case involving predictable problems in democratic deliberation, not simply privacy. Nor was this only true of Roe v. Wade. In privacy cases involving a right of use or access to contraceptives, there was at least a tacit equal protection dimension as well, for women were particularly at risk—far more at risk than men—in the event of an unwanted pregnancy. It does not require much imagination to see this point. When discrimination of this kind is involved, the interest in democratic deliberation legitimately calls for a larger judicial role, so as to counteract predictable problems with ordinary majoritarian processes.

Second, as Alexander Bickel suggested long ago, the outcomes in the early privacy cases could be seen as more minimalist than they were written, for they raised questions of procedural due process, involving as they did laws that were practically unenforced and unenforceable (see Chapter 3).[22] Thus the ban on the use of contraceptives within marriage was not a simple invasion of privacy; it involved a statute enacted long ago, not plausibly representing the considered judgments of the relevant electorate, and enforced only in a selective and discriminatory manner.[23] In this sense the ban presented a case of "desuetude": the lapsing of an old law lacking current support and used, if at all, episodically and discriminatorily. The other privacy cases did not vindicate a broad right to control one's body. They suggested more narrowly that if a state is going to regulate sexual activity, it must do so directly and not through the indirect, at best modestly effective means of making pregnancy the price of that activity. We may thus conclude that the privacy cases generally did not involve a simple identification of a fundamental right and a judgment that the state lacked sufficient justification to intrude. There were important issues involving the democracy-forcing goals of some forms of minimalism and relating to procedural due process and equal protection. And these issues suggest that there were problems in the system of democratic deliberation that contributed to the outcomes in the relevant cases. Hence the Court did not announce a broad right to sexual autonomy. It said more narrowly that any intrusion on that right must be direct, nondiscriminatory, and supported by actual public judgments, rather than indirect, discriminatory, and reflecting no actual judgment from the democratic public.

Along these dimensions, the right to physician-assisted suicide is quite different. In many cases, that right has been considered very recently in the relevant states. Moreover, there is no serious equal protection dimension in these cases. No politically vulnerable group is at risk, at least not in any constitutionally pertinent sense. If the Court is eventually forced to decide the issue, it will make sense to say that when death is imminent and inescapable, the decision whether to live implicates a "liberty" interest for constitutional purposes. But the state has very strong reasons to intrude on that interest. In short, it is perfectly reasonable for citizens, in their capacity as voters, to conclude that state law should allow a right to die. But a decision by the Court, foreclosing diverse solutions in diverse states, would intrude into ongoing deliberative processes in circumstances in which reasonable people may differ. This is so especially insofar as the relevant judgments depend on factual issues not well suited for judicial judgment.

Rejecting the due process claim. Chief Justice Rehnquist—joined by Justices Kennedy, Scalia, and Thomas—would uphold the relevant laws on relatively simple (and nonminimalist) grounds. They would say that under the due process clause there is no fundamental interest, for the traditionalist reasons discussed above. A narrower judgment would be that whether or not the interest is fundamental, the state has sufficient reason to interfere with the choice. There is a great deal to be said on behalf of this conclusion. The distinction between withdrawing treatment and active euthanasia may not be supportable at the level of first principles; but it reflects widely held intuitions and, more fundamentally, the state's justifications for rejecting a right to physician-assisted suicide are stronger at least in degree. Thus the Court might say that the risks of abuse and misapplication might be limited for withdrawal of treatment, but that a state could reasonably decide that those risks are decisive for physician-assisted suicide. The Court might also say that the risks are more limited in cases in which the patient is suffering and recovery highly unlikely, but that a state can reasonably conclude that a right, once granted and even if so limited, will inevitably give rise to sufficient risks to justify a broad prohibition.

Moreover, recognition of the importance of the state's countervailing interests would free up state legislatures to do as they wish with a problem that is very much on the public agenda. And the state does have powerful interests with which to counterpose the claim from decisional autonomy. Notably, those interests are more powerful than in any of the privacy cases vindicating the underlying right. In Roe v. Wade, the state's justification—protection of fetal life—seemed (and seems) to many quite strong. But at least there is a serious question whether, on secular grounds, fetal life deserves the same respect and concern as human life post-viability. The potential abuses introduced by any right to physician-assisted suicide may or may not be sufficient to convince a legislator or a citizen; but they have considerable weight whatever one's convictions about foundational issues. The Court is not in a good position to know whether the likely risks are serious and whether they can be reduced through less restrictive means. For this reason, the question is admirably well suited to a federal system that can conduct a range of experiments.

Institutional notes. It should be clear that the argument I am making depends on the controversial suggestion that when there is no palpable defect in the system of democratic deliberation,[24] courts should respect very reasonable legislative judgments even if a "fundamental interest" is at stake. This is not to say that courts should defer to any minimally plausible legislative judgment; the critical fact here is that fully reasonable people might decide this issue either way, even though the Court might find one view more reasonable than the other as a matter of policy. This view depends on two assumptions. The first is that judicial judgments about how to balance the relevant interests, especially in light of factual and predictive uncertainties, are not always reliable. Judges are aware of this point and they devise doctrines accordingly.

Of course, judges have certain advantages by virtue of their insulation and their ability, perhaps, to be especially systematic and careful with respect to underlying issues of both fact and political morality. But with respect to issues of both fact and value, judicial insulation can be a disadvantage too; it can make it harder for courts to obtain relevant information, and it can make it less legitimate for judges to choose what to do in the face of factual uncertainty. Judicial insulation suggests that courts should not be too sure that they are right, in the sense that they should be reluctant to overturn a legislative judgment when the balance is quite close.

The second assumption is that even if judges are right, they should be aware that their (by hypothesis correct) moral judgments, once announced, may not receive immediate social vindication and may instead produce something very different from what they intend.[25] This is because judicial judgments may truncate ongoing processes of democratic deliberation and, by so doing, may prove futile or even counterproductive. In the context of abortion, this is a plausible view, for the nation may well have been moving reasonably amicably toward a solution not so far from Roe v. Wade and reflecting deliberative compromises in various states.[26] In the current period, the same may well be true with respect to physician-assisted suicide (or, to take an issue that is in some ways similar, the right to same-sex marriage). In these circumstances, a constitutional ruling may embroil the Court in decades of political conflict. Of course this consideration should not be decisive; if the argument for the constitutional right were compelling, as in for example Brown v. Board of Education, a majority or minority that rejects the right should not be allowed to exercise any kind of heckler's veto. The legal system should aspire to justice even if justice is controversial. And in Brown, the existence of political inequality and racial animus suggested that possible disagreement among apparently reasonable people should not be decisive for the Court. But where there is no such inequality and the issue is otherwise very close, institutional considerations of this kind are relevant. They suggest that if democratic processes are not malfunctioning, judges should be cautious about invoking their own moral judgments simply because of the risk of producing unfortunate unintended consequences. The best route is to leave things undecided; the second-best route is to decide that the states can proceed as they wish so long as their judgments are reasonable.

It should be clear from what I have said thus far that most substantive due process cases have some other element involving a democratic failure—excessive role for religious convictions in the public sphere, insufficient connection with considered public judgments, problems of inequality and prejudice. Certainly we could imagine cases calling for substantive due process even without these elements—suppose, for example, that the government imposed a general "one family, one child" policy, or required people to have abortions, or said that randomly chosen people must give their kidneys to those who need them. The fact that these cases are so bizarrely unlikely suggests that the occasions for "pure" substantive due process will be rare indeed. Ordinarily political safeguards are sufficient against such gross abuses, and if they are not sufficient, circumstances (underlying facts and values) are likely to be so entirely different from our own that our present (outraged, uncomprehending) view of them does not produce a strong defense of substantive due process. The central point is that while there may be some cases in which states have no sufficiently powerful grounds for interfering with what is properly characterized as a fundamental interest, the right to physician-assisted suicide is not such a case.

In the context at hand, there is a further point. At least as much as *Roe* itself, a decision on behalf of a right to physician-assisted suicide would put the Court in the exceedingly difficult business of specifying appropriate procedures and boundary lines. It is inevitable that a judicially recognized right would have to be accompanied by guarantees designed to ensure that the patient genuinely wants to die. It is predictable that states that are skeptical of the underlying right would devise correspondingly elaborate procedures, and hence the Court would be in the business of distinguishing among justified and unjustified measures designed to produce certainty about the patient's wishes. And if a ban on suicide is permissible, the Court would have to make fine distinctions between those cases in which physician-assisted suicide is a constitutional right and those in which it is not. These considerations ought not to be decisive if the case for a constitutional guarantee is otherwise compelling. But they suggest that any such guarantee would produce not one judgment but a long line of judgments, not well suited to judicial competence. The Court's difficulties with *Roe* in this regard counsel against a duplication of that experience.

Equal Protection

Rationality review. In Eisenstadt v. Baird,[27] the Court struck down as irrational a law forbidding the distribution of contraceptives to unmarried people. The Court said that it was irrational to prohibit the distribution of contraceptives among unmarried people if such distribution was not prohibited to married people. Of course many questions might be raised about the Court's reasoning; the state's decision was hardly irrational in the technical sense. But *Eisenstadt* can be understood as a rather cautious and modest ruling, one that vindicates a claim that the Court thought convincing without going so far as to announce a general "substantive due process" right to purchase contraceptives.

In one of the right-to-die cases, the Court was asked to do something like this and seek a more modest approach via the generality-requiring requirements of the equal protection clause. The court of appeals attempted a route of just this sort in Quill v. Vacco.[28] The court noticed that New York allowed patients to order the removal of life support systems, but did not allow patients to "take action" to terminate their lives. This inequality, the court said, violated the equal protection clause because it was not rationally related to any legitimate state interest. There is no sufficiently good reason to allow people to terminate their lives in one way while banning them from doing so in another way. Under the decision of the court of appeals, New York might be able to ban both physician-assisted suicide and removal of life support systems (though the latter step would raise substantive due process questions under *Cruzan*). The Supreme Court rejected this challenge on the ground that the law familiarly distinguishes between acts and omissions, and there is nothing irrational about making that distinction. Was the Court right?

The equal protection/rationality approach has an advantage of comparative modesty; it also has a plausible antecedent in *Eisenstadt*. But the Supreme Court was nonetheless right to conclude that the argument is weak. Long-standing traditions, and many reasonable people, have distinguished between killing and letting die. Certainly the action-omission distinction raises many puzzles, and it is far from clear that the distinction makes ultimate sense in distinguishing between administering life-ending drugs and withdrawing aid; but a holding that it is "irrational" runs afoul of both ordinary law and ordinary intuitions.

If the distinction is unconstitutional because irrational in this context, it is unconstitutional in many other contexts as well. Consider, for example, criminal law's distinction between killing and letting die, tort law's absence of liability for bad samaritans, and indeed due process law's own distinction between government actions and omissions.

There is also theoretical support for the distinction. Here are some possible grounds. Without endorsing the distinction for all purposes, we can say that someone who jumps off a building expresses contempt for his own life, whereas someone who disconnects life-saving equipment, and allows nature to take its course, does no such thing. The attitude expressed by what are conventionally labeled "acts" may well be different from the attitude expressed by what are conventionally labeled "omissions." We might think that a doctor who assists in suicide is similarly different from a doctor who withdraws life-saving equipment. In any case, the right to remove life support might be rooted in a desire to allow people to prevent the government from restraining and invading their bodies against their will. The right to physician-assisted suicide is at least plausibly different on this score. I do not argue that these points make sense as a matter of basic principle. But they are sufficient to show that if rationality review is genuinely at work, a state could plausibly allow people to terminate life support while disallowing them from getting doctors to help them administer life-terminating drugs.

In my view, the more important points are empirical and pragmatic. It is reasonable to think that the risks of abuse are far greater in cases of physician-assisted suicide than in cases of withdrawal of life support. The latter set of cases is far easier to cabin; the former set raises in far more instances the various difficulties I have discussed. A central reason is that the withdrawal of life-saving equipment is typically far more justifiable—far more likely to reflect a rational judgment by a competent patient—than is resort to assisted suicide. In the ordinary case, the withdrawal of life-saving equipment will involve a life that a patient reasonably and with adequate information wants to terminate; the act of assisted suicide far more commonly can involve a form of involuntary euthanasia, short-run distortions in judgment, or familial pressure. For this reason, the distinction is an imperfect but fully reasonable proxy for (costly, imperfect) case-by-case inquiries into the reasonableness of the grounds for choosing death in particular instances.

This is not to deny that withdrawal of life support raises risks of abuse too. We can certainly imagine instances in which very dependent patients feel pressured, by family or doctors, to misstate their true wishes in the face of exceptionally expensive medical treatments. But at least some safeguard against widespread abuse comes from the very possibility that the withdrawal would produce death; these are relatively rare cases, mostly involving terrible and terminal illnesses, and allowing the withdrawal of treatment does not risk the sheer number of conceivable instances in which a right to physician-assisted suicide will produce nonautonomous or involuntary deaths, or deaths that more nearly resemble ordinary suicide. The withdrawal of treatment produces death only if the patient suffers from a fatal illness, whereas the right to physician-assisted suicide may well, in theory or practice, apply in much different circumstances even if we attempt to restrict its domain. It is for this reason that this distinction is fully plausible as a way of attempting to protect patient autonomy and to combat risks of abuse. As long as rationality review is genuinely at work, the equal protection challenge is unconvincing.

Equal protection "fundamental rights." In the right-to-die cases, there has also been an effort to root an equal protection argument in the "fundamental rights" branch of equal protection doctrine, and this effort might be made again in future cases; in any event this branch of doctrine has considerable importance. Here is the basic idea. In a number of cases, the Court has said that it will look skeptically at classifications that involve fundamental rights. It might therefore be thought that there is a fundamental interest here and that any discrimination with respect to that interest must be compellingly justified. The distinction between refusing treatment and physician-assisted suicide is rational, to be sure; but perhaps it does not have a compelling argument on its behalf. Thus understood, the case would be like Skinner v. Oklahoma ex rel. Williamson and Zablocki v. Redhail, involving sterilization and marriage, respectively, and using the fundamental rights branch of the equal protection doctrine.

But this branch of doctrine raises many puzzles. At least at first glance, the equal protection clause creates a right to nondiscrimination; it does not create any independent "fundamental rights." The key equal protection "fundamental rights" cases involve voting, and thus should be seen as part of democracy-reinforcing judicial review, not as a kind of junior-varsity substantive due process. It remains to be explained why *Skinner* and *Zablocki* are sensibly treated as equal protection rather than due process cases. If they are to be so treated, it is because they involve issues of discrimination as well as issues of "fundamental rights." *Skinner* is probably best understood as a case in which criminals of a certain social class—poor criminals, in short—were uniquely subject to the punishment of sterilization; *Zablocki* is best understood as a case informed and influenced by the fact that the relevant law prohibited poor people from marrying. Thus both cases can be seen as part of the general line of cases increasing judicial scrutiny where politically weak groups are at risk.

Nor is it clear what might be gained by holding some rights to be fundamental for equal protection purposes though not for purposes of substantive due process. Perhaps the idea is that the fundamental rights branch of equal protection doctrine is more minimalist and less intrusive than substantive due process, because it leaves states more room to maneuver by permitting them to invade the relevant right so long as they do so on a nondiscriminatory basis. In that way a use, for purposes of physician-assisted suicide, of the analysis in Skinner v. Oklahoma would be less intrusive than a rerun of Roe v. Wade. But from the analytic point of view, it is very untidy. If the substantive due process argument is not convincing, the equal protection argument is unconvincing too.

Desuetude

An intriguing possibility, not raised in the cases before the Supreme Court, is for courts to strike down laws forbidding physician-assisted suicide unless they are a product of recent legislative deliberation on the particular issues raised by physician-assisted suicide. This is the solution favored by Judge Calabresi in his intriguing if somewhat adventurous concurring opinion in *Quill*.[29] The solution raises complex issues. To summarize what I will be urging here: Judge Calabresi identifies an important and salutary theme in constitutional law, one that deserves considerable attention, not least because it represents a form of democracy-forcing minimalism. The chief advantage of Judge Calabresi's approach is institutional. It ensures that interferences with important forms of liberty will not be based on law that lacks current political support; in that way, the approach is democracy-supporting. Moreover, it does not preempt but instead catalyzes democratic processes, and in that sense reflects the courts' appropriate caution in dealing with issues of that kind. On the other hand, the case of physician-assisted suicide does not fit the case of desuetude, for the "right to die" has received ample recent consideration in most of the relevant states. I conclude that the idea of desuetude is extremely important and valuable, and deserves a more prominent and explicit place in constitutional law, but that it ought not to be used in the context of physician-assisted suicide.

The general idea. The basic argument is simple. Suppose that the relevant laws—banning people from helping in the commission of suicide—were written long ago, and suppose too that they were not specifically addressed to the problem of physician-assisted suicide. Indeed, that problem is a recent one, made available by new technologies and practices. In light of the novelty of the relevant practice, and (let us assume) the lack of close legislative attention to that practice, we could nearly imagine a state court ruling that state-law bans on assisting suicide do not even cover physician-assisted suicide, on the ground that criminal statutes should be construed narrowly and not applied to a case that is so far afield from the understandings of the enacting legislature. If a state court has not so held, a federal court, faced with a due process challenge, might say something like this: "We do not hold that a state may never forbid physician-assisted suicide. But if a state is going to forbid a decision of this kind, it must demonstrate that it has focused with some particularity on the problem and concluded that its rationale is weighty enough to override the individual's decision. An old statute banning assistance in suicide, enacted long ago in a time of different values and facts, is not sufficient. We will not interpret a general prohibition on assisted suicide to cover the new and distinctive practice of physician-assisted suicide."

This interpretation may seem exotic. But it has roots in the old notion of "desuetude," in accordance with which citizens may not be prosecuted under laws that were enforced long ago, are regularly violated in practice, and are invoked only on a sporadic and highly selective basis. The notion of desuetude does not have explicit support in the decisions of the Supreme Court. But it makes a good deal of constitutional sense. Notably, it is a form of procedural rather than substantive due process; the basic concerns are that there has been no focused legislative deliberation about the particular matter at hand and that rule of law principles are likely to be violated in the enforcement process, which will be ad hoc and episodic. A ruling of this kind is more mini-malist and far less intrusive than one based on ordinary substantive due process principles, for it leaves open the possibility that a current leg-islature might resolve the matter as it chooses. And the principle does have antecedents. It provides a simpler and more compelling basis for *Griswold,* and Justice White's opinion in *Griswold* can be understood to point to concerns of this sort. Other judge-made doctrines have, without using the name, pointed to desuetude-related concerns. Draw-ing on the discussion in Chapter 3, let us isolate several lines of cases.

—In some cases, the Court will uphold a statute only on the basis of a rationale actually at work in the process leading to its enactment. A merely hypothetical purpose is not enough. As we shall see, this was a central part of the Court's reasoning in United States v. Virginia,[30] where the Court invalidated a same-sex program at the Virginia Mili-tary Institute on the ground that no legislature had in fact adopted single-sex education as a way of promoting equality of opportunity and educational diversity. The Court left very much open the possibility that a legislature that actually operated with this purpose might be pro-ceeding constitutionally. We can even understand *Virginia* as a case of desuetude, for the Court treated the relevant statute as embodying an obsolete judgment, one that had not been reaffirmed by a recent leg-islature operating on the basis of constitutionally legitimate principles. In cases of this kind, the Court leaves open the possibility that the same statute, enacted on the basis of a legitimate and sufficiently weighty rationale, will in fact be upheld.

—The Court construes ambiguous statutes so as to avoid raising serious constitutional doubts.[31] This idea has roots in the nondelegation doctrine; indeed, it is a narrow and more targeted version of the non-delegation doctrine, designed to say that the national legislature must focus specifically on the problem at hand. There is a close link with the doctrine of desuetude insofar as both are designed to ensure that the coercive power of law will be brought to bear on citizens only on the basis of evidence of a specific and focused legislative judgment to this effect.

—The void-for-vagueness doctrine is rooted in the same basic con-cern.[32] When the Court strikes down a statute as void, it leaves open the possibility that a more specific version of the legislative judgment—regulating speech or conduct—may be valid. A void-for-vagueness holding leaves that question undecided; it demands a focused legislative determination. It is notable in this regard that *Roe* itself was originally conceived as a void-for-vagueness case[33]—a holding that would have been far more cautious and modest than the opinion that emerged.

—In its intriguing decision in Hampton v. Mow Sun Wong,[34] the Court held that if aliens are going to be deprived of all federal employment, it must be because of a judgment from Congress or the President, not the Civil Service Commission. The Court said that the due process clause renders invalid a wholesale deprivation of employment unless a constitutionally specified official has decided that such a drastic step is desirable. The problem with the relevant regulation was that it faced a "legitimacy deficit" because it had not been embraced by someone with adequate political accountability.

All of these cases have close connections with the notion of desuetude. They suggest that a less intrusive alternative to a substantive due process holding is a conclusion that the state must show sufficient grounds, in democratic judgments, for an intrusion on certain interests and rights.

Problems. As I have noted, an idea of this kind is not a version of substantive due process; rather, it suggests that there is a procedural defect in the laws at hand. Such an approach would have many advantages, but there would be disadvantages as well. What would be wrong with an opinion of this sort? There is an obvious slippery slope problem. Many statutes now in operation were enacted decades ago, when facts and values were different; are all such statutes unconstitutional? Surely they are not, and their long-standing character may well testify to their wisdom and good sense, not to their doubtful legitimacy. A constitutional doctrine would be absurd if it declared all old enactments void. The answer would have to be that the rationale just given applies when (a) a liberty interest of some importance is at stake, (b) the specific arguments brought forward in the law's defense did not play much of a role in the enacting legislature, (c) there is great doubt whether the statute has support in existing convictions, (d) there is a likely or demonstrated problem of sporadic and perhaps discriminatory enforcement, and (e) the relevant arguments, though not made at the time of enactment, may well, once supported by adequate facts and an actual legislative judgment, be sufficient to justify the intrusion on the liberty interest.

There is another objection to an approach based on desuetude. This approach puts courts in the business of setting the legislative agenda. A legislature, of course, has a great deal to do, and its failure to alter a law involving assisted suicide may well signify not indifference or neglect, but something like a considered judgment that the status quo is acceptable. And if the legislature has recently considered the problem and failed to do anything new, the doctrine of desuetude probably does not apply. But for cases that involve an unusually strong liberty interest, and a justification that is post hoc and of questionable relevance to any actual legislative decision, a ruling founded on desuetude makes a great deal of sense as a less restrictive alternative to an equal protection or due process ruling. It should be seen as a kind of democracy-forcing minimalism—an effort to create a more deliberative democracy, one in which certain interests can be compromised only on the basis of a recent deliberative judgment, not as a kind of accident.

Desuetude misapplied? An idea of this kind provides the strongest support for *Griswold* itself, and, as we have seen, it is far from entirely foreign to constitutional law. But of course this rationale could not be used if the statute forbidding physician-assisted suicide were the product of recent and sustained legislative deliberation. And here we find the simplest response to the argument from desuetude: these are not at all cases in which states have been inattentive to the underlying issues of fact and policy. On the contrary, the issue of physician-assisted suicide has received a great deal of attention. In the state of Washington, the relevant law was enacted in 1992. In New York, there has been no recent legislative enactment forbidding physician-assisted suicide, but the issue has been receiving intense consideration at the highest levels of state government. Thus a new enactment specified the conditions for withdrawal of life-saving equipment as recently as 1990, and in 1994, a task force issued a report recommending that things be left as they were.

Judge Calabresi may be taken to be suggesting that intense consideration is not enough, and that a state must not only consider a statute that raises new concerns but also reenact it. The apparent thought is that inertia may reflect something other than approval, and in any case, an intense minority may be able to block consideration, in the sense of an actual vote, without being able to block enactment once a vote occurs. In some ways this is an attractive view; it suggests a possible distinction between New York and Washington, whose laws have somewhat different backgrounds. But if there is good evidence that a state government has actively and intensely considered an issue, as New York has, it seems strained to say that the due process clause requires actual reenactment. The question is whether it would really make sense to invalidate the New York ban while upholding the ban in Washington, when the distinction seems relatively thin in light of the large volume of public attention given to the issue in both states. Nor is this a case like Griswold v. Connecticut, in which a politically intense minority was able to block legislative change that was generally desired. With respect to physician-assisted suicide, politically intense minorities are on all sides of the question, and no particular group faces or creates a systematic barrier to well-functioning democratic deliberation.

I conclude, then, that the general idea of desuetude serves important constitutional values and has significant advantages over the substantive due process route; that we could imagine cases involving physician-assisted suicide that provide a good area for invoking that idea; but that the issue has been under intense discussion in many states, and that Washington and New York have had intense recent deliberations, making it certainly inappropriate to use the idea of desuetude for Washington and probably inappropriate to do so for New York. If the Court is eventually going to accept a version of Judge Calabresi's proposal— and I believe that it ultimately should—it should do so in a simpler and more compelling setting.

There is a further point. American constitutional law lacks, but should have, a kind of "democratic political question doctrine"—a doctrine that would allow the Court to decline to validate or invalidate legislation, and to suspend its judgment about constitutionality until a certain period of democratic deliberation (and clarification of relevant issues) has passed. The Court can deny certiorari, of course, and there are analogues in American law to such a doctrine. An illustration is the idea of abstention, which might have been used in right-to-die cases, and which instructs federal courts to postpone a constitutional ruling until they have received an authoritative interpretation from state courts. These analogies do not, however, give an explicit constitutional foundation to a principle that would allow suspension of constitutional judgment until further time has passed. Such a doctrine would be especially well suited to the right to physician-assisted suicide. In oral argument in the physician-assisted suicide cases, Justice Souter raised exactly this point, suggesting that a constitutional ruling should be suspended pending further developments. Perhaps the Court will be able to develop surrogates for such a timing doctrine, and eventually announce the existence of a doctrine of this kind.

Death and abortion: a note. At several points I have compared the right to physician-assisted suicide with the right to have an abortion, and it will now be useful to bring together the strands of the comparison, since Roe v. Wade looms so clearly in the background of the discussion of a constitutional right to die. A central distinction is that Roe v. Wade is best understood as largely a case about sex equality. It was not simply a due process case, as the Court has come to recognize; it depended centrally on the fact that restrictions on the right to abort are a form of discrimination against women and closely associated with traditional and no longer legitimate ideas about women's appropriate role. The right to die does not have this equal protection dimension.

Along the dimension of justification, there is also a difference between *Roe* and the right to physician-assisted suicide. The principal justification in *Roe* rested on the perceived importance of protecting the fetus. It is possible to think that fetuses are not people and that a commitment to the overriding importance of their survival depends on sectarian claims. Without defending this view, we can see that something of this general sort underlies *Roe* itself. By contrast, the state's justifications for interfering with the right to physician-assisted suicide are perfectly legitimate and largely empirical in nature. To the extent that the state is saying that it fears risks of abuse, it is able to offer a quasi-predictive defense of the sort that was unavailable in *Roe.*

It also follows from what I have said thus far that the Court—as the current Court itself seems to believe—should be very cautious about duplicating the experience of *Roe* and that it is by no means clear that the broad holding of *Roe* was right at the time. At the very least, it is by no means clear that the Court was correct to create so broad a right in its first confrontation with the abortion issue. The Court would have done much better to proceed narrowly, in good minimalist fashion, and to engage in a form of dialogue with the political process. It would have done much better because it would not have caused so much destructive and unnecessary social upheaval, because it would probably have produced a range of creative compromises well adapted to a federal system, and because a more cautious approach would not have deeply compromised the underlying right, as that right is best conceived. In any case, the *Roe* experience is not one that the Court should duplicate, at least when the Court's underlying judgment is subject to reasonable dispute and when there is no particular reason to distrust political processes.

Minimalism and Death

In this chapter I have made four claims. First, I have suggested that to the extent possible, minimalism—a form of both narrowness and shallowness—is the appropriate path in cases involving physician-assisted suicide. The Court does best to leave the most fundamental issues undecided, and neither to invalidate nor to validate existing laws in the most difficult cases. This was the path followed by five justices in the physician-assisted suicide cases, and it is an appropriate use of minimalism.

Second, courts should be reluctant to invalidate legislation under the due process clause in its "substantive" dimension when there is no defect in the system of democratic deliberation and when reasonable people might decide the underlying questions of value and fact either way. I have also suggested that this idea plays a large and underappreciated role in existing law. The key privacy cases, though decided as a matter of substantive due process, had important dimensions of desuetude and equal protection. The equal protection "fundamental rights" cases had large dimensions of democracy-reinforcement, involving as they did political rights or groups at particular risk in democratic processes. Thus these cases were more minimalist than they appear; in fact they can be taken to reflect an appealing brand of democracy-forcing minimalism.

Third, I have argued that when conditions are or appear to be medically hopeless, the individual's interest in physician-assisted suicide should probably qualify as one on which the state may intrude only with special justification. This is an issue that the Court has left undecided. But—and this is the fourth claim—I have also suggested that this principle should not be understood to invalidate state efforts to prevent people from taking their own lives, on their own or with the assistance of others. There are palpable risks of abuse, and the weight to be given to these risks depends on hard predictive judgments and complex assessments of how to handle factual uncertainty. A reasonable legislature, even giving great weight to the interests of patients, might decide that those risks are sufficient to justify a prohibition. A state could decide, with sufficient reason, that a ban on physician-assisted suicide actually promotes the autonomy of many or most people and in the process has salutary effects on the norms and practices of the medical profession. There is a general lesson here: it is not at all clear that respect for individual choice promotes individual freedom. In some circumstances, a decision to override choice can actually enhance freedom—yet another reason for the Court to be cautious in invoking the due process clause as a basis for striking down statutes that interfere with choice. Probably the simplest opinion would assume for purposes of argument that the right to physician-assisted suicide qualifies as a "fundamental right" while finding that the state has sufficient reason to override that right.

It is hard to be comfortable with this conclusion. In actual cases, fully competent people, joined by their loved ones, are seeking to terminate their lives amid hopeless conditions and an inevitable period of helplessness, despair, and perhaps intense emotional or physical pain. Those of us who are healthy are not unlikely to have known people in such situations; those of us who are healthy may eventually find ourselves in such situations. In such cases, an insistence on the abstract "right to life" can be an egregious and unnecessary cruelty, and the notion of "death with dignity" acquires immense force. Lawyers and citizens should be aware that a judgment that people have no constitutional right to commit some act does not mean that they do not deserve, in the deepest moral sense, that very right. Probably doctors should consult closely with patients, friends, and family members, and in that process all will conclude, on occasion, that physician-assisted suicide is a merciful and fully legitimate act. Sometimes they will reach this conclusion whatever the technical content of state law, and in such cases prosecutors should tread very cautiously indeed. And here we arrive at the heart of the matter. The argument I have offered is institutional rather than substantive: it is not the Supreme Court but these arenas— state legislatures, prosecutors' offices, hospitals, and private homes— that should decide whether, when, and how to legitimate a "right to die."

6

Affirmative Action Casuistry

The minimal substance of the equal protection clause is a ban on the subordination of African Americans. More particularly, everyone agrees that a law that discriminates on the basis of race, and that has the effect of treating African Americans worse than whites, violates the equal protection clause. Almost everyone agrees, of course, that the equal protection clause forbids more than this. But there is a great deal of disagreement about plausible analogies to the core or defining cases.

My purpose in this chapter is to venture a simple and somewhat impressionistic argument. I start with the suggestion that the issue of affirmative action should be settled democratically, not judicially. Certainly the Supreme Court should not invalidate all or most race-conscious remedial programs. But until relatively recently, there has been little or no sustained democratic deliberation on the issue. Affirmative action programs have not been adopted as a result of sustained public support, and the arguments for and against such programs have not received much in the way of a public airing until the last several years. The citizenry's ambivalence about—or hostility toward—affirmative action has been expressed mostly in private and not in public arenas.

In particular, the enormous diversity of affirmative action programs, not to mention the separable justifications for and variable efficacy of each program, has not received much public attention. Some programs work well; some do not; and neither empirical data nor public judgments about their content and value have been reflected in program design. In these circumstances, the Supreme Court's apparently odd behavior in the affirmative action context—its meandering course, its refusal to issue rules, its minimalism—might be defended as performing a valuable *catalytic* function. One of the distinctive goals of the Court's approach has been to spur, but not to preempt, effective public debate. The Court's willingness to hear a number of affirmative action cases and its complex, rule-free, highly particularistic opinions have had the salutary consequence of helping to stimulate public processes and directing the citizenry toward more open discussion of underlying questions of policy and principle. In these ways, the Court's route has been far preferable to the most obvious and less minimalist alternatives: validation or invalidation of most affirmative action programs pursuant to clear doctrinal categories.

That, in a nutshell, is the argument to follow. I do not claim that the Court has always been self-conscious about the virtues of casuistry thus described. But if the point is correct, it bears a great deal on the relations between the Court and a well-functioning system of political deliberation. There are, however, serious questions about whether current public processes are sufficiently deliberative, especially in the area of affirmative action.

Social Norms and Public Debate

People often think one thing but say another, because of the effects of social pressures and social norms on what can be said in public.[1] For example, in most contemporary American circles, there is a strong social stigma against anti-Semitic statements; people who hold anti-Semitic views are unlikely to make such statements on television or in a public debate. In many groups where religious convictions are both deep and widespread, people cannot confess their uncertainty about whether God exists; they may attend church regularly despite their doubts on that score. In other places, people cannot acknowledge that they are deeply religious; in such places, social norms punish public declarations of religious conviction. People may pretend to be, or not to be, feminist, just because of the intense feelings about feminism in the relevant community. The general point is simple: social norms drive a wedge between public statements and private beliefs, hopes, and convictions. From this point, it emerges that "political correctness" is no isolated phenomenon limited to left-leaning intellectuals. It is a pervasive fact of social life. It appears whenever prevailing norms discourage people from taking issue with a widely held social belief. Norms can even operate as taxes on, or subsidies to, both talk and action. People saying and doing popular things are subsidized by existing norms; people saying and doing unpopular things are taxed. Following John Stuart Mill, those interested in democratic politics should notice the omnipresent role of public constraints on public statements.

Is the existence of such constraints something to be lamented? No simple answer would make sense. Sometimes, by imposing sanctions on malicious or invidious judgments, social norms have a healthy "laundering" effect.[2] The existence of social sanctions can make people embarrassed about those judgments and eventually make them recede or even disappear. If "[h]ypocrisy is the homage that vice pays to virtue,"[3] then social norms can identify both vice and virtue as such, and enable citizens to tell which is which. Hypocrisy can therefore have valuable social uses. It has a civilizing effect.[4] It can produce justice by making unjust behavior seem vicious or otherwise unacceptable. In the recent past, social norms have made it less likely that people will express racist sentiments, and this is in many ways an important social good.

But social norms of the kind I am discussing can cause damage in two different ways. First, they may prevent people from offering arguments that are productive, reasonable, or even right. If prevailing norms are invidious or rooted in confusion, they may even perpetuate invidious or confused practices. Consider the fact that for decades, social norms prevented public criticism of communism in Soviet-bloc countries. Or consider the many areas in the world where social norms strongly discourage advocacy of sex equality: many women who indicate their belief in equality run enormous risks. Second, social norms may discourage the expression of doubt, even when doubt exists and when debate is, partly for that very reason, desirable and potentially productive. In that way, prevailing norms can damage processes of public deliberation. And even if prevailing norms are not invidious on their merits—even if they reflect clear thinking or hard-won wisdom—their effects can be pernicious when they prevent public deliberation on issues about which there is in fact social uncertainty. In a well-functioning democracy, facts and options are clarified through doubt, and people have an accurate, not distorted, sense of what their fellow citizens think.

Of course, a certain suppression of issues and opinions stems from practical necessities. Not everything can be discussed at once. At any time, many things must be taken for granted. Some things are properly taken as so obvious that they "go without saying." But in many areas, one can safely say that democratic processes would be better if public debate focused on what really concerns, and separates, people.

From the standpoint of both law and democratic theory, a great deal needs to be done on this important topic. We do not know the extent to which actual private judgments are not expressed publicly, even when they are quite widespread and when the reason for silence is that social norms impose sanctions on the public expression of those judgments. It is therefore important to take account of possible disparities between what is said and what is thought. It is also important to know how wide such disparities are, whether the disparities reflect biases, and whether some social institutions or practices facilitate or inhibit open discussion.

Court as Catalyst

It seems obvious to say that when the Supreme Court faces a constitutional attack on a law, it has three basic options: it might uphold the law, it might invalidate the law, or it might refuse to address the issue by denying certiorari or by taking advantage of various avoidance strategies. On a familiar view, the Court should often permit issues to "percolate" in lower courts and in the nation as a whole. Through this route, it can allow many forms of legal and political discussion and debate; in that way, the Court avoids premature judicial foreclosure of hard questions. The Court might take this route for practical reasons or for reasons of principle. Perhaps a firm judicial resolution would be poorly received by the community. Surely this point bears on possible judicial foreclosure of affirmative action programs, say, twenty-five years ago. Perhaps a judicial resolution would disserve the very cause that the Court is seeking to promote. This point has been vigorously urged in the context of abortion, where (it is said) the Court's early judicial decision in Roe v. Wade helped undermine the movement for sex equality.[5] Certainly judicial decisions can have unintended social consequences, and this practical point argues in favor of judicial caution. As we have seen, the Court might also avoid premature foreclosure because of its own humility. The Court might lack relevant information and wait to see how a certain practice works out in reality. Or the Court might believe that certain issues are difficult from the standpoint of (legally relevant) morality and that therefore, in principle, it is important to ensure that a good deal of public deliberation occurs before the Court acts.

As we shall see, these points bear a great deal on the issues raised by affirmative action. But the Court actually has a fourth option: it can issue a minimalist decision, one that resolves little beyond the single case, but that operates as a catalyst for public discussion. By assuming jurisdiction, by offering a ruling, but by issuing a ruling that is case-specific and along crucial dimensions not authoritative for the future, it can call public attention to a problem without foreclosing public judgment. This fourth option is especially appropriate when the Court is uncertain about whether general rules would be satisfactory, and when it believes that differences of fact and content are highly relevant to constitutional outcomes. There is, of course, a large debate within the Court and within the scholarly community about the virtues of case-by-case particularism (see Chapter 9). Defenders of particularism often speak of the need to proceed cautiously in the midst of ignorance about issues not before the Court. But particularism, in the form of narrowness, and theoretical caution, in the form of shallowness, also have a democratic function, and this is so in two different ways. Judicial minimalists can promote democratic virtues of participation and responsiveness, by ensuring that people are not foreclosed by rulings involving previous litigants who have somewhat different complaints. The process of judicial minimalism allows each person to have a day in court, invoking the distinctive features of his or her case. But—and this is the second point—minimalist decisions allow people, through democratic processes, to continue to debate issues, secure in the knowledge that courts have not attempted to have a final say. In this respect, case-specific and theoretically unambitious judgments operate as a kind of "remand" to the public for further proceedings, at least in the sense that they do not foreclose those proceedings and may even spur them through the visibility of court decisions.

In administrative law, a remand to the agency for further proceedings is an exceedingly common phenomenon.[6] In the remand, the agency is permitted to do as it originally did, but it must offer a new and better justification. The court's decision is case-specific; it can easily be "distinguished" by a resourceful administrator, even on the same set of facts. It is possible to debate whether this process generally tends to work out well. But when it does, the remand promotes better public deliberation by drawing attention to difficulties that have not yet received adequate attention, and by helping to produce better processes of deliberation for the future.

Much of constitutional law has a structure similar to the administrative law remand. Sometimes the Court effectively "remands" issues for fresh deliberation. Many of the modern privacy cases involving sexual autonomy can be understood accordingly. In these cases, the state defended laws restricting the availability of contraception by reference to the goal of preventing premarital or extramarital activity. The Court did not deny that the state has a legitimate interest in preventing nonmarital sexual activity. It did not say that a law directly punishing such activity is unconstitutional. It concluded instead that the state may not attempt to promote the underlying interest through the indirect means of preventing contraception. If the state is genuinely interested in preventing nonmarital sexual relations, it must pursue that policy in a way that receives meaningful democratic scrutiny and reflects actual democratic approval of the underlying judgment of policy and principle— through the criminal sanction. The more indirect and discriminatory route of preventing contraception is an unacceptable means of pursuing the relevant end. Because of its indirection, a ban on contraceptives does not accurately reflect a democratic judgment that extramarital relations should not be permitted. In fact, no such judgment followed the Court's cases, because the public was unwilling to use the criminal sanction to punish extramarital relations directly.

This account of the privacy cases helps make sense of rulings that are otherwise very puzzling. And at the very least, it suggests the possibility of a judicial role in catalyzing public debate through narrow rulings designed to focus public attention on the more fundamental questions.

The Affirmative Action Muddle

It is easy to be skeptical about the Supreme Court's affirmative action cases. From the standpoint of the rule of law, the cases are truly a mess. This was so from the very start. In Regents of the University of California v. Bakke,[7] the Court was badly divided and could not produce a majority opinion. Of course, the often-criticized "rule" of the case was that universities may use race "as a factor" in admissions, but may not create quotas. While this rule has played a crucial role in American society and debate, it represented the view of Justice Powell alone. The other eight participating justices explicitly rejected that rule. Ironically, the case stands for a proposition that only one justice thought sensible. The outcome in *Bakke* was both narrow and shallow. In particular, the Court did not settle the question whether affirmative action plans would have to survive "strict scrutiny" (the greatest degree of judicial skepticism, almost always producing invalidation), or something closer to "rational basis" review (the most lenient form of judicial scrutiny, almost always producing validation).

Bakke was not an auspicious beginning for those seeking clear rules. The Court's second affirmative action case, Fullilove v. Klutznick, compounded the problem.[8] In that case, no majority spoke for the Court, no standard of review was selected for affirmative action cases, and by the plurality's own admission, its decision was highly dependent on the facts of the particular case. In a case with slightly different facts, the outcome might be different. Remarkably, during the next nine years, the Court's decisions developed no clear standard of review and seemed to turn not on rules, but instead on a large set of factors:[9] whether official findings of past discrimination had been made; whether the relevant program was rigid or flexible; whether the relevant program operated as a quota; whether the relevant program had been issued by Congress, by another politically accountable body, by a court, or by some other institution; whether innocent victims were injured, and if so in a severe way; and more.

The use of these numerous factors led to surprising decisions in particular cases, and outcomes were hard to predict in advance. Notably, some of these factors relate to the nature of the deliberative process itself. The relevant cases received a good deal of public attention, but the constitutional position of affirmative action programs remained quite obscure.[10]

It was not until 1989 that the Court finally settled on a standard of review. In City of Richmond v. J. A. Croson Co.,[11] a plurality of the Court held that affirmative action programs would be subject to "strict scrutiny," at least if they had not been enacted by the federal government. But even while announcing a standard of review, it did so in such a way as to leave the law exceptionally obscure, and to leave the many decisions that preceded *Croson* in an uncertain state. *Croson* was widely taken to signal a general refusal to permit affirmative action programs; but the decision did not reject the Court's casuistical approach to affirmative action. In Adarand Constructors, Inc. v. Pena,[12] the Court finally announced that the same standard of review applied to the nation as to the states, and *Adarand* has been read to suggest that the Court will strike down affirmative action programs in all but the most unusual cases (involving limited remedies for proven past discrimination). This, however, is an unnecessary reading of the opinion, for the Court went out of its way to make clear that the standard would not lead to automatic invalidation, that outcomes would turn on particular facts, and thus that we could not foresee certain results in future cases. Justice O'Connor, a minimalist in areas of this kind, wrote for the Court: "We wish to dispel the notion that strict scrutiny is 'strict in theory, but fatal in fact.' The unhappy persistence of both the practice and the lingering effects of racial discrimination against minority groups in this country is an unfortunate reality, and government is not disqualified from acting in response to it. . . . When race-based action is necessary to further a compelling interest, such action is within constitutional constraints if it satisfies the 'narrow tailoring' test this Court has set out in previous cases."

As a result, there is still—about two decades and numerous Supreme Court cases after *Bakke*—a high degree of uncertainty about the law governing affirmative action. The public reaction to the key cases shows that a great deal of doubt about whether affirmative action is constitutionally permissible still remains. Now, as before, the validity of an affirmative action program greatly depends on the details of the particular case.

What has the Court achieved? Perhaps the Court has succeeded in invalidating the most indefensible affirmative action plans and in upholding the most legitimate. This would certainly be the optimist's view, and it would be pleasing if it were so. But if we step back a bit, we might conclude that the Court has helped keep the nation's eye on the affirmative action issue—on the questions of policy and principle that lie behind the debate—while at the same time failing to preempt processes of public discussion and debate. Above all, the Court has done this because it has decided a large number of cases, but proceeded in a minimalist manner.

Affirmative Action and Public Debate

The Constitutional Attack on Affirmative Action

The question of affirmative action should be settled democratically, not judicially. Despite frequent arguments to the contrary, the Constitution imposes no clear textual ban on affirmative action. In fact, the textual arguments are laughably inadequate. To be sure, the Constitution calls for "equal" protection of the laws. But whether affirmative action programs violate a requirement of equality cannot be settled by the text alone; the question is what "equal" means. Everyone agrees, for example, that a state university may favor students who have done well in high school. This does not violate equality. Hence the term "equal" cannot possibly mean "the same," if "the same" is intended to suggest a ban on all classifications. By their very nature, laws classify, and whether they violate a requirement of "equality" depends on how we specify that contested ideal. Even the law of equal protection classifies, by treating some groups, and some classifications, differently from others (how could it be otherwise?). Thus it is no offense to the equal protection clause if courts scrutinize sex-based classifications more skeptically than they scrutinize age-based classifications—even though this difference does not treat people "the same." The question is what the word "equal" requires in this context. Dictionaries are unhelpful here. The only way to make progress is to go outside of the bare text; we must look there to find possible understandings of the Constitution's equality principle.

Nor is it helpful to insist that the Constitution speaks in terms of individuals—"nor shall any state deny any person the equal protection of the laws"—rather than of groups. The Supreme Court, together with many others, appears to think that the reference to "any person" means that the clause requires attention to individuals rather than to groups, and that this point counts decisively against affirmative action. This claim contains some truth, but it is misleading, and the conclusion does not follow. To be sure, "any person" may complain that a classification is constitutionally unacceptable. But on what grounds can "any person" seek special judicial assistance? Under the equal protection clause, all claims of unconstitutional discrimination are necessarily based on complaints about treatment that singles out a characteristic *shared by a group*. A glance at the cases, or at any imaginable set of cases, shows that anyone who complains of unconstitutional discrimination is necessarily complaining about the government's use, for purposes of classification, of some characteristic (race, gender, age, disability, scores on a test) that is shared by some number of group members. The issue is whether the government's use of that particular shared characteristic is disfavored from the constitutional point of view. There is no serious question about whether the characteristics of which "any person" may complain are shared characteristics; of course they are. In this sense, claims of unconstitutional discrimination are always claims about the government's impermissible use of some group-based characteristic, even if those claims are made by "any person."

For example, suppose that Smith has been denied a government job. As a "person," she certainly has a right to make a complaint under the equal protection clause. But whether her complaint has any force depends on the characteristic on which the government has allegedly seized in denying her the job. If the government has decided that Smith is incompetent, there is no problem, since discrimination against incompetent people raises no constitutional issue. But if the government denies jobs to Catholics, and if Smith is Catholic, the equal protection clause is certainly implicated. These examples show that for Smith to claim special judicial protection under the equal protection clause, she has to specify the classification that the government has used; and she must say that the classification treats her, as a member of a certain group, in a "suspect" way. Under current law, the same plaintiff Smith has a right to heightened judicial scrutiny of the relevant laws if they classify on the basis of sex, but no right to heightened judicial scrutiny if those laws classify on the basis of age. She is thus entitled to a degree of judicial protection corresponding to the basis of the classification of which she complains.

In short, almost all classifications involve "groups." The issue is whether heightened judicial scrutiny represents the appropriate standard of review for the particular classification that the government has used. The fact that the Constitution refers to "any person" is utterly uninformative about whether any particular grounds for classification should, or does, meet heightened judicial scrutiny. We may conclude that the Court's use of the constitutional text as a justification for heightened scrutiny is a dishonorable version of legal formalism—the pretense that the legal text resolves the question when the judgment must actually be based on other grounds.

If the text of the Constitution does not ban affirmative action, what of the Constitution's history? It might be tempting to say that the lesson of the Civil War is that all racial classifications are unacceptable. But the history shows no such particular understanding on the part of those who ratified the Fourteenth Amendment. On the contrary, it tends to suggest that affirmative action policies were regarded as legitimate. Hence there is no historical warrant for a maximalist ruling that affirmative action is generally unconstitutional. The Reconstruction Congress that approved the Fourteenth Amendment concurrently enacted a number of race-specific programs for African Americans.[13] A substantial debate about whether such programs were legitimate occurred, and the people who controlled Congress after the Civil War concluded that they were. There is no evidence in the Fourteenth Amendment ratification debates that race-conscious programs would be impermissible.[14]

History need not be decisive, at least to nonoriginalists (see Chapter 9). Perhaps the Constitution is best taken to establish a moral argument that justifies the Court in reading the text to ban affirmative action. But this moral argument would call for a high degree of theoretical ambition, and no clear argument authorizes courts to treat affirmative action policies with great skepticism. Many critics of affirmative action claim that the moral argument lay at the heart of the work of Martin Luther King, Jr., and others in the civil rights movement of the 1960s; but this is a historical error. Asked in 1965 whether he thought it was "fair to request a multibillion-dollar program of preferential treatment for the Negro, or for any other minority group," King flatly replied, "I do indeed."[15] In 1966, King wrote, "It is impossible to create a formula for the future which does not take into account that our society has been doing something special against the Negro for hundreds of years. How then can he be absorbed into the mainstream of American life if we do not do something special for him now, in order to balance the equation and equip him to compete on a just and equal basis?"[16] In fact, King's 1964 book, *Why We Can't Wait*, criticized the idea that once African Americans had been granted simple equality before the law, no further action should be taken. He wrote, "On the surface, this appears reasonable, but it is not realistic. For it is obvious that if a man is entered at the starting line in a race three hundred years after another man, the first would have to perform some impossible feat in order to catch up with his fellow runner."[17]

For constitutional purposes, of course, the views of Martin Luther King, Jr., need hardly be decisive; they may well be irrelevant. Perhaps a moral principle of color-blindness deserves constitutional recognition whatever was thought by civil rights advocates in the nineteenth and twentieth centuries; certainly this is so if it is the only intelligible principle behind the constitutional concern for racial equality. But if it is necessary to identify a competing moral principle of some ambition, it is not difficult to find one, and indeed that alternative principle has actually been responsible for most of the movement for racial equality in America, both during the Civil War and thereafter. In the area of race, a large target of the Civil War amendments was the preexisting system of racial caste: a system that turned the highly visible and morally irrelevant characteristic of race into a systemic basis for second-class citizenship.[18] The Fourteenth Amendment is best conceived of as opposing that caste system—as ensuring that characteristics that have been a basis for second-class citizenship may no longer have that function. And if this represents the best conception of the Fourteenth Amendment, then there is nothing fundamentally illegitimate, or constitutionally out of bounds, about affirmative action programs. Such programs are designed to overcome caste-like features of existing practice. This does not mean that they are a good idea, nor does it mean that they always have this effect. It may be that they are bad on grounds of policy and should be rejected, or wholly eliminated, in democratic and administrative arenas. But that possibility does not make them constitutionally objectionable.

In fact, the Supreme Court has yet to provide a clear explanation of the principle that requires affirmative action programs to be treated so skeptically. Most of its argument depends on a false claim of symmetry: if discrimination against African Americans is presumptively forbidden, how can discrimination against whites be presumptively legitimate? This question is more rhetoric than argument. It is no better than the question, if discrimination on the basis of sex is presumed illegitimate, how can the same not be true for discrimination on the basis of age? The anticaste principle helps provide an answer to both questions, and that answer suggests that different forms of discrimination or unequal treatment are utterly different. To be sure, the Court has referred to a set of legitimate concerns about affirmative action policies: the social divisiveness of affirmative action, the ordinary moral irrelevance of race, the fact that race is not chosen voluntarily, and the possibility that affirmative action programs will stigmatize their intended beneficiaries. But none of these points supports a convincing constitutional complaint about affirmative action. Many things that the government does are divisive, yet they are not unconstitutional for that reason. Many characteristics that are morally irrelevant, and that are not voluntarily chosen, are used by the government as classifying devices; consider height, strength, and intelligence. Affirmative action programs may well stigmatize their intended beneficiaries. But this form of stigma does not create a constitutional objection. A stigma might also be created by programs that benefit children of alumni or people from underrepresented regions, and those programs are not, because of their stigmatizing effects, unconstitutional under the Fourteenth Amendment.

Democratic Debate and Affirmative Action

These remarks certainly do not mean that affirmative action programs are a good idea. The range of such programs is very wide, and to make a judgment on their merits, it is important to have a sense of their variety and of their consequences. Such programs include relatively uncontroversial efforts to increase the pool of applicants by ensuring that the candidates are diverse; these efforts are certainly race-conscious, but at the stage of recruitment rather than actual appointment. It is hard to see why such efforts are objectionable. Other affirmative action programs include race as a modest factor among many others. Some programs seem to create a system of racial spoils, as in the set-aside of a specified percentage of government contracts for minority-owned businesses; other programs appear to be efforts to ensure that government offices can actually do their work well, as in efforts to ensure that police forces in African-American communities include a significant number of African-American officers. Some programs give a minor boost to highly qualified candidates, and some allow people entry into programs for which they are ill suited. Still other programs amount to rigid quota systems. Evaluation of such programs should depend partly on their content and their consequences, and the term "affirmative action programs" is far too imprecise to speak adequately on that score. Above all, we need to know how such programs are operating in the real world. Undoubtedly, many affirmative action programs are successful and perceived as such.

It is striking but true that until the very recent past, the nation had yet to have a sustained discussion about the legitimacy and variety of affirmative action programs and of possible alternatives. When Congress adopted the Civil Rights Act in 1964, discrimination against African Americans was of course the central focus of the debate. Affirmative action programs were in an embryonic state and did not receive much, if any, consideration. The first important affirmative action program was actually adopted by Executive Order.[19] The proliferation of such programs at the national, state, and local levels has proceeded without sustained attention to the underlying issues of principle and policy. Whatever one thinks about the legitimacy of affirmative action, this lack of deliberation and public attention is quite disturbing. In fact, it is plausible to think that some of the public backlash against affirmative action is attributable to the perception that the relevant programs have never been debated and defended publicly. It is not at all true to say, as many do, that affirmative action programs are a creation of federal courts; many such programs have their origins in private decisions or in decisions of politically accountable bodies. But the widespread perception that affirmative action programs are court-generated is illuminating insofar as it suggests a belief that such programs have not been debated and ratified publicly.

The Court as Catalyst in Affirmative Action

We are now in a position to discuss the possible catalytic role of the Supreme Court insofar as that role bears on the affirmative action debate. Suppose that it is agreed that the issue of affirmative action should be decided democratically rather than judicially—but suppose, too, that public institutions are operating in such a way as to ensure that any public decisions are taken in an unaccountable way, and are not really a product of democratic judgments. The Supreme Court's meandering, casuistical, minimalist, rule-free path may well be a salutary way of sig-naling the existence of large questions of policy and principle, at least with constitutional dimensions, when those questions would otherwise receive far less attention than they deserve. Hence the participants in Supreme Court cases have become familiar "characters" in the national debate, helping to frame discussion: people like Alan Bakke, Brian Web-er, Meredith Johnson, minority construction contractors, and others.

Judicial signaling is especially important in a context where social norms are having an adverse effect on open public discussion. Suppose that a policy persists not because people are in favor of it, but because social norms prevent people from voicing their complaints publicly. Suppose too that these complaints, though rarely articulated in public places, are widespread. If this is so, there is a democratic problem that requires attention. At least as a general rule, something should be done to ensure that the issue receives public consideration. Private actors can help to remedy the situation. We might even describe as "norm entre-preneurs" those people who try to activate private beliefs and judg-ments in favor of a shift in existing social norms. Consider, as diverse examples, Martin Luther King, Jr., Jerry Falwell, Billy Graham, Louis Farrakhan, and Catharine MacKinnon. Private norm entrepreneurs can signal the existence of a generally held but unarticulated view; they can solve the collective action problem faced by individuals who have re-mained silent because of existing norms. But official institutions can play a role as well. In particular, the Supreme Court can signal the existence of hard questions of political morality and public policy, by taking cases, drawing public attention to the underlying questions, and refusing to issue authoritative pronouncements. And if we examine the Court's practice in the area of affirmative action, we can see that the Court has operated in precisely this way. It has helped keep the affir-mative action issue in the public domain without foreclosing public deliberation. In this way, the Court has served a valuable catalytic func-tion, partly in virtue of its minimalism.

I do not claim that the Court has been self-conscious about its role. But some of the justices who tend to eschew broad rules, especially Justices O'Connor and Powell, have undoubtedly been aware of the difficulty and variety of the affirmative action problem and have chosen a minimalist approach for this reason. Nor do I claim that the current public attention to affirmative action owes its origin mostly to Supreme

Court decisions. The causal issues are complex, and undoubtedly a wide range of factors could be said to have played a catalytic role. All I contend is that the Court's decisions have been among the factors that have both kept affirmative action in the public eye and helped focus the public on issues of principle and policy. And to the extent that those effects have been salutary, the Court's practice here bears on other meandering paths in the past, and also on future practices where a degree of casuistry makes a good deal of sense.

The argument for minimalism, as a catalytic approach, would be much strengthened by evidence that judicial decisions will in fact spur, or at least be a healthy part of, ongoing processes of public deliberation. The argument would become even stronger if those processes have the potential to function well. If this is so, judicial minimalism may promote, rather than undermine, the system of democratic deliberation. If, on the other hand, public deliberation is unlikely in any event, or likely to operate very badly, a more rule-bound approach to the Constitution would be better. Obviously there are empirical issues here that I have not resolved.

On these grounds, we can see how the Court's minimalist decisions, defended in the way I have here, might best be criticized. Perhaps the Constitution is sensibly interpreted to ban all affirmative action programs (though I have suggested that this would be a most adventurous reading). Perhaps the Constitution is best understood not to draw such programs into question at all; the substantive argument I have offered suggests that this view has considerable weight. Or perhaps democratic processes have been working very well without the Court, and the Court's decisions have been marginally relevant, or have even helped to facilitate distortions of democratic deliberation. I do not believe this judgment could be supported, but it suggests the direction in which a challenge to the Court's approach might move. It suggests, too, how judicial minimalism might be evaluated in the context of other issues.

Deliberative Government and the Referendum

The suggestion that the Court has helped catalyze public debate should not by any means be taken as a claim that with respect to affirmative action, the democratic process has been or is now working well. With "norm cascades"—large shifts in current norms—there is a risk that outcomes will be based on sensationalistic anecdotes, on factual misperceptions, or, worse, on simple racism and hatred. Undoubtedly, objections to affirmative action programs are often well motivated; it would be ludicrous to think that such objections are necessarily or generally rooted in racial prejudice. But appeals to racism, usually tacit, are an unmistakable part of the debate. Some people might think that affirmative action is an unpromising area for public deliberation precisely because of the likelihood that racist motivations will be at work. If this is an unpromising area for public deliberation, the argument for a catalytic effort from the Court is of course weakened, and judges might attempt to resolve the problem on other grounds.

The relevant risks are especially severe in the context of a referendum, which bypasses the ordinary (and constitutionally central) filters of political representation and hence raises special dangers. Referenda may well be based on inadequate information and on popular passions that are insufficiently influenced by reason-giving and understanding of context. This was of course a relevant concern in the Constitution's framing period, for the framers rejected populist models in favor of a republican effort to promote more considered reflection through mechanisms designed, in James Madison's words, to "refine and enlarge" the public view. In the mid-1990s, for example, much national attention was focused on a successful referendum proposal in California, Proposition 209, designed to eliminate preferential treatment based on race. Political processes in California on this issue did not appear to be deliberative. The American system is one of representative rather than direct democracy, partly because of a judgment that political deliberation can be best promoted through a representative system. If judicial decisions stimulate poorly functioning referendum processes, little will be gained.

In the context of affirmative action in particular, there is a danger that referendum outcomes will not be based on a careful assessment of facts and values, but instead on crude "we-they" thinking. This is a particular danger in the context of race. It is not my purpose here to evaluate that risk. But if a catalytic role from the Court serves to intensify poorly functioning majoritarian processes, that role may be nothing to celebrate. Both exercises of statesmanship and institutional correctives—displacing the referendum process with more insulated bodies—may be in order. Hence it is appropriate to assemble politically insulated groups to try to compile information about the actual effects of affirmative action programs.

Unfortunately, it is unclear whether the Supreme Court can do a great deal to make things better. Perhaps the Court should review the outcomes of referenda with an unusually high degree of skepticism. There is some sense in this suggestion. An approach of this kind can find structural support in the Constitution, which is rooted in faith in representation, and in the Constitution's most fundamental underlying concerns. It is plausible to say that the Court should be mildly more receptive to a constitutional challenge when legislation has come through referenda. But no provision of the Constitution specifically authorizes judges to regard the outcomes of referenda as less legitimate than the outcomes of representative processes, and in any case it is not, under current law, easy to see how someone might challenge a ban on affirmative action on these constitutional grounds.

But there is a genuine constitutional difficulty with California's Proposition 209 and with any effort to ban affirmative action across the board. A constitutional ban on affirmative action at the state level has something in common with other measures, previously invalidated by the Supreme Court, that take racial issues outside of ordinary political processes and impose a special burden on civil rights groups seeking remedies for race-related harms.[20] Thus the Court invalidated a city charter amendment forbidding fair housing legislation; in a separate case, it held that a state may not adopt a statewide initiative barring localities from requiring students to attend schools other than those nearest or next nearest their place of residence. In both cases, the Court said that the relevant measure "uses the racial nature of an issue to define the governmental decisionmaking structure, and thus imposes substantial and unique burdens on racial minorities." In both cases, the invalidated law prevented measures that "inure primarily to the benefit of the minority." Thus "when the political process or the decision-making mechanism used to address racially conscious legislation—and only such legislation—is singled out for peculiar and disadvantageous treatment, the governmental action plainly rests on distinctions based on race." Hence the Court will be suspicious of any allocation of power "that places unusual burdens on the ability of racial groups to enact legislation specifically designed to overcome the 'special condition' of prejudice."

These precedents are quite complex, but the foregoing passages show that they do raise serious doubts about the California initiative insofar as that measure creates unusual barriers to ordinary political processes involving affirmative action. It would have been an intriguing irony if the Court, committed to a minimalist path with respect to affirmative action, chose to strike down a referendum in part with the knowledge that it contained a ban that prevented the kind of careful analysis of particulars that has stood behind the Court's own decisions. In 1997, however, the Supreme Court refused to hear a constitutional challenge to the California initiative, probably in an effort to exercise the "passive virtues." We can understand the Court's refusal to hear the case as rooted in an understanding that the judiciary ought not to disrupt ongoing processes of political debate over the status of affirmative action. Hence the Court's refusal to intervene is a coherent part of the Court's minimalist approach to the general area.

Norms and Minimalism

In this chapter I have tried to connect two ideas. The first involves the disjunction between private beliefs and public statements—a disjunction that stems from social norms that can discourage honest public argument about public issues and in that way undermine values that animate the First Amendment itself. The second involves the catalytic role of the Supreme Court. This role is ordinarily thought to involve three principal powers: validating laws, invalidating laws, and refusing to hear cases. But the Court has a fourth power—the authority to issue minimalist rulings that do not settle much, but that operate as a kind of "remand" to the public, alerting people to the existence of hard issues of principle and policy. In the affirmative action context, the Court, whether or not intentionally, has done precisely this. It has said little that is authoritative. It has endorsed no rule and no theory. It has, however, attempted to help trigger public debate, with, perhaps, an understanding on the part of some of the justices that until recently, the debate was neither broadly inclusive nor properly deliberative—and that it did not honestly reflect people's underlying concerns. In other words, the Court can be taken to have responded to the fact that social norms have helped prevent open public discussion, and to have tried to promote such a discussion.

From these points, it would be possible to celebrate what many have seen as the Court's indefensible course of rule-free judgment. Perhaps the Court has refused to foreclose an issue on which the political branches should have the final say, but nonetheless played a valuable role in ensuring that the political branches actually give the issue the attention that it warrants. Certainly the Court's decisions have inspired a great deal of media attention and placed a kind of public spotlight on affirmative action. And the Court's approach may even be seen as modeling the kind of close engagement with particulars that the area of affirmative action seems to require.

Ideas of this sort generally support minimalism in many domains of constitutional law, and minimalism makes a great deal of sense in the context of hard issues on which the nation is sharply divided. But the approach may be too optimistic in the particular context of affirmative action. If it is too optimistic, this is so either because affirmative action is not problematic from the standpoint of policy and principle, or because the political process, realistically speaking, is not deliberative at all, but instead serves as a forum for sloganeering, mutual suspicion, and racial prejudice.

Neither of these reservations can be easily dismissed. But in light of the wide range of programs labeled "affirmative action," the first reservation seems too starkly stated. Even those who approve of affirmative action should recognize that some programs are unfair and do not fulfill their intended purposes. In any case, a better public discussion would serve many valuable functions. It is much too soon to know whether the second reservation is warranted. But it does seem safe to say that the area of affirmative action casts a new light on the role of the Supreme Court. It shows that the Court's catalytic role can help trigger public debate and heretofore silent protest where debate might otherwise be absent. It shows that a form of minimalism—even one that occasionally invalidates outcomes of political processes—may well promote, rather than undermine, democratic deliberation. And because this is an area in which social norms have sometimes had harmful effects on political discussion, it shows, once again, that there is no simple opposition between majoritarian politics and judicial review.

7

Sex and Sexual Orientation

Outside of the context of race, what practices should the equal protection clause be understood to forbid? For what principle should it be taken to stand? And how aggressive should the Supreme Court be in invoking that principle? What is the role of minimalism in answering that question?

These issues have become especially pressing in the context of discrimination on the basis of sex and sexual orientation. In the highly publicized 1996 decision in Romer v. Evans,[1] the Supreme Court held, for the first time in its history, that discrimination against homosexuals violates the equal protection clause. The Court's use of the equal protection clause in the context of sex discrimination is far less recent, having begun in 1971 with the minimalist decision in Reed v. Reed.[2] But the issue has become newly heated in connection with discrimination in the military and same-sex education. In these areas, the key case is the Supreme Court's invalidation of same-sex education at Virginia Military Institute in United States v. Virginia.[3] As we will see, that invalidation, like the decision in Romer v. Evans, was quite narrow, in the sense that it resolved few issues other than those necessary to decide the case. But unlike the (emphatically shallow) decision in *Romer*, it was quite deep, in the sense that it offered an ambitious understanding of the objective of the equal protection clause.

The two cases therefore provide a good occasion for exploring both the uses of minimalism and the substantive issues raised by equal protection law. My basic argument is that the Court proceeded properly in both cases. The Court's decision in Romer v. Evans was sparsely reasoned—somewhat too sparsely—but the Court was right to strike down the discrimination involved in the case, and the minimalist character of the opinion makes sense in light of the complexity, and novelty, of the issues raised by constitutional attacks on discrimination against homosexuals. Because those issues are so new, and because they are a part of continuing political deliberation, the Court was right to provide a narrow and incompletely theorized judgment, one that allows room for future political and judicial debate. The Court was also correct to invalidate the state's exclusion of women from Virginia Military Institute. It was right to give an ambitious account of what is wrong with discrimination on the basis of sex; and it was right to leave open the status of other same-sex programs. And in both cases, the Court was correct to offer a distinctive understanding of the equal protection clause, one that bans second-class citizenship and that forbids the state from acting in accordance with an "animus" against any group.

Possible Worlds

Amendment 2 to the Colorado Constitution was enacted by popular referendum. It was responsive to, and an effort to outlaw, local ordinances forbidding discrimination on the basis of sexual orientation. As enacted, Amendment 2 provided that "[n]either the State of Colorado . . . nor any of its agencies . . . shall enact, adopt or enforce any statute, regulation, ordinance or policy whereby homosexual, lesbian or bisexual orientation, conduct, practices, or relationships shall be the basis of or entitle any person or class of persons to have or claim any minority status, quota preferences, protected status or claim of discrimination."

In Romer v. Evans, the Supreme Court was asked to decide whether this provision was a violation of the equal protection clause. In answering that question, the Court had various obvious options.

- It could have concluded that this was not a form of discrimination at all, and hence that there was no equal protection issue.
- It could have concluded that this was a form of discrimination against homosexuals, but that discrimination of that kind would be subject to "rational basis" review, and that Amendment 2, like almost all forms of discrimination subject to rational basis review, should be upheld.
- It could have concluded that discrimination on the basis of sexual orientation should be subject to special judicial scrutiny, like dis-

crimination on the basis of race and sex, and that Amendment 2 should therefore be invalidated.

- It could have emphasized that some of the amendment was targeted not against conduct at all but against status—the status of homosexuality—and that it was unconstitutional because it created a kind of "status" offense, in violation of the due process clause. It is generally agreed that under that clause, the government may punish behavior (disorderly conduct, driving while drunk) but may not punish status (aggressive tendencies, alcoholism). Perhaps Amendment 2 created a status offense.
- It could have said that the amendment was unconstitutional because it involved a disability in the political process, as the Colorado Supreme Court had concluded.

The Court adopted none of these options. In an extremely unusual ruling, the Court held that Amendment 2 violated rational basis review because it was based not on a legitimate public purpose but on a form of "animus"—with the apparent suggestion that statutes rooted in "animus" represent core offenses of the equal protection guarantee. This claim is more minimalist than any of the others. It also raises more complex issues, not least because the Court did not say a word about Bowers v. Hardwick,[4] the only other Supreme Court decision involving homosexuality, in which the Court upheld a Georgia law making consensual homosexual sodomy a crime.

The Court began its analysis by rejecting the view that Amendment 2 merely puts homosexuals in the same position as everyone else. It said that by enacting a special prohibition against any protective measures, the amendment actually put homosexuals in a distinctive and worse position. "The amendment withdraws from homosexuals, but no others, specific legal protection from the injuries caused by discrimination, and it forbids reinstatement of these laws and policies." Understood as a special disability, the amendment, in the Court's view, failed "rationality" review, since it did not bear a rational relation to a legitimate statutory end. The Court offered two different (but evidently overlapping) explanations.

First, it said that Amendment 2 "is at once too narrow and too broad," because it takes people with "a single trait and then denies them protection across the board." Thus it did not show an adequate connection between the classification and the object to be attained. "A law declaring that in general it shall be more difficult for one group of citizens than for all others to seek aid from the government is itself a denial of equal protection of the laws in the most literal sense." A measure that disqualifies a class of people "from the right to seek specific protection from the law" violates the requirement of impartiality.[5]

Second, the Court said that that law is too broad to be justifiable by reference to the reasons invoked on its behalf, such as recognition of the associational liberty of those with religious objections to homosexuals and homosexuality. Hence it "seems inexplicable by anything but animus toward the class it affects." Thus Amendment 2 "in making a general announcement that gays and lesbians shall not have any particular protections from the law, inflicts on them immediate, continuing, and real injuries that outrun and belie any legitimate justifications that can be claimed for it." The interest in associational liberty for people with religious convictions could be protected by different and narrower means, such as an exemption from any antidiscrimination law for those having religious objections. The state also said that it wanted to conserve its resources to protect other forms of discrimination. But Amendment 2 was far too broad to be justified by reference to that purpose. Thus it stands (and falls) as "a status-based classification of persons undertaken for its own sake."[6]

Subminimalism? An Initial Evaluation

At first glance, neither of the Court's two arguments is convincing. Let us assume that rationality review is the appropriate standard. As we have seen, rationality review ordinarily means that a state law will be upheld if it has any plausible connection to a legitimate goal. If this is so, Amendment 2 seems constitutional, as an effort either (1) to prevent or discourage the social legitimation of homosexuality or (2) to conserve scarce enforcement resources and to protect associational privacy. The first interest may seem of doubtful legitimacy—I will discuss this possibility below—but rationality review by itself does not rule out any interests as illegitimate, and thus for the Court to say that (1) is illegitimate, it has to speak somewhat ambitiously, and controversially, about what the state may properly say or do. The Court was reluctant to do this in the *Romer* case.

The second and third interests do seem crudely adapted to the measure itself, for they are both overinclusive and underinclusive. As the Court said, a state could promote those interests by better means than forbidding antidiscrimination laws. But this fact does not doom a statute under rational basis review; overinclusive and underinclusive legislation is perfectly acceptable, indeed, quite common. For example, a mandatory retirement law is overinclusive, because it eliminates good workers, but it is not unconstitutional for that reason. Do the Court's two arguments contain any response to this challenge?

Recall the Court's first argument: that Colorado had eliminated "protection" of homosexuals and thus created a kind of per se violation of the equal protection clause. As offered by the Court, the argument seems to be a confusing amalgam of a claim based on means-ends scrutiny and an argument based on the "literal" meaning of the words "equal protection." The means-ends concern is identical to the Court's second argument, to be taken up shortly, so let us focus on the Court's suggestion—a variation on one offered in an ingenious and widely discussed amicus brief written by law professor Laurence Tribe—to the effect that Amendment 2 is a "literal" denial of equal protection of the law. What does this mean? Perhaps Amendment 2 is akin to a law declaring certain people to be *outlaws*—as in a provision that murderers, the elderly, felons, or people with blue eyes cannot claim the protection of the laws. Such a law would—it might be urged—amount to a per se or "literal" violation of the equal protection clause, since it deprives some people of the power to seek state protection through the law. A state may not say that some people are unable to invoke the "protection" of the law; under the equal protection clause, all citizens, equally, may claim the law's protection.

This is a simple and appealingly minimalist argument; it would permit the Court to strike down Amendment 2 without saying anything else about the relationship between homosexuality and the Constitution. And we may agree that a state could not say that certain people (smokers, the elderly, homosexuals) are literally unprotected by the law. But there are serious problems with this argument in the context of Amendment 2, for it is not at all clear that Amendment 2 is really akin to the hypothesized law. Amendment 2 does not declare homosexuals to be outlaws. Most important, the Court was willing to assume that they remain protected by the ordinary civil (contract, tort, property) and criminal law. Homosexuals may seek protection from the ordinary civil courts if someone has breached a contractual duty, or committed a tort, or trespassed on their property. Amendment 2 says only that homosexuals cannot claim the (unusual, in a sense "special") protection of antidiscrimination law simply by virtue of their status as homosexuals; it added the (unusual, in a sense "special" and admittedly somewhat bizarre) idea that homosexuals cannot get such protection without amending the Constitution. However unusual, this does not make anyone into an outlaw. If Colorado enacted a constitutional amendment saying that unwed mothers, or unwed mothers who refuse work, or unwed mothers who live with a man out of wedlock, may not claim the protection of the welfare statutes, it would not be committing a literal or per se violation of the equal protection clause. The fact that some people do not get statutory protection, while others do, is not a constitutional problem. To know whether there has been a violation of the right to "equal" protection, we have to know about the grounds for differential treatment. The technical question would be whether the provision faced rational basis review or heightened scrutiny, and whether it was valid or invalid under the appropriate standard of review.

In other words, Amendment 2 appears to be akin to one that makes certain people (constitutionally) unable to invoke the protection of laws granting welfare benefits. If the analogy is correct, the claim of "literal" denial of equal protection is really a kind of verbal trick, a play on the word "protection." It is a pun, not an argument. My conclusion is that the Court's first argument adds nothing, and the real argument is the second.

Is the Court's second argument persuasive? As I have indicated, the state had two possible responses. To offer a bit more detail, let us suppose that the state responded in either or both of the following ways.

1. "The interest in conserving enforcement resources is, to be sure, crudely connected to Amendment 2. But there is some connection. We believe that if a locality is spending its time on preventing discrimination against homosexuals, it will spend less of its time on preventing discrimination against blacks and women, which we think are more important concerns. In any case many people have strong religious or other reasons to discriminate on grounds of sexual orientation. We want

to respect their convictions. Amendment 2 may be imperfectly matched to our goals—we acknowledge that it covers many contexts in which those goals are not involved—but so long as rationality review is the appropriate standard, we think we have said more than enough."

2. "We do not want to legitimate homosexuality as a social practice. In fact we are not tyrants and we do not seek to subject homosexual acts to criminal punishment (as we are permitted to do under Bowers v. Hardwick). But we do want to make a statement to the effect that homosexuality is not officially sponsored, in the sense that homosexuals do not have a way of life that, as such, qualifies its members for legal protection against discrimination. We are trying to express a widely held moral commitment, to the effect that homosexuality is not to be approved even if it is to be tolerated; and we choose to express that view through a prohibition on special protections against discrimination. Of course our law applies to people with homosexual tendencies who do not engage in homosexual activity. But people with tendencies are likely to engage in acts. We do not punish through criminal law the tendencies alone; we think our basic goal is well enough matched to what we have done here."

The Court did not offer much of a response to these arguments. The most troubling (sub)minimalism of the opinion lies in this failure. Let us try to approach the issue through a question that received particular attention in the case: Was Amendment 2 a unique disability, or a denial of special privileges? And how, if at all, is this a relevant question?

Special Benefits and Unique Disabilities

We find nothing special in the protections Amendment 2 withholds. These are protections taken for granted by most people either because they already have them or do not need them.

—Romer v. Evans

The Court thought that Amendment 2 was a unique disability because it "withdraws from homosexuals, but no others, specific legal protection from the injuries caused by discrimination, and it forbids reinstatement of these laws and policies." Writing in dissent, Justice Scalia thought that on the contrary, Amendment 2 was a denial of "special privileges" because most characteristics are not a basis for statutory protection from discrimination. In Justice Scalia's view, what Amendment 2 did was to restore the status quo ante—a situation in which only a few groups receive that protection.

Let us try to sort out these issues by noting that there was a sense in which both sides were right. It is true to say that states do not consider most group-based characteristics to be a basis for statutory protection against discrimination. Short people, tall people, movie-makers, singers, horse riders, dog owners—all these, and innumerable others, receive no special legal protection against discrimination. In this sense it is fair to say that Amendment 2 simply restored homosexuals to a status like that of nearly everyone else. On the other hand, there is also a sense in which Amendment 2 imposed on homosexuals a unique disability. Short people, tall people, movie-makers, singers, horse riders, dog owners—all these can petition relevant legislatures for protection against discrimination. Homosexuals are subject to a unique disability in the sense that they are uniquely required to amend the Colorado Constitution to obtain such protection. In this sense there is indeed discrimination.

Thus Justice Scalia and the Court are both right. The weakness of Justice Scalia's opinion is that it does not come to terms with the respect in which Amendment 2 puts homosexuals at a special disadvantage. There is such a respect. In the striking quotation at the beginning of this section, the Court embraced a baseline of nondiscrimination. But this special disadvantage is not necessarily fatal to the legislation. A unique disability of this kind may not violate the equal protection clause. If, for example, Colorado said—in, say, Amendment 3—that no governmental body may allow cigarette smokers to claim minority status, quota preferences, or protected status for any claim of discrimination, it would probably be acting constitutionally, at least if Amendment 3 were understood in the narrow way the Supreme Court was willing to understand Amendment 2. Amendment 3 would be constitutional because a state could legitimately decide that it would want to prevent itself and its subdivisions from giving special safeguards to smokers. It could make that decision because it is legitimate to think that smokers create serious risks to themselves and to others. Perhaps some localities reject this position and want to treat smokers as the functional equivalent of blacks and women; this is hardly an unimaginable view. But a state could reasonably choose to override this view.

Could smokers, thus disadvantaged, complain that they had been deprived of equal protection of the laws? It seems clear that they would face a unique disability. But this burden would not fail rationality review, because it would be reasonably related to the legitimate interest in decreasing risks to life and health. Thus a finding that Amendment 2 imposes a unique disability is not fatal to its constitutionality. The question is whether there is a legitimate justification for the imposition of the disability.

What distinguishes *Romer* from the smokers' case? The only possible answer is that there is no legitimate reason for a state to constitutionalize a judgment that homosexuals cannot be protected from discrimination, because there is no legitimate reason to think that homosexuals pose a risk in the way that smokers do, or because the state has no legitimate interest in deciding that localities should not protect homosexuals from discrimination. Thus the case seems not at all to turn on whether we have a removal of special benefit or a unique disability, but instead whether the state has legitimate reasons for doing what it has done. An understanding of this kind seems to underlie the Court's suggestion that what makes Amendment 2 unconstitutional is that it is undergirded by a "bare desire to harm a politically unpopular group."

But on this point Justice Scalia has a seemingly powerful response. In this context, at least, the "bare desire to harm" can be translated into one side in a "culture war." Those who take that side believe that homosexuality should not be approved through antidiscrimination law, and "surely it is rational to deny special favor and protection to those with a self-avowed tendency or desire to engage in the conduct." The relevant animus here is not a bare desire to harm but a product of a widespread "moral disapproval of homosexual conduct." In Justice Scalia's eyes, that kind of animus is hardly objectionable from the constitutional point of view.

The majority must be taken to be saying the opposite. It must be taken to be saying that any such animus is illegitimate at least if it is the source of an unusual, blunderbuss prohibition on any antidiscrimination measures. In this way the debate is joined. Here, then, is the crux of the *Romer* case.

The Moreno-Cleburne-Romer Trilogy

[L]aws of the kind now before us raise the inevitable inference that the disadvantage imposed is born of animosity toward the class of persons affected.
—Romer v. Evans

[T]he deliberative conception of democracy . . . restricts the reasons citizens may use in supporting legislation to reasons consistent with the recognition of other citizens as equals. Here lies the difficulty with arguments for laws supporting discrimination. . . . The point is that no institutional procedure without such substantive guidelines for admissible reasons can cancel the maxim "garbage in, garbage out."
—John Rawls[7]

In a handful of cases, rationality review has actually meant something; it has resulted in judicial invalidation of laws. Each of these cases has been minimalist in character. The Court has found an inadequate connection with statutory means and ends; in doing so, it has attempted to "flush out" impermissible purposes.

A number of the key cases have involved issues of federalism.[8] The Court has struck down state statutes that purport to protect public-regarding goals and that actually seem to reflect protectionism—a desire to protect in-staters at the expense of out-of-staters. If the federal system is understood to ban protectionism, these cases are not at all hard to understand. Rationality review means something here because it serves as an effort to "flush out" the constitutionally prohibited end of protectionism. The Court looks beyond the articulated justifications, which typically bear a weak though not wholly implausible relation to the classification. What it sees is illegitimate protectionism. These cases are not entirely minimalist—they depend on an account of a prohibited end, an account that leads to a degree of width and depth—but they tend toward the minimalist end of the continuum. They offer narrow, targeted bans on certain kinds of reasons for law.

But there is a more puzzling set of cases; we may now refer to them as the "Moreno-Cleburne-Romer trilogy." In these cases, the Court ruled off-limits a constitutionally unacceptable "animus" not involving federalism or discrimination on the basis of race or sex. The hard question is whether we can identify the impermissible goal and see how it links the three cases. What precisely is "animus"?

The problem in *Moreno*[9] arose from Congress's decision to exclude from the food stamp program any household containing any individual who was unrelated to any other member of the household. Thus the statute required that any household receiving food stamps must consist solely of related individuals. The Court invalidated the statute. The Court said that the articulated justification—minimizing fraud in the food stamp program—seemed weakly connected to the statutory classification; in this way its opinion is a clear precursor of the Court's skeptical approach in *Romer* with respect to conservation of enforcement resources and protection of association. The Court noted that the legislative history suggested a congressional desire to exclude "hippies" and "hippie communes." To this the Court said, in words echoed in *Romer:* "[I]f the constitutional conception of 'equal protection of the laws' means anything, it must at the very least mean that a bare congressional desire to harm a politically unpopular group cannot constitute a legitimate governmental interest. . . ." Justice Rehnquist dissented on the ground that Congress could reasonably decide that it wanted to support, with taxpayer funds, only those units that are a "variation on the family as we know it." Justice Rehnquist's strategy—like Justice Scalia's in *Romer*—was to describe the "bare desire to harm" as an effort to promote a moral commitment, by funding traditional rather than untraditional families.

In the *Cleburne* case,[10] a city in Texas denied a special use permit for the operation of a group home for the mentally retarded. The Court rejected the view that discrimination against mentally retarded people should be subject to "heightened scrutiny." But applying rational basis review, it nonetheless found the city's denial of the permit unacceptable. It appeared to think that the city was operating on the basis of prejudice, or "animus," rather than any legitimate public purpose. The city had pointed to the fears of elderly residents, the negative attitudes of property owners, the concern that students nearby might harass the residents, the size of the home and the number of people who would occupy it, and the fact that the home would be located on a flood plain. Unquestionably these concerns would satisfy ordinary rationality review. For purposes of that standard, it is not decisive—it is not even relevant—that there is a poor fit between these ends and the means chosen by Cleburne. But the *Cleburne* Court was clearly concerned that something illegitimate underlay the city's decision. It signaled these illegitimate purposes by admonishing that "mere negative attitudes, or fear, unsubstantiated by factors which are properly cognizable in a zoning proceeding, are not permissible bases for" unequal treatment. Thus the Court concluded that the discriminatory action under review was based "on an irrational prejudice." (It should be plain that *Romer* was rooted in the same basic concern.)

Notably, each case in the Moreno-Cleburne-Romer trilogy partakes of decisional minimalism. None of the three cases establishes a new "tier" of scrutiny. *Cleburne* and *Romer* are notable for having failed to do so, for many people have urged that discrimination on the basis of disability or homosexuality should give rise to some kind of heightened scrutiny. All three cases reflect the possible use of rationality review as a kind of magical trump card, or perhaps joker, hidden in the pack and used on special occasions. In this way too they are minimalist; they need have no progeny.

The trilogy is also linked with the federalism cases in the sense that all of them involved a judicial suspicion of a constitutionally illicit purpose. But there is a substantial difference. In the federalism cases, the illicitness of the purpose is easy to understand. It is not controversial to say that the Constitution makes it illegitimate for states to disfavor citizens of other states, when the reason is simply that the disfavored citizens are citizens of other states. But what is constitutionally illicit about the purposes in the trilogy? This is the question pressed by Justice Scalia in *Romer*. If we are seeking a theoretically adequate opinion, Justice Scalia was owed a better answer.

In both *Cleburne* and *Romer*, the Court was concerned that a politically unpopular group was being punished as a result of irrational hatred and fear. Many people appear to think that mental retardation (like homosexuality) is contagious and frightening. The mentally retarded are frequently subject to irrational hatred, rooted in an absence of empathetic identification, a belief that they are not entirely human and should be avoided and sealed off. The use of rationality review to invalidate the law depended on the Court's understanding of all this and in particular its explicit belief that irrational hatred was likely to be at work. And if *Cleburne* is to make sense, it must be because the state cannot discriminate against the mentally retarded simply because people are frightened by them.

But we have seen enough to be able to say that hatred and fear can always be translated into public-regarding justifications. Thus in *Cle-*

burne the city was able to point to neutral-sounding grounds—students might harass the residents, property values might drop. Thus in *Romer*, it might have been said that the state was attempting to protect associational liberty or not to legitimate homosexual behavior, just as in *Moreno*, it was attempting not to promote nontraditional living arrangements. Along this dimension *Romer* and *Moreno* are very close. Food stamps can be seen as a form of "subsidy"; so too for antidiscrimination laws. And so too in *Cleburne*, involving a denial of a "special" use permit. Thus in all three cases there were poorly fitting but probably rational justifications (harassment by students in *Cleburne*, discouragement of fraud in *Moreno*, conservation of resources and protection of association in *Romer*) and also well-fitting justifications whose legitimacy was in doubt (response to private fears in *Cleburne*, desire to exclude nontraditional families in *Moreno*, desire not to legitimate homosexuality in *Romer*).

With this we come close to the heart of the matter. The underlying judgment in *Romer* must be that at least for purposes of the equal protection clause, it is no longer legitimate to discriminate against homosexuals simply because the state wants to discourage homosexuality. Discrimination must be justified on some other, public-regarding ground. The underlying concern must be that a measure discriminating against homosexuals, like a measure discriminating against the mentally retarded, is likely to reflect sharp "we/they" distinctions and irrational hatred and fear, directed at who they are as much as at what they do. It is for this reason that measures directed against homosexuals are not only or not fundamentally about actions.[11] Here, as with the mentally retarded, we can find a desire to fence off and seal off members of a despised group whose characteristics are thought to be in some sense contaminating, corrosive, or contagious. In its most virulent forms, this desire is rooted in a belief that members of the relevant group are not fully human.[12] On this count *Cleburne* and *Romer* are at one. And because the proffered justifications were so weakly connected with the measures at issue, the Court was right to do what it did in both cases.

Moreno is the harder case, because there was less reason to believe that hatred and fear were at work. Perhaps the case was wrongly decided. But the reference to "hippie communes," taken in the context of the time, may be taken to suggest a similar kind of "we-they" antagonism. And if we see the three cases in these terms, we can link them not only with each other but with the defining case of discrimination against the newly free slaves. *Moreno, Cleburne,* and *Romer* reflect an understanding that other groups, and not merely African Americans, may be subject to unreasoning hatred and suspicion. Hence the *Romer* Court's remarkable opening reference to Justice Harlan's dissenting opinion ("there is no caste here") in Plessy v. Ferguson.

With this point we can see that the outcome in *Romer* was not minimalist in the less controversial way that Kent v. Dulles and Hampton v. Mow Sun Wong were minimalist (see Chapter 3). The outcome turned on a substantive judgment about what grounds for state law are legitimate. For this reason we can understand Justice Scalia's complaint that *Romer* did not promote but instead usurped democratic deliberation. If *Romer* is to be defended, it must be because the grounds for Amendment 2 are, in a deliberative democracy, properly ruled off-limits, because they reflect a judgment that certain citizens are and are properly treated as social outcasts. The argument for *Romer* must in this way associate Amendment 2 with measures like those in Plessy v. Ferguson, upholding racial segregation, and Bradwell v. Illinois,[13] upholding the exclusion of women from the practice of law (which is not to suggest that the harms of Amendment 2 are the same in degree). *Romer* must in this way be treated as embodying a ban on laws motivated by a desire to create second-class citizenship, a point that connects the outcome with United States v. Virginia as well. This was the forbidden motivation that the Court described as "animus."

Subminimalism versus Minimalism

Should the Court have been clearer on these points? From the standpoint of traditional judicial craft, the answer is yes. Such an opinion would be more coherent. Though it would be more deeply theorized, it need not have been very wide; it could have left open the status of many other forms of discrimination against homosexuals, including the ban on same-sex marriage. We could certainly imagine an opinion saying that if the government is going to discriminate against homosexuals, it must do so on some ground other than its dislike of homosexuals and homosexuality. We could certainly imagine an opinion linking this form of discrimination with discrimination on the basis of sex and race. If that argument is correct, it would be hard to object to its judicial adoption. But perhaps at this early stage, it makes sense for the Court to have been even more minimalist than that—to have rendered an opinion lying somewhere between a denial of certiorari and a fully articulated defense. It may have made sense to do this partly because of the simple practical difficulties in obtaining a more ambitious majority opinion; partly because of the justices' lack of confidence in their own understandings of exactly what the Constitution requires in this setting; and partly because of strategic considerations having to do with the timing of judicial interventions into politics in this highly contested area. Perhaps Romer v. Evans is like Reed v. Reed, the Court's first decision striking down a law on grounds of sex discrimination—a subminimalist beginning to a set of judicial developments that go hand in hand with processes of democratic deliberation.

What the Court did had the vice of its own distinctive brand of minimalism—the failure even to do what is minimally necessary for self-defense. This is a genuine vice. But if we consider the entire context, it may also be an act of statesmanship. The narrow and shallow decision may turn out to symbolize something broader and deeper; ultimately analogical reasoning and applicable principles of stare decisis will resolve that question. *Romer* imposes unusually few constraints on its own interpretation. One of the central issues here has to do with the fate of Bowers v. Hardwick.

Equal Protection versus Due Process

We have not yet explored an obvious question: what about *Hardwick*, which—it will be recalled—upheld a ban on consensual homosexual sodomy? Astonishingly, the *Romer* Court did not discuss or even cite *Hardwick*. Its failure to do so is remarkable in light of the fact that *Hardwick* seemed to belie the argument just offered. That is, *Hardwick* seemed to say that it is legitimate for the state to express disapproval of homosexual conduct, indeed that it is legitimate for the state to express that disapproval via the criminal law. If it is acceptable for the state to *criminalize* homosexual activity, why does it not follow that it is acceptable for the state to ban localities from providing special legal protection against discrimination against homosexuals? Criminal punishment is a far more severe response to moral opprobrium than a ban on antidiscrimination claims.

We have encountered subminimalism in the *Romer* Court's failure to identify the illegitimate purpose that it detected and to explain why that purpose is illegitimate. An additional aspect of the Court's subminimalism consists in its failure to answer the question just posed, or indeed to say anything about how *Romer* and *Hardwick* fit together. We might even say that the Court's silence on *Hardwick* is under ordinary circumstances an unacceptable exercise of judicial power. An apparently relevant precedent ought to receive at least some discussion, especially if it is raised seriously in dissent. If the Court's silence is legitimate, it is because these are far from ordinary circumstances.

Let us attempt an answer to a simple factual issue first: why did the Court say nothing about *Hardwick?* I speculate that the Court's silence about *Hardwick* stemmed from the fact that a majority could not be gotten to (a) distinguish *Hardwick,* (b) approve *Hardwick,* or (c) overrule *Hardwick*. If each of these options was unavailable, silence was the only alternative. No discussion of *Hardwick* could have garnered majority support. The Court's silence may therefore have been a product of the fact that a multimember tribunal could not converge on any rationale.

But what, then, is the current status of *Hardwick?* This is a pressing question. Justice Scalia is certainly correct to suggest that there is a severe tension between the two cases. The tension lies in the fact that *Hardwick* says that disapproval of homosexual sodomy is a sufficient reason for criminal prohibition, whereas *Romer* denies that disapproval of homosexuality is a sufficient reason to bar use of antidiscrimination law. It follows that if *Hardwick* is taken as settled law, if we put to one side possible differences between the due process and equal protection clauses, and if *Romer* is understood as a true rationality case, *Romer* was wrongly decided. It also follows that if these conditions are met, and if *Romer* is taken as settled law, *Hardwick* has been overruled.

The Court could have dealt with *Hardwick* in various ways. Each of these possibilities bears on what lower courts, or the Court itself, might say or do in the future.

1. It could have said that *Hardwick* was wrong and is therefore overruled. This would certainly not have been minimalist; it would have involved rejecting a precedent that is fairly long-standing and that has helped stake out an important position on the meaning and future of the due process clause. A decision to overrule *Hardwick* would be an

especially troubling result in light of the fact that the due process clause was not at issue in *Romer*. If anything like decisional minimalism is appropriate in this context, the Court was properly reluctant to overrule *Hardwick* in a case in which it was not necessary to do so.

2. It could have said that *Hardwick* was different from *Romer* because it involved the due process clause, whereas *Romer* involved the equal protection clause.

3. It could have said that there is a large difference between (a) a narrow, targeted prohibition on certain activity via the criminal law and (b) an indiscriminate, blunderbuss prohibition on all laws helping a certain group (whose members may or may not have engaged in the relevant activity). On this view, it is acceptable to ban sodomy if a society finds that form of conduct reprehensible. But it is not acceptable for government to ban people of homosexual orientation *or* engaging in homosexual conduct, in an open-ended way, from seeking the protections of antidiscrimination law. The reason is that the ban on sodomy reflects a long-standing, targeted, and hence legitimate social judgment, whereas the ban on antidiscrimination laws is a novel, broad-gauged measure inexplicable in terms that reflect anything other than animus. Perhaps this argument could or should be combined with the argument immediately above; perhaps it could be freestanding.

4. It could have said that the law in *Hardwick* was supported by tradition, whereas the law in *Romer* was not. In fact the *Romer* Court emphasized the novelty of Amendment 2, whereas the *Hardwick* Court emphasized the time-honored character of the ban on homosexual sodomy. On this view both decisions could be understood as reflecting the perceived legitimacy of tradition.

5. It could have said that the key point in *Romer* is that many of those who could not seek antidiscrimination had engaged in no homosexual behavior, and that *Romer* involved something like a status offense. Hence the Court's suggestion that this is "a status-based classification of persons undertaken for its own sake."

Let us briefly evaluate these possibilities. Argument (5) does connect with some of the Court's statements in *Romer*. Amendment 2 had the most peculiar feature of targeting people regardless of their actions. *Hardwick* says that the government can legitimately act against homosexual sodomy; but it does not follow that it can punish mere homosexual status. In fact it would certainly be unconstitutional to make "homosexual status" a crime. But these points do not suggest that (5) is right. There was no criminal ban in *Romer*. The Court's opinion did not principally stress the status offense issue; if it had, it might well have invalidated Amendment 2 only insofar as it targeted the mere status of homosexual orientation and preserved the rest. In any case, Justice Scalia plausibly argued that it follows from *Hardwick* not that government can make homosexual status a crime, but that government can prohibit the use of the antidiscrimination law to protect people who have an inclination to engage in the conduct it disfavors. In other words, it is not clear that a government disabled from creating "status offenses" is also disabled from saying that people inclined to engage in disfavored activity cannot, because of that inclination, seek the protection of antidiscrimination laws. The analogy is not perfect, but consider a law defining alcoholics or smokers to be addicts, or people inclined to heavy drinking and smoking, and saying that alcoholics and smokers cannot as such claim the protection of antidiscrimination law.

Argument (4) has some truth to it. The Court did refer to the novelty of Amendment 2, with the apparent thought that the novelty helped signal that something odd and perhaps untoward was at work. But novelty is not synonymous with unconstitutionality. Even if tradition helps give content to the due process clause, and even if novelty gives rise to suspicion, tradition does not have the constitutional weight that argument (4) attempts to give it (see the discussion in Chapter 5). In any case the Court's emphasis on the unusual nature of Amendment 2 was a bit odd. It is only recently that localities have started to forbid discrimination on the basis of sexual orientation; tradition is hardly inconsistent with that form of discrimination; and thus Colorado might have said that it was restoring the traditional status quo ante by undoing those laws.

Argument (3) is more plausible. The law in *Hardwick* was hardly over- or underinclusive, and this was the Court's objection to Amendment 2. Hence it could be said that *Romer*, invalidating a poorly fitting law, falls in the protectionism-*Moreno-Cleburne* line of equal protection cases, whereas *Hardwick*, upholding a nicely fitting law, is like any case upholding a statute against substantive due process attack. This is not an unreasonable position. But it is not convincing. The key question, uniting *Hardwick* and *Romer*, is whether it is permissible for the state to try to delegitimate, or to decide not to legitimate, homosexual relations. If it is, *Hardwick* is right and *Romer* is wrong, even if Amendment 2 was over- and underinclusive. Thus it seems that argument (3) does not work unless it is accompanied by argument (2).

It may well be that *Hardwick* is now very fragile and that eventually argument (1) will prevail. We could certainly imagine worse outcomes than the overruling of *Hardwick*, a casually written (subminimalist) opinion and one of the most vilified decisions since World War II. But it is right to insist that the equal protection and due process clauses have very different offices, and that *Hardwick* is in no tension with *Romer* so long as those different offices are kept in mind. The *Hardwick* Court was careful to say that no equal protection challenge had been raised, and this is important, for the category of legitimate state interests is provision-specific rather than Constitution-general.[14] A set of judgments honored by tradition may be immune from due process challenge; perhaps the rights protected by the due process clause must grow out of long-standing practices. But the same cannot be said of the equal protection clause, which has a different purpose and a different function.

As it has come to be understood, the equal protection clause is tradition-correcting, whereas the due process clause is at least generally tradition-protecting. The equal protection clause sets out a normative ideal that operates as a critique of existing practices; the due process clause safeguards rights long established in Anglo-American law. Part of the explanation for this understanding is historical. The textual and interpretive difficulties in the whole notion of substantive due process have pressed the Court to embrace "tradition" as the source of constitutionally protected rights. This is a controversial step (see Chapter 5); but it is certainly understandable as an effort to constrain judicial discretion.

Equal protection law is very different. It can proceed more or less sensibly from the paradigm case of discrimination against the newly free slaves, a paradigm case from which equal protection cases, not excluding Romer v. Evans, have indeed developed. On this view, *Romer* leaves *Hardwick* untouched, simply because different provisions were at issue. And on this view, Justice Scalia is wrong to think it anomalous that the state can prohibit homosexual sodomy while being banned from enacting Amendment 2. The Constitution includes a number of provisions, not just one. Everything depends on the particular constitutional

challenge that is being mounted and the particular constitutional provision that is being invoked. The equal protection clause, for example,
makes animus against African Americans constitutionally unacceptable,
even though there is nothing specifically objectionable about that animus under the contracts clause. Consider as an illustration the maximalist opinion in Loving v. Virginia, in which a ban on miscegenation
was struck down on both equal protection and due process grounds.
If the ban had been upheld against due process attack in *Loving*, it
would not follow that an equal protection challenge would be unavailable. Indeed, if the *Loving* Court had held that the due process clause
is purely procedural, the equal protection attack would not be affected
in the least.

If we insist on the distinction between equal protection and due
process, we can say that *Romer* was right even if *Hardwick* remains
good law, and it will not be clear that *Hardwick* should be overruled if
it is taken as a simple substantive due process case. This is because the
Court should be cautious about overruling its own decisions, even
those a majority thinks wrong, and because as a substantive due process
case, perhaps *Hardwick* is not so clearly or egregiously wrong as to be
overruled ten years later. But there is good reason to think that *Hardwick* was indeed wrong; at least it is not easy to imagine the Court
upholding a law imposing criminal punishment on someone for consensual sexual activity. Probably *Hardwick* should have been decided
(if it was to be decided by the Court at all)[15] the other way and very
narrowly—as a case involving the old and nicely minimalist idea, with
democratic foundations, of desuetude (see Chapter 5). A challenge of
this sort was not raised or passed on by the Court, and hence it could
be accepted without overruling *Hardwick*'s substantive due process
holding.

To summarize a lengthy discussion, a minimalist (as opposed to subminimalist) opinion in *Romer* would have said the following:

> *Hardwick* held only that the ban on homosexual sodomy did not
> violate the Due Process Clause, whose content has been defined at
> least partly by reference to tradition. This case involves the Equal
> Protection Clause, which was not at issue in *Hardwick*. The content
> of the Equal Protection Clause is not given by tradition; that Clause
> is rooted in a principle that rejects many traditional practices and in

any case subjects them to critical scrutiny. Our narrow conclusion today is that when a state discriminates against homosexuals, the Equal Protection Clause requires that the discrimination must be rational in the sense that it must be connected with a legitimate public purpose, rather than fear and prejudice or a bare desire to state public opposition to homosexuality as such. In this case, Colorado has been unable to show any such connection. Its reference to associational liberty is an implausible justification for its broad ban, a judgment fortified by Amendment 2's reference to "orientation" as well as "conduct." To reach this conclusion, it is unnecessary for us to say whether and when other, less unusual forms of discrimination on the basis of sexual orientation are connected with legitimate public purposes.

A Note on Meaning and the Expressive Function of Law

> [I]n making a general announcement that gays and lesbians shall not have any particular protections from the law, Amendment 2 inflicts on them immediate, continuing, and real injuries that outrun and belie any legitimate justifications that can be claimed for it.
> —Romer v. Evans

It is frequently observed that the Supreme Court's decisions may have educative effects. The nature and extent of these effects raise serious empirical questions, and these should be investigated empirically. But short of such an investigation, it can be said that Supreme Court decisions seem to have at least short-term effects in communicating certain messages containing prestigious national judgments about what is and what is not legitimate. Official pronouncements about law—from the national legislature and the Supreme Court—have an expressive function. They communicate social commitments, and these acts of communication may well have major social effects just by virtue of their status as communication. Consider, for example, debates about whether the Constitution should be amended to allow the criminalization of flag-burning, or whether universities should be permitted to regulate hate speech. Measures of this kind are debated largely because of their expressive effects, not primarily because of their more direct consequences. By communicating certain messages, law may affect social norms. It may also humiliate people, or say that people may not be humiliated. In fact a central object of the law of equality is to ensure against official expressions of contempt, or attempts, by government institutions, to humiliate people.[16]

Much of the debate about measures relating to equality, or about "animus," relates to this question. We do not get an adequate handle on such debates by asking about the empirically observable consequences of law. There are, for example, vigorous debates about the impact of Brown v. Board of Education and the Civil Rights Act of 1964. These debates are extremely illuminating; it is important to know whether *Brown* actually produced school desegregation and whether the Civil Rights Act of 1964 had good effects on the employment prospects of blacks and women. But part of the importance of *Brown* and the Civil Rights Act of 1964 lay in their expressive effects. When *Brown* was announced, it had immediate consequences for the attitude of black Americans toward their nation and their role in it. The Civil Rights Act of 1964 had immediate importance for what it said, quite apart from what it did or from what it would turn out to do. This is not to say that "statements" are most of what matters, or that law should be celebrated if it makes good statements regardless of what it actually does. But it is to say that one thing that law does is to make statements, and these statements matter, partly because of their potential effect on social norms and partly because of their immediate effects on both self-esteem and self-respect.

What did the Court mean with its suggestion that the "general announcement" in Amendment 2 inflicts on gays and lesbians "immediate, continuing, and real injuries"? The answer may well lie in the expressive content of the amendment. How could the injuries otherwise be "immediate" and a function of the mere "announcement"? And if the Court is understood in this way, Romer v. Evans is important in large part because of its expressive effects too, effects that are directly counter to those of Amendment 2. It is hard to understand the immediate, intense public reaction to *Romer* without stressing this point.

In the same way, we might say that the importance of Bowers v. Hardwick does not lie in its direct effects on the criminal law. The decision probably did not spur many prosecutions of homosexuals (though it may well have helped serve as a basis for legal disabilities in various noncriminal areas). But *Hardwick* can be counted as one of the few genuinely humiliating decisions in American constitutional law,[17] joining Plessy v. Ferguson and Bradwell v. Illinois. At least in the short run, the importance of Romer v. Evans may lie more in its expressive function than in its concrete effects on law and policy. It says something large about the place of homosexuals in society. Whatever the doctrinal complexities, it claims, and is understood to claim, that they are citizens like anyone else. In fact this may be the meaning of the Court's stunning first sentence: "One century ago, the first Justice Harlan admonished this Court that the Constitution 'neither knows nor tolerates classes among citizens.' "

The point goes well beyond the Court's analysis of the technical issues. It does not suggest that the Court did well on that count. To be sure, some sort of minimalist approach seems right in this context. I have suggested that the *Romer* decision, to make sense, must be rooted in a judgment that a state may not defend discrimination on the basis of sexual orientation solely by reference to a desire to discourage, to delegitimate, or not to legitimate homosexuality. Perhaps the Court should have made this point clearer. But if what I have said here is correct, the inadequate treatment of the technical issue may actually be a virtue, because an adequate treatment would have required the Court to write with a breadth and a depth that could not easily have commanded a majority opinion, and because that breadth and depth may have foreclosed the future and limited democratic debate about a series of issues that are currently engaging the nation, and that deserve, broadly speaking, a democratic rather than a judicial solution. Attention to the expressive functions of law thus shows how even a minimalist opinion may have large social effects, by "making statements" about the legitimacy or illegitimacy of certain widespread social attitudes and practices.

Homosexuality and the Constitution's Future

After *Romer,* when does the Constitution forbid discrimination on the basis of sexual orientation? Lawyers are now invoking a principle of constitutional equality to persuade courts to invalidate democratic outcomes in many areas, including the ban on same-sex marriage. It is often insisted that a properly capacious notion of constitutional equality justifies an aggressive judicial role.

I will assert, without defending the point here, that this notion of equality does indeed connect very well with the best understanding of the equality principle that underlies the Civil War amendments. Simply as a matter of abstract constitutional theory, the anticaste principle (see Chapter 6) draws discrimination on the basis of sexual orientation into considerable doubt. Minimalist though it is, Romer v. Evans, with its opening reference to Plessy v. Ferguson, recognizes this point. Let us simply assume that this claim is right. We might even assume, at least for purposes of argument, that the rightness of the constitutional claim is very clear. And then—having made things especially hard for minimalism—let us ask about the Court's appropriate role.[18]

Abraham Lincoln always insisted that slavery was wrong. On the basic principle, Lincoln allowed no compromises. No justification was available for chattel slavery. But on the question of means, Lincoln was quite equivocal—flexible, strategic, open to compromise, aware of doubt. The fact that slavery was wrong did not mean that it had to be eliminated immediately, or that blacks and whites had to be placed immediately on a plane of equality. On Lincoln's view, the feeling of "the great mass of white people" would not permit this result. In his most striking formulation: "Whether this feeling accords with justice and sound argument, is not the sole question, if indeed, it is any part of it. A universal feeling, whether well or ill-founded, can not be safely disregarded."[19] What is most striking about this claim is the view that the inconsistency of a "feeling" with justice or sound argument may be *irrelevant* to the question of what to do at any particular point in time.

On Lincoln's view, efforts to create immediate social change in this especially sensitive area could have disastrous unintended consequences or backfire, even if those efforts were founded on entirely sound principles. It was necessary first to educate people about the reasons for the change. Important interests had to be accommodated or persuaded to come on board. Issues of timing were crucial. Critics had to be heard and respected. For Lincoln, rigidity about the principle would always be combined with caution about the means by which the just outcome would be brought about. For this reason it is a mistake to see Lincoln's caution with respect to abolition as indicating uncertainty about the underlying principle. But it is equally mistaken to think that Lincoln's certainty about the principle entailed immediate implementation of racial equality.

The point is highly relevant to constitutional law, especially in the area of social reform. Good minimalists know that as it operates in the courts, constitutional law is a peculiar mixture of substantive theory and institutional constraint. Suppose, for example, that the ban on same-sex marriage is challenged on equal protection grounds. Even if judges find the challenge plausible in its substance, there is much reason for caution on the part of the courts. An immediate judicial vindication of the principle could well jeopardize important interests. It could galvanize opposition. It could weaken the antidiscrimination movement itself as that movement is operating in democratic arenas. (Compare Roe v. Wade.) It could provoke more hostility and even violence against homosexuals. It would certainly jeopardize the authority of the judiciary. And the very same debates are occurring in democratic arenas, where there is a great deal of discernible movement.

Is it too pragmatic and strategic, too obtusely unprincipled, to suggest that judges should take account of these considerations? I do not believe so. Prudence is not the only virtue; it is certainly not the master virtue. But it is a virtue nonetheless. At a minimum, it seems plausible to suggest that courts should generally use their discretion over their docket in order to limit the timing of relevant intrusions into the political process. It also seems plausible to suggest that courts should be reluctant to vindicate even good principles when the vindication would compromise other interests, at least if those interests include, ultimately, the principles themselves. This consideration argues in favor of both shallowness and narrowness.

In the area of homosexuality, we might make some distinctions. If the Supreme Court of the United States accepted the view that all states must authorize same-sex marriages in 2001, or even 2003, we might well expect a constitutional crisis, a weakening of the legitimacy of the Court, an intensifying of hatred of homosexuals, a constitutional amendment overturning the Court's decision, and much more. Any Court should hesitate in the face of such prospects. It would be far better for the Court to do nothing—or better still, to start cautiously and to proceed incrementally.

The Court might, for example, follow its path in *Romer*, and conclude that the equal protection clause invalidates state constitutional amendments that forbid ordinary democratic processes to outlaw discrimination on the basis of sexual orientation. And the Court might say—as some lower courts have done—that the government cannot rationally discriminate against people of homosexual orientation, without showing that those people have engaged in acts that harm some legitimate government interest. The military is of course an area requiring special sensitivity, because the stakes are so high and courts know so little; but if forced to confront the issue, courts might invalidate discrimination unless the government can show that there is some reason other than "animus" to justify exclusion of homosexuals from employment. Narrow and incompletely theorized rulings of this sort would allow room for public discussion and debate before obtaining a centralized national ruling that preempts ordinary political process.

We can go much further. Constitutional law is not only for the courts; it is for all public officials. The original understanding was that deliberation about the Constitution's meaning would be part of the function of the President and legislators as well. The post–Warren Court identification of the Constitution with the decisions of the Supreme Court has badly disserved the traditional American commitment to deliberative democracy. In that system, all officials—not only the judges—have a duty of fidelity to the founding document. And in that system, we should expect that elected officials will have a degree of interpretive independence from the judiciary. We should even expect that they will sometimes fill the institutional gap created by the courts' lack of fact-finding ability and policy-making competence. For this reason, they may conclude that practices are unconstitutional even if the Court would uphold them, or that practices are valid even if the Court would invalidate them. Lincoln is an important example here as well. Often he invoked constitutional principles to challenge chattel slavery, even though the Supreme Court had rejected that reading of the Constitution in the *Dred Scott* case. Thus elected representatives might well move in the direction of more width and depth even if courts are reluctant to do so. It is through this process that the nation, with catalytic participation from the courts, might ultimately arrive at the constitutionally appropriate solution: a general ban on discrimination on the basis of sexual orientation.

VMI and "Actual Purpose"

There is no caste here.
> —Plessy v. Ferguson (Justice Harlan, dissenting)

It is fair to infer that habit, rather than analysis or actual reflection, made it seem acceptable to equate the terms "widow" and "dependent surviving spouse." . . . I am therefore persuaded that this discrimination . . . is merely the accidental byproduct of a traditional way of thinking about females.
> —Califano v. Goldfarb (Justice Stevens, concurring)

It will certainly be possible for this Court to write a future opinion that ignores the broad principles of law set forth today, and that characterizes as utterly dispositive the opinion's perceptions that VMI was a uniquely prestigious all-male institution, conceived in chauvinism, etc., etc. I will not join that opinion.
> —United States v. Virginia (Justice Scalia, dissenting)

At first glance, the Court's decision in United States v. Virginia seems at the opposite pole from Romer v. Evans. In United States v. Virginia, the Court said a great deal about the appropriate approach to sex equality and about the foundations of sex equality doctrine. This is true and important. But United States v. Virginia had distinctive minimalist dimensions. It was democracy-forcing as well.

The Virginia Military Institute has long been the only single-sex school among Virginia's public colleges and universities. Having been found in violation of the Constitution, Virginia proposed to create a parallel program for women. The Supreme Court held that the operation of VMI as a single-sex school was unconstitutional and that the parallel program would be an inadequate remedy.

The Court's opinion, written by Justice Ruth Bader Ginsburg, came in three simple steps. First, the Court said that those who seek to defend gender-based discrimination must show an "exceedingly persuasive justification." Before United States v. Virginia, it had seemed well settled that gender discrimination would face "intermediate scrutiny," that is, the state would have to show that the classification serves important objectives and that the discriminatory means are substantially related to the achievement of those objectives. This is a standard between "strict scrutiny," applied to racial classifications, and "rational basis" review, applied generally. United States v. Virginia seeks to increase the level of scrutiny for gender discrimination and to bring it closer to the "strict scrutiny" that is applied to discrimination on the basis of race. Thus the Court said that the state must show "at least" what intermediate scrutiny requires, and the Court placed a great emphasis on the need for an "exceedingly persuasive justification," which now seems to have become the basic test for sex discrimination.

Second, the Court said that the state could not justify the single-sex military institution by pointing to the educational benefits of single-sex schooling or to the unique VMI "adversitive" approach and its suitability for men alone. The most interesting aspect of the opinion involved single-sex schooling. The Court acknowledged that this form of schooling could improve education for some students. Its emphasis was on the need to show that the state had actually sought to promote this legitimate purpose. In exploring the background, the Court found no evidence that this goal was actually at work. Instead higher education was initially considered too "dangerous" for women, "reflecting widely held views about women's proper place." With respect to Virginia in particular: "the historical record indicates action more deliberate than anomalous: First, protection of women against high education; next, schools for women far from equal in resources and stature to schools for men; finally, conversion of the separate schools to coeducation." Thus the Court suggested that a self-conscious effort to promote educational diversity through same-sex schools, at least if it was committed to equality of opportunity, could indeed be constitutional. But it was implausible to think that Virginia's course of action fell in that category. "A purpose genuinely to advance an array of educational options . . . is not served by VMI's historic and constant plan— a plan to 'affor[d] a unique educational benefit only to males.' "[20]

The Court acknowledged that VMI had a distinctive method of training, which VMI labels (a bit ominously) "adversitive." It also acknowledged the possibility that most women would not choose this method. But it rejected the view that the adversitive method was by itself incompatible with the presence of women. It did so partly because of the absence of sufficient evidence and because the same argument had been made in a number of other contexts, including admission of women to the practices of law and medicine. Thus the Court referred to past " 'self-fulfilling prophecies' once routinely used to deny rights or opportunities" to women. Even if many women were ill suited to the VMI method, the same would be true for many men, and VMI would have to rely on individualized assessments.

Third, the Court rejected Virginia's remedial plan, consisting of a parallel program for women. The parallel program would be inferior in academic offerings, methods of education, and financial resources. The state attempted to justify the absence of the adversitive method on grounds of what best suited women; but this stereotypical generalization was inadequate even if it was accurate. In any case the new program was separate and unequal, not least because of its inferior prestige. Thus it failed to provide an adequate remedy.

There is no question that like Romer v. Evans, the VMI case should be understood partly with reference to the expressive function of law. The maintenance of an all-male military school in Virginia was probably more important for its expressive effects than for its actual deprivation of educational opportunities. And the intense public debate over the case, and over the place of women in the military, is intelligible only if we see it in its expressive capacity, as embodying judgments about the extent to which social roles, as between men and women, are prescribed by nature. And the outcome in the case, together with its language, is important in large part because of the statement the Court made about the relationship between government and sex-role stereotyping.

Deep but Narrow

In several ways, United States v. Virginia was an ambitious, nonminimalist opinion. First, the Court offered a particular understanding of sex equality. The problem with the Virginia system was not that the state noticed a difference between men and women but that it turned that difference into a disadvantage. Differences "remain cause for celebration, but not for denigration of the members of either sex or for artificial constraints on an individual's opportunity."[21] Thus the Court understood the equality principle to mean that the difference between men and women could not be used as a basis for deprivation of educational opportunities. Similarly, the Court noticed that some "differences" may be a product of past practices, and thus sometimes differences become a kind of "self-fulfilling prophecy." The Court was clearly concerned that this was true with respect to women's capacity to participate in the adversitive method.

Second, the Court did not merely restate the intermediate scrutiny standard but pressed in closer to strict scrutiny. After United States v. Virginia, it is not simple to describe the appropriate standard of review. The state must "at least" satisfy intermediate scrutiny, and the Court's description of what the state must do suggests that the standard is now somewhere between intermediate scrutiny and strict—rather like the place that affirmative action, realistically speaking, now occupies.

In these ways, the Court said more than it needed in order to justify its decision in the case, just as the *Romer* Court said less than it needed for that purpose. The Court deepened the foundations of sex equality law by giving a clearer sense of its point. The modest revision of the standard of review is less important, because the revision is unlikely to produce different results from those that would follow from intermediate scrutiny. It may be an overstatement to say that the outcome in United States v. Virginia was compelled by prior cases. But the far more natural reading of those cases was that the maintenance of an all-male school in higher education, without a plausibly equal school for females, was a violation of the equal protection clause. What is notable is the comparative depth of the opinion.

What is the reach of United States v. Virginia? Was the decision narrow or wide? It would be altogether wrong to conclude that the Court has by its rationale committed future courts to the invalidation of all programs, public and private, that separate the sexes. The Court was careful to emphasize that Virginia could not claim to have attempted to promote educational diversity and that its programs could not, in purpose or in effect, ensure equality of opportunity. This particularistic judgment was pivotal to the case. Thus the Court left open the possibility that a new legislature, acting on the basis of a concern for the well-being of both men and women, could separate the sexes as long as it provided equal opportunity.

In this way United States v. Virginia can be linked, along different dimensions, with both *Romer* and Kent v. Dulles, where the Court said that the secretary of state could not, without an explicit judgment from Congress, ban communists from traveling outside of the country (see Chapter 2). United States v. Virginia is linked with *Romer* insofar as it shows skepticism about the state's articulated justification and seeks to "flush out" an actual, illegitimate motivation—here, a belief that women are legitimately treated as less well suited for certain educational practices than men as a class. The link with *Romer* is even deeper than this: both cases rest on a judgment that "animus," connected with prejudice and stereotyping, is an illegitimate basis for law. United States v. Virginia is linked with Kent v. Dulles insofar as it requires a current legislative judgment that same-sex education or programs are necessary to promote educational diversity. Thus, for example, we can imagine an educational institution ensuring separate sports teams simply in order to ensure equal opportunities for both girls and boys. United States v. Virginia certainly does not invalidate a decision of this kind. Such a decision may well promote, rather than undermine, equal opportunity. Or suppose that a school system decided that girls and boys learn best if they are educated in separate places. If this decision were reached deliberatively and without infection from stereotypes about the appropriate role of men and women, it might be upheld.

It also follows that federal funding of private, same-sex educational institutions, even at the level of colleges and universities, is likely to be constitutional after United States v. Virginia. Such funding may itself be neutral and therefore nondiscriminatory; the national government is not itself engaged in discrimination. Even if private institutions, not subject to the Constitution, face certain legal bans on discrimination, it is not clear that those bans must be interpreted to require them to admit both men and women. In particular, educational institutions for women alone seem to have potential benefits for women, benefits that are connected with the promotion of equality.

I do not mean to specify what United States v. Virginia will be understood to require. It is too early for that. I suggest only that there are a variety of same-sex schools and institutions, and that the Court was therefore correct to proceed narrowly. No general rule would make sense. For this reason, the Court's decision was far more minimalist than it seemed, and properly so.

Was *VMI* Wrongly Decided?

Many people have doubted whether the Court was right to invalidate same-sex education at VMI. The issues raised by sex segregation in the military context involve disputed questions of fact and issues of value on which the nation remains sharply divided. Thus Judge Posner has urged, in an argument overlapping with some of the concerns of this book, that the *VMI* decision was a form of hubris—judicial over-reaching based on little understanding of the underlying problem.[22] In his view, the role of sex segregation in the military is a complex, consequence-dependent question, and it is by no means clear that experiments in an integrated military have always been successful. Here too the nation is in a period of moral flux, with the relevant questions receiving a great deal of public attention. Since military preparedness is at issue, the stakes are unusually high. And the Court is in an extremely poor position to untangle the relevant factual issues. Why wasn't the *VMI* case, like the physician-assisted suicide cases, a good one for judicial deference to political processes? Doesn't approval of the physician-assisted suicide cases argue against the outcome in *VMI?*

The best answer invokes two points. First, the underlying political processes were unreliable. When a state discriminates on the basis of sex, prejudice or habitual thinking is unusually likely to be at work. There is therefore a reason for judicial skepticism, a reason not found in the substantive due process cases. To say this is not to say that all sex discrimination is unconstitutional; the Court properly left open the possibility that some segregation would be acceptable. But this raises the second point: in the *VMI* case itself Virginia was able to offer little basis for upholding the practice of segregation. Virginia came up with little evidence that anyone would be harmed by admitting qualified female students to VMI. Judge Posner is right to say that consequences count and that in the military context, the Court should give the government the benefit of the doubt if the case is otherwise in equipoise. But in *VMI,* there was no sufficient showing of bad consequences to put the case in equipoise. The decision was therefore correct.

The Path of the Law

In the area of sex discrimination, the law has taken a steady and revealing path. In Reed v. Reed, decided in 1972, the Court struck a law giving preference to men over women as administrators of estates; the Court said that it was employing rational basis review, but nonetheless struck down the law as "arbitrary." In 1973 a plurality of the Court attempted, but failed, to achieve consensus on strict scrutiny for sex discrimination; Justice Powell refused to take this step, writing in minimalist fashion that the Supreme Court should proceed cautiously and incrementally because the nation was engaged in a debate over the Equal Rights Amendment.[23] After a series of additional cases, both narrow and shallow, the Court settled in 1976 on the standard of intermediate scrutiny, thus making the law of sex equality a bit clearer and more systematic.[24] At the same time, the law has remained complex rather than simple, as the Court has upheld sex discrimination with respect to the age for statutory rape and in the registration requirements for the military draft.[25] The theoretical foundations of the law of sex equality deepened in the 1980s and early 1990s, with cases suggesting that the question was not whether men and women are different, but whether the state has made impermissible use of the difference, in a way that helped produce second-class citizenship.[26] This deepening of the law was accompanied by some widening, as the Court suggested that any form of legal discrimination would likely be struck down. But the Court allowed the possibility of rebuttal to a presumption against such discrimination, if the state could show that it was actually promoting equality or otherwise serving important goals unrelated to the perpetuation of second-class citizenship.[27]

I have offered a defense of the Court's narrow approach in United States v. Virginia; but what of its comparative depth? Has the Court been right to converge on some relatively ambitious abstractions? The depth of the *Virginia* opinion can be found in the Court's understanding of the principle of equality in the context of gender. The Court emphasizes that there are indeed differences between men and women, some of them biological, some of them social. Its claim is that differences are to be "celebrated," and not turned into a source of inequality. Thus the opinion suggests that the problem of sex inequality is a problem of second-class citizenship, in which women's differences from men are used, by the state, as a reason for prescribing gender roles in a way that deprives women of equal opportunity.

Notice what this conception of sex equality avoids. It avoids a claim that women are not different from men, biologically or socially. It avoids a claim that those differences necessarily justify unequal treatment. And it avoids a claim that equal treatment is necessarily required in all contexts. The Court left open the possibility that a law that promotes both educational diversity and equal opportunity might be upheld. The question is whether the state is acting from a kind of "animus," or instead trying to promote equality, or responding to differences in a way that has nothing to do with the perpetuation of illegitimate stereotypes.

It would be possible to criticize the Court for adopting a contentious understanding of the equality principle when a less contentious understanding would suffice. A thoroughgoing minimalist would certainly urge this criticism. And if we think that the Court's understanding was misconceived, we might also think that it was hubristic for the Court to announce it. But—a qualification to my basic claim in this chapter— a deep understanding of a constitutional provision is nothing to lament when a variety of justices can converge on it and when they (and we) have good reason to believe that it is right. Both of these conditions were met in United States v. Virginia. The case was far from the first constitutional judgment involving sex discrimination. After so many encounters with so many contexts, the Court was entitled to have confidence in its understanding of the point of the equality guarantee; and the particular setting of a wholesale exclusion of women from a top-flight military academy was a good occasion on which to announce that point. The Court's understanding was right and the Court was right to have confidence in it.

Thus this was a relatively rare occasion on which it was appropriate to give an ambitious account of the underlying principle. It is parallel to Brown v. Board of Education, when the Court also spoke ambitiously after encountering the basic problem for a period of years. The difference is that *Virginia* was properly narrow while *Brown* was properly broad in view of the differences between sex and race segregation in education.

Equality's Source

As I have noted, there is a clear connection between the conception of "animus" in *Romer* and the concern about sex-role stereotyping in United States v. Virginia. Both cases seem inspired by Justice Harlan's suggestion in Plessy v. Ferguson that "[t]here is no caste here," an idea recalled both by the opening words of *Romer* and implicitly by the *Virginia* Court's discussion of "volumes of history" demonstrating "official action denying rights or opportunities based on sex." In the case of homosexuals, "animus" typically takes the form of hatred and fear, whereas for women the motivation for discrimination has often been a kind of "chivalry" associated with perceptions of women's appropriate role. But in both cases, the central equality concern is that government ought not to be permitted to turn a morally irrelevant characteristic into a basis for second-class citizenship. This was the basic problem in both *Romer* and United States v. Virginia. In the end it unites the two cases.

I have argued that both *Romer* and United States v. Virginia were rightly decided; that *Romer* was properly both narrow and shallow; that United States v. Virginia was properly narrow but deep; and that the two cases reflect the right conception of the equal protection clause, involving a ban on measures that produce second-class citizenship, or that reflect an "animus," or a form of contempt, directed against certain social groups.

Of course these propositions leave many questions open. In the area of discrimination on the basis of sex, the Court has adopted a clear conception of the underlying problem and an aggressive standard of review. In the area of discrimination on the basis of sexual orientation, the Court has taken neither step. But the *Romer* Court's emphasis on "animus" is a promising place to start. While leaving a great deal of room for future development, it appropriately places a constitutional obstacle to the most illegitimate measures, and it helps explain why those measures deserve to be branded as especially illegitimate. Romer v. Evans therefore stands as a remarkable case—one that reflects the correct understanding of the equality principle alongside an appropriate view about the Court's institutional role.

8

The First Amendment and
New Technologies

The minimal content of the First Amendment consists of a ban on government suppression of political dissent. The government may not insulate itself by silencing opposition; it must allow all points of view to have their say.

Of course these claims leave many ambiguities. An incompletely theorized agreement supports them, and they are themselves incompletely specified. How do these claims bear on the regulation of new technologies? How might they be supplemented in the modern era? These are the principal questions with which I deal in this chapter; in the process I will defend a form of free speech minimalism.

Government Failure and Constitutional Failure

Begin with a platitude: When the government attempts to regulate the market, many things may go wrong. In the familiar litany, regulation may be counterproductive, producing outcomes that defeat the aspirations of well-meaning reformers and make things even worse from their point of view. Or regulation may be futile, as the market adapts to the initiatives and prevents them from accomplishing their purpose. Or regulation may produce unanticipated harmful consequences. All of these results may follow from the regulators' incomplete understanding of the system into which they are attempting to intervene. This is not an argument that the government should never intervene in markets; sometimes interventions can do a great deal of good. But it is certainly a reason for caution, for attempting to acquire a good deal of information, and for proceeding in an experimental, empirical, and non-dogmatic way.

172

It is less often recognized that constitutional law can have similar problems. Supreme Court decisions may be counterproductive. If it is understood as a case about gender equality, Roe v. Wade is a possible example, for the Court's decision may well have damaged the effort to produce gender equality, by demobilizing women's groups and by activating their opponents. Or Supreme Court decisions may be futile. Sometimes Fourth Amendment decisions seem to have this feature; to say the least, it is far from clear that police officers comply as a matter of course with Supreme Court pronouncements about Fourth Amendment requirements. Supreme Court decisions may also have harmful unanticipated consequences. This is true of many efforts in the area of judge-led social reform.

Justice Oliver Wendell Holmes's opinions in constitutional law were built largely on seeing the political process as a kind of market, subject, like other markets, to forces of supply and demand.[1] As a regulator of the political market, the Supreme Court may reach decisions that reflect ignorance of relevant factors. Because they interfere with the political market, Supreme Court decisions may also disturb some kind of social equilibrium. It is ironic but true that many people alert to the problems with government interference with economic markets are quite sanguine about Supreme Court interference with political markets.[2] This was true in the 1920s when constitutional law assumed center stage in debates over the regulation of new and old markets. It is true as the twenty-first century approaches, as constitutional law takes center stage in debates over new communications markets, prominently including the Internet and novel innovations involving television.

We have seen a number of areas in which the Supreme Court endorses a form of minimalism. Very strikingly, the Court has proceeded in a minimalist manner in no fewer than four important decisions involving new communications technologies (including the Internet) and the First Amendment.[3] In upholding a legal grant of permission for cable operators to exclude "indecent" programming, the Court referred to a set of factors and expressly avoided any rule. In invalidating a ban on "indecent" speech on the Internet, the Court did little more than to stress the vagueness of the ban, vagueness that was intolerable in the context of a legal prohibition on speech. And in two important cases, the Court narrowly upheld statutory requirements that cable operators "must carry" local programming. The Court emphasized that

the "must carry" rules were an attempt to promote broad dissemination of ideas and opinions, especially by ensuring continued programming for people without access to cable.

In this chapter I defend a form of free speech minimalism. This approach is focused on the goal of ensuring the preconditions of a well-
functioning deliberative democracy; it argues in favor of judicial caution
in invalidating regulatory controls. I urge that a form of minimalism
makes particular sense for the new communications technologies, including the Internet. The most important reason is that the relevant
facts are in flux and changing very rapidly, and the consequences of
current developments are hard to foresee. At the moment, courts are
in a position to know relatively little about the effects of possible interventions. Would a requirement of free air time for candidates make
the political process work better? Would a requirement of educational
programs help children? If cable television flourishes, will ordinary
broadcasters be at risk in a way that threatens free programming? What
are the effects of the Internet on children, and what mechanisms are
available to protect children from possible harm, including sexually harassing behavior? Is violent programming dangerous for children? The
underlying predictive issues are poorly suited to judicial resolution. In
such circumstances the Court does best if it proceeds cautiously and
with humility, allowing some room for political judgment and (it must
be acknowledged) maneuvering.

It is also important that the legally relevant values are also in flux and
not at all simple to sort out. There is, of course, a continuing social
debate about the regulation of pornography, especially pornography
about and for children, on the Internet. Reasonable people disagree
about the relationships among the Internet, children, and parental control; must government rely on parents, or can it stand in their place?
There is also a large debate over the legitimacy of efforts to improve
public discussion through regulation of the mass media. It is increasingly unclear whether the Court's current free speech doctrine—
founded on the categories of viewpoint-based, content-based, and
content-neutral regulation—makes complete sense in this context. If,
for example, the government attempts to promote educational and
public-affairs programming, it is acting on the basis of content. Are its
actions for that reason illegitimate? I do not believe so. Or suppose that

the government proceeds on the basis of content through efforts that fall short of regulation, as, for example, by exempting broadcasters from the antitrust law so as to enable them to reduce violence on television. It is hardly clear that the First Amendment should be read to preclude a step of this kind.

In the area of new communications technologies, there is a related but more general issue. In some areas, the First Amendment is sometimes playing the same (unfortunate) role with respect to the communications market as did the Fourteenth Amendment with respect to the labor market in the period from 1905 through 1936. In that period, questions about minimum-wage and maximum-hour laws, or efforts to protect labor unions, were answered in significant part by asking: what does the due process clause say about such questions? In retrospect we can see that this was an exceedingly bad way to proceed—that it would have been much better to dispense with lawyers and cases and to focus instead on underlying questions of fact and value, questions for which purely legal tools are inadequate. The problems of policy should be solved by people who understand problems of policy, not by lawyers skilled in reading Supreme Court opinions.

To a discouragingly large extent, the same is true for modern communications technologies. Too often, hard questions are answered by consulting previous cases, as if the First Amendment, judicially understood, supplies the foundations for choosing regulatory policy for the emerging speech market. Of course the First Amendment has a good deal to say about legitimate regulatory strategies. Obviously some such strategies would violate the First Amendment. But for the most part, the relevant questions are first and foremost ones of policy rather than of constitutional law. Courts and judges will do well if they remember this point.

Markets and Madison

Even minimalists should agree that it is difficult to make progress on First Amendment issues without having some ideas about the point of the free speech guarantee. To orient the discussion, let us notice, then, that there are two free speech traditions in the United States, not simply one. There have been two models of the First Amendment, corresponding to these two traditions. The first emphasizes well-functioning speech markets. It can be traced to Justice Holmes's great *Abrams* dissent,[4] where the notion of a "market in ideas" received its preeminent exposition. The market model emerges as well from Miami Herald Publishing Company v. Tornillo,[5] invalidating a "right of reply" law as applied to candidates for elected office. It finds its most recent defining statement not in judicial decisions, but in a Federal Communications Commission opinion rejecting the fairness doctrine,[6] which required attention to public issues and an opportunity for diverse views to have access to the airwaves.

The second tradition, and the second model, focuses on public deliberation. The second model can be traced from its origins in the work of James Madison, with his attack on the idea of seditious libel, to Justice Louis Brandeis, with his suggestion that "the greatest menace to freedom is an inert people,"[7] through the work of Alexander Meiklejohn, who associated the free speech principle not with laissez-faire economics but with ideals of democratic deliberation.[8] The Madisonian tradition culminated in the (maximalist) invalidation of broad libel laws in New York Times v. Sullivan[9] and the reaffirmation of the fairness doctrine in the *Red Lion* case,[10] with the Supreme Court's suggestion that governmental efforts to encourage diverse views and attention to public issues are compatible with the free speech principle—even if they result in regulatory controls on the owners of speech sources.

Under the marketplace metaphor, the First Amendment requires—at least as a presumption—a system of unrestricted economic markets in speech. Government must respect the forces of supply and demand. At the very least, it may not regulate the content of speech so as to push the speech market in its preferred directions. Certainly it must be neutral with respect to viewpoint. A key point for marketplace advocates is that government cannot be trusted when speech is at risk. Illicit motives are far too likely to underlie regulatory initiatives. The FCC has at times come close to endorsing the market model, above all in its decision abandoning the fairness doctrine. When the FCC did this, it referred to the operation of the forces of supply and demand and suggested that those forces would produce an optimal mix of entertainment options. Hence former FCC chair Mark Fowler described television as "just another appliance. It's a toaster with pictures."[11] The rise of new communications technologies is often taken to fortify this claim.

Those who endorse the marketplace model do not claim that government may not do anything at all. Of course government may set up the basic rules of property and contract; it is these rules that make markets feasible. Government is also permitted to protect against market failures, especially by preventing monopolies and monopolistic practices. Structural regulation is acceptable as long as it is a content-neutral attempt to ensure competition. It is therefore important to note that advocates of marketplaces and democracy might work together in seeking to curtail monopoly. Of course, the prevention of monopoly is a precondition for well-functioning information markets.

Government has a final authority, though this authority does not easily fall within the marketplace model itself. Most people who accept the marketplace model acknowledge that government is permitted to regulate the various well-defined categories of controllable speech, such as obscenity, false or misleading commercial speech, and libel. This acknowledgment will have large consequences for government controls on new information technologies. Perhaps the government's power to control obscene, threatening, or libelous speech will justify special rules for cyberspace. But with these qualifications, the commitment to free economic markets is the basic constitutional creed.

Many people think that there is now nothing distinctive about the electronic media or about modern communications technologies that justifies an additional governmental role. If such a role was ever justified, they argue, it was because of problems of scarcity. When only three television networks exhausted the available options, a market failure may have called for regulation designed to ensure that significant numbers of people were not left without their preferred programming. But this is no longer a problem. With so dramatic a proliferation of stations, most people can obtain the programming they want. With new technologies, including the potential merger of television and the Internet, people will be able to make or to participate in their own preferred programming in their own preferred "locations." With new technologies, perhaps there are no real problems calling for governmental controls, except for those designed to establish the basic framework.

The second model emphasizes that our constitutional system is one of deliberative democracy. This system prizes both political (not eco-

nomic) equality and a shared civic culture. It seeks to promote, as a
central democratic goal, reflective and deliberative debate about possible courses of action. The Madisonian model sees the right of free
expression as a key part of the system of public deliberation.

On this view, even a well-functioning information market is not immune from government controls. Government is certainly not permitted to regulate speech however it wants; it may not censor political
dissent or restrict speech on the basis of viewpoint. But it may regulate
the electronic media or even the Internet to promote, in a sufficiently
neutral way, a well-functioning democratic regime. It may attempt to
promote attention to public issues. It may try to ensure diversity of
view. It may promote political speech at the expense of other forms of
speech. In particular, educational and public-affairs programming, on
the Madisonian view, has a special place.

I cannot attempt in this chapter to defend the proposition that the
Madisonian conception is superior to the marketplace alternative as a
matter of constitutional law.[12] A thoroughgoing minimalist would attempt to bracket that question, and indeed I will suggest that a large
degree of bracketing, as part of free speech minimalism, is appropriate.
But a few brief notes may be helpful. The argument for the Madisonian
conception is partly historical; the American free speech tradition owes
much of its origin and shape to a conception of democratic self-
government. The marketplace conception is a creation of the twentieth
century, not of the eighteenth. As a matter of history, it confuses modern notions of consumer sovereignty in the marketplace with democratic understandings of political sovereignty, symbolized by the trans-
fer of sovereignty from the King to "We the People." The American
free speech tradition finds its origin in that conception of sovereignty,
which, in Madison's view, doomed the Sedition Act on constitutional
grounds.

But the argument for Madisonianism does not rest only on history.
We are unlikely to be able to make sense of free speech problems without insisting that the free speech principle is centrally (though certainly
not exclusively) connected with democratic goals, and without ac-
knowledging that marketplace thinking is inadequately connected with
the point and function of a system of free expression. A well-functioning democracy requires a degree of citizen participation, which requires

a degree of information; and large disparities in political (as opposed to economic) equality are damaging to democratic aspirations. To the extent that the Madisonian view prizes education, democratic deliberation, and political equality, it is connected, as the marketplace conception is not, with the highest ideals of American constitutionalism.

Some people think that the distinction between marketplace and Madisonian models is now an anachronism. Perhaps the two models conflicted at an earlier stage in history; but in one view, Madison has no place in an era of limitless broadcasting options and cyberspace. Perhaps new technologies now mean that Madisonian goals can best be satisfied in a system of free markets. Now that so many channels, Internet sites, e-mail options, and discussion "places" are available, can't all people read or see what they wish? If people want to spend their time on public issues, are there not countless available opportunities? Is this not especially true with the emergence of the Internet? Is it not hopelessly paternalistic, or anachronistic, for government to regulate for Madisonian reasons?

I do not believe that these questions are rhetorical. We know enough to know that even in a period of limitless options, our communications system may fail to promote an educated citizenry and political equality. Madisonian goals may be severely compromised even under technologically extraordinary conditions. There is no logical or a priori connection between a well-functioning system of free expression and limitless broadcasting or Internet options. We could well imagine a science fiction story in which a wide range of options coexisted with sensationalistic fare, with a nonexistent line between news and gossip, with little or no high-quality fare for children, with widespread political apathy or ignorance, and with social balkanization in which most people's consumption choices simply reinforced their own prejudices and platitudes, or even worse.

Quite outside of science fiction, it is foreseeable that free markets in communications will be a mixed blessing. Of course they create enormous opportunities and carry extraordinary benefits, not least from the Madisonian point of view; they greatly increase the opportunities for more in the way of both learning and citizenship. But they can also create a kind of accelerating "race to the bottom," in which many or most people see low-quality programming involving trumped-up scandals or sensationalistic anecdotes calling for little in terms of quality or quantity of attention. It is imaginable that well-functioning markets in communications will bring about a situation in which many of those interested in politics merely fortify their own unreflective judgments, and are exposed to little or nothing in the way of competing views. It is imaginable that the content of the most widely viewed programming will represent a bland, watered-down version of conventional morality and will not engage serious issues in a serious way. From the standpoint of the present, it is imaginable that the television—or the personal computer carrying out communications functions—will indeed become "just another appliance . . . a toaster with pictures," and that the educative or aspirational goals of the First Amendment will be lost or even forgotten. At least this would be so if the Supreme Court converged on the marketplace conception of the free speech principle.

An Era of First Amendment Minimalism?

As I have suggested, minimalists are cautious about adopting the Madisonian model; they are reluctant to choose between Madisonians and marketplace enthusiasts. Often the two ideals will lead in similar directions, and hence incompletely theorized agreements are possible between the opposing camps, or among those who dislike the whole idea of camps. And people who think that the First Amendment is centered on democratic deliberation need not deny that the free speech principle serves a wide range of goals, not limited to politics. The interest in autonomy, for example, suggests that government ought not to be permitted to restrict speech because people are offended by the ideas that it contains, or because government thinks that people will be persuaded by those ideas. So, too, the interest in self-expression suggests that government needs to have a good reason if it seeks to regulate artistic or literary expression. For purposes of most First Amendment questions, it is not necessary to choose among the theoretical abstractions, and it is possible to proceed in a way that is relatively shallow whether or not narrow.

Consider, for example, the Supreme Court's most recent decisions, which are emphatically minimalist in character. The Court has approached First Amendment issues with considerable caution in light of the characteristics of new technologies; thus the Court has studiously avoided either width or depth. The four crucial cases leave most of the central issues undecided, while at the same time reaffirming a firm commitment to freedom of political expression and to a requirement that regulatory controls be clear and precise.

In two cases involving Turner Broadcasting Company, the Court upheld a controversial statutory requirement that cable television operators "must carry" local broadcast television stations.[13] In both cases, the Court concluded that the must-carry rule was content-neutral, in the sense that the rule's requirements did not depend on the content of speech. In the first case, *Turner I,* the Court said that the key question was whether Congress had an adequate basis to believe that the restriction on the freedom of cable operators was really necessary to protect legitimate interests. After a set of factual findings by a lower court, the Supreme Court said, in *Turner II,* that the restriction could be justified as a way of promoting fair competition in the television market, maintaining the benefits of free local broadcast television, and promoting the widespread dissemination of information from multiple sources. In so saying the Court rejected the view that the government had the same power over cable that it does over broadcasting (where the scarcity rationale has more force).

In both *Turner* cases, the Court emphasized Congress's judgment that local broadcasting is at some risk because of the advent of cable. In the Court's view, it was reasonable to think that without the must-carry rule, many viewers would be deprived of the current level of programming, especially in light of cable's economic interest in disadvantaging its broadcast competition. Since so many viewers do not have cable, this was a serious problem in light of the government's legitimate interest in ensuring that citizens generally have access to a good deal of information from varied sources. Justice Breyer, the crucial fifth vote to uphold the must-carry rules, was even more explicit and in a way less minimalist, because deeper. In Justice Breyer's view, there were important First Amendment interests on both sides, for the First Amendment would be disserved by a sharp decline in the "quality and quantity of programming choice for an ever-shrinking non-cable-subscribing segment of the public." What was especially important was that this policy "seeks to facilitate the public discussion and informed deliberation, which, as Justice Brandeis pointed out many years ago, democratic government presupposes and the First Amendment seeks to achieve."

The majority opinions in the *Turner* cases are minimalist in the sense that they are relatively narrow and relatively shallow. The implications of the two cases for other kinds of speech regulation are unclear; the Court said almost nothing about how it would treat content-based regulation, and while it indicated that some structural regulation might be upheld if it promoted free speech goals, it left most of the key questions undecided. The decisions seem to endorse some Madisonian ideas. But free market enthusiasts need not be terribly alarmed, for the Court also stressed the market-enhancing goals of the relevant regulations.

Even less ambitious was the Court's complex decision in *Denver Area Educational Telecommunications Consortium*.[14] There the Court was asked to assess three provisions of the 1992 act regulating cable television. Section 10(b) of the act required cable operators to segregate "patently offensive" programming on a single channel, to block that channel from viewer access, and to unblock it within thirty days of a subscriber's written request. Section 10(a) regulated leased access channels, that is, channels reserved under federal law for commercial lease by parties unaffiliated with the cable operator; it permitted the operator to prohibit "programming" that it "reasonably believes . . . depicts sexual . . . activities or organs in a patently offensive manner." Section 10(c) granted the same permission to "public access" channels, that is, channels required by local government to be reserved for public, educational, and governmental programming.

The Court struck down section 10(b). The plurality opinion said that this provision was mandatory rather than permissive, and that it was far more restrictive than necessary to protect children. Other legislation already required cable operators to honor a subscriber's request to block programming. In the near future, the "v-chip" device will allow automatic blocking of material that people do not want in their homes. And cable operators were already required, by separate provisions of law, to scramble or block "patently offensive" material. The Court did not say whether these methods of protecting children were constitutional. But they were less restrictive than 10(b), and hence the Court thought that the "segregate and block" requirement was an overly restrictive way of jeopardizing free speech interests for a speculative gain.

Things were different with section 10(a). The Court emphasized that this provision was permissive rather than mandatory. The provision also operated in an unusual context, granting permission for cable operators to exclude programming that, without previous law, would have no path of access to cable channels free of the operator's control. In addition, the provision was directed to protecting children, an important interest. The problem Congress was attempting to address was similar to that involved in the *Pacifica*[15] case, where the Court had upheld the FCC's decision to ban "seven dirty words" from the airwaves during certain times in the day; this permissive provision was less restrictive than that in *Pacifica*. The plurality emphasized the narrowness of this holding, refusing to defend the outcome by reference to rule and insisting that "aware as we are of the changes taking place in the law, the technology, and the industrial structure, related to communications, we believe it unwise and unnecessary definitively to pick one analogy or one specific set of words now."

But the Court struck down section 10(c). For the plurality, the first point was that cable operators historically reserved channels for public, governmental, and educational programming; hence these were not channels over which operators have historically exercised control, and thus 10(c) did not restore to cable operators the editorial control that they once had. In any case existing regulations already controlled offensive programming on these channels. It was unlikely that an operator's veto would be necessary. Thus the function of 10(c) would be not to protect children, but to "increase the risk that certain categories of programming (say, borderline offensive programs) would not appear."

Taken as a whole, these three rulings are remarkably narrow. They depend on a set of factors, not on any rule. They reflect the plurality's explicit desire to leave a range of questions undecided.

Of the Court's decisions involving new communications technologies, the most ambitious was Reno v. ACLU,[16] where the Court struck down the Communications Decency Act. The relevant provision criminalizes the "knowing" transmission of "obscene or indecent" messages to anyone under eighteen. It also bans the "knowing" sending or display, to anyone under eighteen, of a message "that, in context, depicts or describes, in terms patently offensive as measured by contemporary community standards, sexual or excretory activities or organs." Insofar as the act attempted to regulate not merely obscenity but also "indecent" speech, the Court struck down these provisions on First Amendment grounds. The Court's major complaint was that there were far too many ambiguities in the act's coverage. "Could a speaker confidently assume that a serious discussion about birth control practices, homosexuality, . . . or the consequences of prison rape would not violate the CDA?" At least in the context of a content-based regulation of speech carrying criminal penalties, this degree of vagueness was unacceptable.

The Court acknowledged the legitimacy of the government's interest in protecting children, but it said that this vague and broad prohibition would greatly burden adult speech as well, and there were other, narrower techniques for protecting children from inappropriate material. The district court found, for example, that it might be possible to "tag" indecent material for parental control, and there were also methods for limiting a computer's access to an approved list of sources, or for blocking inappropriate material. Here Congress had made no findings and held no hearings to deal with the issue in a more careful and responsible fashion. The Court particularly emphasized the speed with which the act was passed and the absence of much in the way of legislative deliberation. Indeed, the Court went so far as to suggest that unlike the regulation upheld in *Pacifica,* the act did not come from "any evaluation by an agency familiar with the unique characteristics of the Internet."

Several important themes emerge from these cases. The most conspicuous is the Court's caution, manifesting itself in narrow and incompletely theorized judgments. In addition, the Court has insisted on a high degree of clarity from Congress, in order to ensure that Congress has focused on particular problems and given them appropriate deliberation. A primary difference between the must-carry rules upheld in both *Turner* cases and the ban struck down in *Reno* is the far greater degree of legislative care in the former cases. A final theme, of considerable importance for the future, is the emphasis, in *Turner,* on the need to ensure broad dissemination of information and ideas, and in particular the emphasis, in the Court's opinion and especially Justice Breyer's, on the Madisonian goals of the free speech principle.

A Minimalist First Amendment: The Core

A minimalist First Amendment requires a "core"—an agreed-upon set of understandings about what kinds of practices would constitute a violation of the free speech principle. The core may or may not be a product of agreement on ambitious claims about theoretical foundations. Without making such claims, I suggest that for the next generation of free speech law, the Court should proceed confidently in three kinds of cases. With respect to the regulation of new technologies, this confidence generates the core of the minimalist First Amendment.

The first involves cases in which the government is discriminating on the basis of viewpoint. Suppose, for example, that the government imposes special restrictions on antifeminist speech, or antiabortion speech, or speech that speaks for or against the performance of the American government in a certain historical period. The prohibition on viewpoint discrimination is the most simple and straightforward inference from the First Amendment's ban on governmental favoritism. Despite its breadth, it attracts support from a variety of theoretical positions; it can command agreement from those who believe that the free speech principle is rooted in principles of democracy, autonomy, and self-expression.

It follows that if the government regulates the Internet or cable television so as to preclude or prefer viewpoints of the government's liking, the First Amendment requires invalidation. But several clarifications are important. There is a difference between regulation of content and regulation of viewpoint; a requirement of educational programming, or coverage of an election, discriminates on the basis of content, but it does not punish or favor any point of view. To say that viewpoint discrimination is illegitimate is not to say the same for content discrimination. Some laws that discriminate on the basis of content are invalid, but some are entirely permissible; with respect to content regulation, a presumption of invalidity may make sense, but there is no basis for a rule to the effect. Perfectly legitimate interests may underlie content regulation.

The second category includes cases in which government is regulating political speech. Whenever the government regulates political speech, there is special basis for suspicion: the government's motives may well be illicit, and the system of democratic deliberation is not, when political speech is regulated, likely to be self-correcting. Madisonians insist that the heart of the First Amendment lies in democratic self-governance; others believe that this view is too narrow; but no one disagrees that courts must be quite skeptical of government efforts to regulate political speech. Of course the question whether speech qualifies as "political" is not always simple to answer, and special issues are raised by government regulation of political "speech" that comes in the form of money. Here the government may be attempting to promote the goal, internal to the democratic ideal, of political equality, and such attempts may well be constitutionally acceptable even though political speech is involved.

The third category of clear cases, signaled by Reno v. ACLU, involves restrictions that are vague or overbroad. In the area of speech, statutes that produce guessing games for regulated parties create an unacceptable risk. Congress should be expected to regulate with a reasonable degree of clarity. The requirement of clarity is—we have seen in Chapter 3—democracy-forcing in an important way, since it is an effort to ensure legislative deliberation on issues that raise constitutional difficulty. Nonpolitical speech may certainly be regulated in a constitutionally unacceptable manner, and laws that are vague or overbroad are core cases of unacceptable regulation.

Future Areas of Regulation

In this section I discuss how a First Amendment minimalist might respond to a series of actual or imaginable laws that raise First Amendment issues. The general themes are that in the hard cases, no simple rule will make much sense, and that an appreciation of the range of possible cases leads toward more modest rulings and presumptions.

Free speech minimalism, of the sort endorsed here, is highly sympathetic to congressional efforts to promote Madisonian goals, with an understanding that the economic ideal of "consumer sovereignty" is not a First Amendment mandate. Free speech minimalism is also willing to allow Congress to promote voluntary action on the part of those who produce or "consume" offerings on television or the computer, even if the resulting efforts have the purpose and effect of altering the nature and content of what is available.

Voluntary Means

Mutually Destructive Races

Some of the problems with the mass media are conspicuously a product of pressures imposed by the marketplace. Cable or broadcasting operators may well offer programming that is excessively violent, or sensationalistic, or grotesque, simply in order to keep up with the competition. They may well regret this fact; undoubtedly they often do. It is certainly imaginable that good journalists would prefer to be permitted to relax market pressures so as to offer programming that better fits with their goals and aspirations.

In 1992, Congress enacted, for a three-year period, a statute exempting broadcasters from the antitrust laws, to enable them to come up with voluntary guidelines about programming content. The particular goal of the law was to permit the development of guidelines for televised violence, so as to reduce the exposure of children to especially violent programming. Congress proposed to extend this idea via the Television Improvement Act of 1997. The key provision of the bill (which has not yet been enacted) is section 4, which would exempt from the antitrust laws agreements by "persons in the television industry for the purpose of developing and disseminating voluntary guidelines designed—(1) to alleviate the negative impact of telecast material such as, but not limited to, violence, sexual conduct, criminal behavior, or profane language; or (2) to promote telecast material that is educational, informational, or otherwise beneficial to the development of children."

At least in general, a law of this kind ought not to be thought to raise serious constitutional questions. The bill would not regulate or prohibit speech. Its only effect is to authorize voluntary action by broadcasters. In this particular way, it increases rather than decreases their freedom, by reducing the pressures of the marketplace with respect to educational programming, television violence, and related issues. In an important sense, the bill enhances the freedom of speech of broadcasters, by removing a governmental constraint (the antitrust laws) that prohibits broadcasters from acting as they wish and from speaking to one another about their action. If the bill does in fact have its intended effects, by increasing educational programming and reducing the amount of violence on television, it will be largely because the bill eliminates the competitive pressures that force broadcasters to produce violent shows even though (and this is the key point) broadcasters would in a sense prefer not to produce such shows. The creation of an antitrust exemption would merely free broadcasters from competitive pressures in this context.[17]

There are, however, two possible objections to the conclusion that voluntary measures of this kind raise no constitutional problem. The first objection is that the bill is less permissive and innocuous than it seems, because it is undergirded by an implied threat on government's part: to regulate if voluntary measures are not taken. In these circumstances, any voluntary measures do not really qualify as such; they are a product of the coercive force of government. But no commission is given authority to pressure distributors to remove particular items that it dislikes. Indeed, the FCC has no role to play here.

The second and more substantial objection is that the bill amounts to impermissible content regulation. On this view, government cannot enact selective exemptions from the antitrust laws in order to encourage speech that it prefers or discourage speech that it dislikes. For example, it would be impermissible to manipulate the antitrust exemption to allow cooperative behavior to ensure against criticism of governmental policy, of Republicans, or of the Supreme Court. This objection properly points to the fact that a viewpoint-based grant of immunity would be illegitimate; but it is not a persuasive objection to the bill in the forms in which it has been discussed. Crucially, the bill is viewpoint-neutral. And strictly speaking, an exemption from the antitrust laws is not content "regulation" at all. It bans no speech; it requires no speech. This fact is not decisive in its favor. But it makes the case for its constitutionality significantly stronger.

The strongest precedent in this regard—and it is a strong one indeed—is *Denver Area Educational Telecommunications Consortium* and in particular the Court's decision to uphold a provision by which Congress granted cable operators "permission" to exclude indecent programming from the airwaves. A content-based exemption from the antitrust laws would be objectionable if it were actually an effort to suppress a point of view. But insofar as the exemption is designed to promote educational programming for children, or to reduce violence (with its demonstrated harmful effects on children), it is unobjectionable. To the First Amendment minimalist, the bill raises serious problems only insofar as it goes beyond these goals.

Ratings

Recently Congress has gone somewhat further than provision of an antitrust exemption, via a statutory requirement of "ratings" by those who present programming to the public. Under this requirement, the content of any ratings system is devised not by government itself but by the private sector. The ratings system is already substantially in place, with simple information now provided about appropriate ages for programming.

Is a compulsory system of ratings unconstitutional? From the analysis thus far, it should be deemed entirely valid—as long as the government does not make particular decisions about the operation of the system. Such a system is viewpoint-neutral. It does not favor or disfavor any kind of speech. Moreover, it imposes no punishment, civil or criminal, on speakers. It is designed to provide information for the viewing public, and in that sense to increase consumer choice, in a way that should meet with the approval of both Madisonians and free marketeers. To be sure, it is also a form of compulsory speech, requiring programmers to provide information that perhaps they would prefer not to provide. But this kind of information-promoting provision is not unconstitutional for that reason. It is very different from a requirement that speakers include substantive messages that they disfavor. In minimalist spirit, courts should be cautious before raising serious doubts about consumer protection measures of this kind.

Facilitating Parental Control

In the last decade, there has been a great deal of concern about the risk that children will be exposed to obscene or violent material. Direct regulation is of course imaginable, and the ratings system just described is partly an effort to come to terms with this problem. Suppose, however, that the government attempts to assist parental control by allowing families to "block" certain material and to prevent it from entering the home. This is the idea behind the controversial "v-chip" proposal enacted by Congress in 1996. Through this enactment, Congress is requiring new televisions to be equipped with technology enabling parents to block certain programming. The goal of the requirement is to allow people to monitor what comes into their homes. By itself the v-chip requirement does not impose a ratings system of any kind. What it does impose is a requirement that technology allow people to stop programming in certain categories from appearing on their sets; and it is clear that Congress's fundamental motivation is to allow people to protect their families from violent programming. The v-chip requirement does, however, interact with any ratings requirement, by enabling people to have a sense of what programming to "block."

Some people believe that courts should strike down the v-chip requirement, on the theory that government cannot interfere with the communications market simply because it is concerned about the social effects of certain kinds of programming. (The original motivation was to ensure parental control of violent programs; "v" stands for violence.) But in keeping with a spirit of constitutional minimalism, courts should not disturb legislation of this kind. To be sure, a v-chip requirement may have a substantial effect on programming because of anticipated parental blocking; perhaps some broadcasters will not put on shows that are likely to be blocked by a large number of households, partly because of the lower consumer demand, partly because of social norms and public pressures. But it is not at all clear that the v-chip, accompanied by ratings, would decrease the demand for shows that some people wish to "block"; the very fact of identification of some programming as violent or highly sexual might even increase demand. In any case a diminished demand is not by itself constitutionally decisive. Any such effect would result from the voluntary behavior of those who watch and monitor television, which is an inevitable and acceptable aspect of a well-functioning market. From the constitutional point of view, the central point is that proposals of this sort would facilitate parental control but would not involve federal content regulation; they would not involve direct governmental control or censorship of the speech market. Because they are noncensorial and facilitative, courts should treat them more leniently.

The only serious questions involve selectivity and bias: is the government facilitating the exclusion of material of which it disapproves? If so, the fact that no direct regulation is involved is not enough; impermissible selectivity would be objectionable by itself. This is the concern invoked by those who emphasize that violent material is the specific motivation for the v-chip requirement. Certainly it would be troublesome if the government enabled people to screen out material of a certain, governmentally disapproved content; imagine a governmentally mandated "Democrat chip" or "Republican chip" or "liberal chip." But the "v-chip" lacks this feature. On its face, it is content-neutral. The most that can be said against it is that it is motivated by concern about violent material. But this suggests that it is founded on a desire to discriminate on the basis of content, not on the basis of viewpoint. As we have seen, the concern with violent content is perfectly legitimate. For this reason the v-chip requirement should be upheld. At least this is so in light of the existence of an ample factual record demonstrating that the government is attempting to combat harm rather than viewpoint. What I am emphasizing, consistent with the spirit of free speech minimalism, is that preexisting categories do not give clear guidance and that it is best for the courts to proceed in a cautious manner.

Violence

Thus far the discussion has focused on largely voluntary and minimally intrusive measures on the government's part—measures that create information and incentives rather than coercion. But it is also necessary to ask whether the First Amendment allows direct regulation of speech that plays a causal role in producing real-world violence. The question received considerable public attention in the wake of the Oklahoma City bombing in 1996, and it is likely to receive far more attention in the future, as new technologies make it easy to engage in speech that may well lead to violence. Applying ordinary standards, constitutional lawyers may well believe that this is a simple issue, settled by the key decision in Brandenburg v. Ohio, where the Court held that speech cannot be regulated unless the speaker both intends to produce, and is likely to produce, imminent lawless action.[18] As we saw in Chapter 4, this idea has become part of minimalism's current system. But the underlying issues are anything but simple.

Let us try to make the discussion as concrete as possible. The controversy produced a good deal of public concern in the spring of 1996, when talk-show host G. Gordon Liddy, speaking on the radio to millions of people, explained how to shoot agents of the Bureau of Alcohol, Tobacco, and Firearms: "Head shots, head shots. . . . Kill the sons of bitches." Later Liddy said, "[s]hoot twice to the belly and if that does not work, shoot to the groin area." On March 23, the full text of the Terrorist's Handbook was posted on the Internet, including instructions on how to make a bomb (the same bomb, as it happens, that was used in Oklahoma City). By the time of the Oklahoma bombing on April 19, three more people had posted bomb-making instructions, which could also be found on the Internet in the Anarchist's Cookbook. On the National Rifle Association's Internet "Bullet 'N' Board," someone calling himself "Warmaster" explained how to make bombs using baby-food jars. Warmaster wrote, "These simple, powerful bombs are not very well known even though all the materials can be easily obtained by anyone (including minors)." After the Oklahoma bombing, an anonymous notice was posted to dozens of Usenet news groups listing all the materials in the Oklahoma City bomb, explaining why the bomb allegedly did not fully explode and exploring ways to improve future bombs.

More than fifty hate groups are reported to be communicating on the Internet, sometimes about conspiracies and (by now this will come as no surprise) formulas for making bombs. On shortwave radio, people talk about bizarre United Nations plots and urge that "the American people ought to go there bodily, rip down the United Nations building and kick those bastards right off our soil." In fact, radio talk-show host Rush Limbaugh, who does not advocate violence, said to his audience, "The second violent American revolution is just about, I got my fingers about a fourth of an inch apart, is just about that far away. Because these people are sick and tired of a bunch of bureaucrats in Washington driving into town and telling them what they can and can't do."

In particular, there has been a series of national debates about speech over the Internet counseling violence or inciting hatred of public officials. Of course it is unclear whether such speech has had a causal role in any act of bombing. But new technologies, and particularly the Internet, have put the problem of incitement into sharp relief. It is likely, perhaps inevitable, that hateful and violent messages carried over the airwaves and the Internet will someday be responsible for acts of violence. This is simply a statement of probability. The questions raised for constitutional lawyers are these: Is that probability grounds for restricting such speech? Would restrictions on speech advocating violence or showing how to engage in violent acts be acceptable under the First Amendment? And how do preexisting categories bear on the current issue?

The Clear and Present Danger Doctrine and Its Evolution

It should go without saying that recent events should not be a pretext for allowing the government to control political dissent, including extremist speech and legitimate hyperbole (a large and important category). But let us explore the narrowest question, a new and unanswered one: the constitutionality of restrictions on speech that expressly advocates illegal, murderous violence in messages to mass audiences. For most of American history, the courts have held that no one has a right to advocate violations of the law.[19] They ruled that advocacy of crime is wholly outside of the First Amendment—akin to a criminal attempt and punishable as such. Indeed, many of the judges revered as the strongest champions of free speech believed that express advocacy of crime was punishable. Judge Learned Hand, in his great 1917 opinion in Masses Publishing Co. v Patten,[20] established himself as a true hero of free speech when he said that even dangerous dissident speech was generally protected against government regulation. But Hand himself agreed that government could regulate any speaker who would "counsel or advise a man" to commit an unlawful act.

In the same period the Supreme Court concluded that government could punish all speech, including advocacy of illegality, that had a "tendency" to produce illegality. Justices Holmes and Brandeis, the dissenters from this conclusion, took a different approach, saying that speech could be subjected to regulation only if it was likely to produce imminent harm;[21] thus they produced the famous "clear and present danger" test. But even Holmes and Brandeis suggested that the government could punish speakers who had the explicit intention of encouraging crime.

After the great Holmes and Brandeis dissents, modern First Amendment law was developed by a series of narrow, incompletely theorized steps. For many years, the Supreme Court tried to distinguish between speech that was meant as a contribution to democratic deliberation and speech that was designed to encourage illegality. The former was protected; the latter was not. In 1951 the Court concluded in Dennis v. United States[22] that a danger need not be so "clear and present" if the ultimate harm was very grave. The break in the doctrine did not come until the Court's 1969 decision in Brandenburg v. Ohio. There the Court said the government could not take action against a member of the Ku Klux Klan who said, among other things, "[W]e're not a revengent organization, but if our President, our Congress, our Supreme Court, continues to suppress the white, Caucasian race, it's possible that there might have to be some revengence taken." The speaker did not explicitly advocate illegal acts or illegal violence. But in its decision the Court announced a broad principle, ruling that the right to free speech does "not permit a State to forbid or proscribe advocacy of the use of force or of law violation except where such advocacy is directed to inciting or producing imminent lawless action and is likely to incite or produce such action."

The *Brandenburg* principle was not deeply theorized, and it can attract support from different foundations; but it was very wide. Offering broad protection to political dissent, the Court required the government to meet three different criteria to regulate speech. First, the speaker must promote not just any lawless action but "imminent" lawless action. Second, the imminent lawless action must be "likely" to occur. Third, the speaker must intend to produce imminent lawless action. The *Brandenburg* test borrows something from Hand and something from Holmes and produces a standard even more protective of speech than either of theirs. We might even see *Brandenburg* as analogous to Brown v. Board of Education: a broad ruling that emerged after years of narrower judgments, an area for which breadth had been shown, through repeated encounters with a variety of situations, to be entirely appropriate.

Old Standards, New Technology

Applied straightforwardly, the *Brandenburg* test seems to protect most speech that can be heard on television or found on the Internet. It suggests that a simple rule can resolve all cases. And in general, the *Brandenburg* test makes a great deal of sense. Remarks like those quoted from Rush Limbaugh unquestionably qualify for protection; such remarks are not likely to incite imminent lawless action, and in any case they are not "directed to" producing such action. They should also qualify as legitimate hyperbole, a category recognized in a 1969 decision allowing a war protester to say, "If they ever make me carry a rifle the first man I want to get in my sights is L.B.J."[23] Even Liddy's irresponsible statements might receive protection insofar as they could be viewed as unlikely to produce imminent illegality. A high degree of protection and breathing space makes a great deal of sense whenever the speech at issue is political protest, which lies at the core of the First Amendment. The appropriate remedy is not regulation but more in the way of speech.

But there is some ambiguity in the *Brandenburg* test, especially in the context of modern technologies, and it is here that a high degree of judicial caution is appropriate. Suppose that an incendiary speech, expressly advocating illegal violence in the form of murder, is not likely to produce lawlessness in any particular listener or viewer. But suppose too that of the millions of listeners, one or two, or ten, may well be provoked to act, and perhaps to imminent, illegal violence. Might the government ban advocacy of criminal violence in mass communications when it is reasonable to think that one person, or a few, will take action? *Brandenburg* offers a reasonable approach to the somewhat vague speech in question in that case, which was made in a setting where relatively few people were in earshot. But the case offers unclear guid-ance on the express advocacy of criminal violence via the airwaves or the Internet.

When messages advocating murderous violence are sent to large numbers of people, it is sensible to wonder whether the constitutional calculus changes: government may well have the authority to stop speakers from expressly advocating the illegal use of force, at least if it is designed to kill people. The calculus changes when the risk of harm increases because of the sheer number of people exposed. Hence the requirement of causation might be loosened, at least for explicit ad-vocacy of murder. There is little democratic value in protecting simple counsels of murder, and the ordinary *Brandenburg* requirements might be weakened where the risks are great. Consider, for example, the fact that Congress has made it a crime to threaten to assassinate the Presi-dent, and the Court has cast no doubt on that restriction of speech. It would be a short step, not threatening legitimate public dissent, for the Federal Communications Commission to impose civil sanctions on those who expressly advocate illegal acts aimed at killing people. Courts might well conclude that the government may use its power over the airwaves to ensure that this sort of advocacy does not occur.

Of course, there are serious problems in drawing the line between counsels of violence that should be subject to regulation and those that should not. We might begin (and perhaps we should end) with restrictions on express advocacy of unlawful killing; this is the clearest case. I am not trying to draw conclusions so much as I am trying to suggest reasons for courts to be cautious in invoking the Constitution. In any case, we can now see that existing doctrine does not justify a simple conclusion. It was built on different factual circumstances; it was designed for what was, with respect to communications, a quite different world. The degree of danger from counsels of murder has increased with the rise of the Internet.

Authorizing the restriction of any speech, even counsels of violent crime, creates serious risks. It is unnecessary to emphasize that the government often overreacts to short-term events, and the Oklahoma City tragedy, for example, should not be the occasion for an attack on extremist political dissent. Vigorous, even hateful, criticism of government is very much at the heart of the right to free speech. Certainly advocacy of law violation can be an appropriate part of democratic debate. As the example of Martin Luther King, Jr., testifies, there is an honorable tradition of civil disobedience. We should sharply distinguish, however, King's form of nonviolent civil disobedience from counsels or acts of murder. The principle condemning government regulation of political opinions, including the advocacy of illegal acts, need not be interpreted to bar the government from restricting advocacy of unlawful killing on the mass media. These are hard cases, and courts should be reluctant to conclude that the First Amendment forbids well-designed legislative initiatives.

Bombs

Does the government have the power to limit speech containing instructions on how to build weapons of mass destruction? The *Brandenburg* test was designed mostly to protect unpopular points of view from government controls; it need not protect the publication of bomb manuals, at least if these manuals are being transmitted to millions of people. Instructions for building bombs are not by themselves a point of view, and if government wants to stop the mass dissemination of this material, it should probably be allowed to do so. A lower court so ruled in a 1979 case involving an article in *The Progressive* that described how to make a hydrogen bomb.[24]

The court's argument is even stronger as applied to the speech on the Internet, where so many people can be reached so easily. In such a case, the potential harm from the relevant materials is significantly increased. And bomb manuals, qua bomb manuals, do not deserve the highest degree of constitutional protection. Regulation of instructions on how to commit terrorist acts does not place the government in a position where it does not belong.

Libel, Threats, Privacy, and Harassment

New technologies have greatly expanded the opportunity to communicate obscene, libelous, violent, or harassing messages—perhaps to general groups via stations on (for example) cable television, perhaps to particular people via electronic mail. Invasions of privacy are far more likely. The Internet poses special problems on these counts. As a general rule, any restrictions should be treated like those governing ordinary speech, with ordinary mail providing the best analogy. If restrictions are narrowly tailored, and supported by a sufficiently strong record, they should be upheld.

Consider in this regard a highly publicized effort to bring suit against the television talk-show host Oprah Winfrey under laws allowing people to seek compensation for "disparagement" of agricultural products. The impetus for these laws is not obscure. Sensationalistic stories about supposedly dangerous products (apples? beef?) can circulate widely and cause great damage to the economy. If the stories are false, the results are hardly laughable. Ordinary people can be hurt: the employees in the relevant industries, whose wages may be cut and who may even face unemployment, and consumers, who may be terrified, itself a harm, and unwilling to buy entirely safe products, a harm of a different sort. Product disparagement laws can also prevent a destructive kind of "race" within the news media, where the search for a superior competitive position may make a sensationalistic story travel far and wide whether or not it is true. Existing law provides a good start toward analyzing the constitutionality of these measures. Hyperbole is entirely legitimate; so too with good-faith mistakes. Under libel law as applied to public figures, statements must be shown to be false or made with reckless indifference to the matter of truth or falsity. Even negligently made statements are protected. The product "disparagement" laws should be interpreted, if this is possible, to allow a plaintiff to recover compensatory damages if he can prove that false statements were made on purpose. So interpreted, the laws should probably be upheld.

Or consider another well-publicized case, involving "cyberporn" at the University of Michigan. A student is alleged to have distributed a fictional story involving a fellow student, explicitly named, who was, in the story, raped, tortured, and finally killed. The first question raised here is whether state or federal law provides a cause of action for conduct of this sort. Perhaps the story amounts to a threat, or a form of libel, or perhaps the most plausible state-law claim would be based on intentional infliction of emotional distress; perhaps there is no legal claim at all. The next question is whether, if a state-law claim is available, the award of damages would violate the First Amendment. At first glance it seems that the question should be resolved in the same way as any case in which a writer uses a real person's name in fiction of this sort. And it certainly does not seem obvious that the First Amendment should prohibit states from awarding damages for conduct of this kind, as long as a particular person is being targeted and as long as no political issue is involved. Perhaps the ease of massive distribution of such materials, which can be sent to much of the world with the touch of a button, argues in favor of loosening the constitutional constraints on compensatory damages.

What of a regulatory regime designed to prevent invasion of privacy, libel, unwanted commercial messages, obscenity, harassment, or infliction of emotional distress? Some such regulatory regime will ultimately make a great deal of sense. The principal obstacles are that the regulations should be both clear and narrow. It is easy to imagine a broad or vague regulation, one that would seize upon the sexually explicit or violent nature of communication to justify regulation that is far broader than necessary. Moreover, it is possible to imagine a situation in which liability was extended to any owner or operator who could have no knowledge of the particular materials being sent. The underlying question, having to do with efficient risk allocation, involves the extent to which a carrier might be expected to find and to stop unlawful messages; that question depends upon the relevant technology.

Consider more particularly possible efforts to control the distribution of libelous or sexually explicit materials on the Internet. Insofar as the government seeks to ban materials that are technically libelous or obscene, and imposes civil or criminal liability on someone with specific intent to distribute such materials, there should be no constitutional problem. By hypothesis, these materials lack constitutional protection, and materials lacking constitutional protection can be banned in cyberspace as everywhere else. On the other hand, many actual and imaginable laws would extend beyond the technically obscene, to include (for example) materials that are "indecent," or "lewd," or "filthy." Terms of this sort create a serious risk of unconstitutional vagueness or overbreadth. At least at first glance, they appear unconstitutional for that reason.

The best justification for expansive terms of this kind would be to protect children from harmful materials. It is true that the Internet contains pornography accessible to children, some of it coming from adults explicitly seeking sexual relations with children. There is in fact material on the Internet containing requests to children for their home addresses. Solicitations to engage in unlawful activity are unprotected by the First Amendment, whether they occur on the Internet or anywhere else. For this reason, regulation designed to prevent these sorts of requests should not be held unconstitutional. But when the government goes beyond solicitation, and bans sexually explicit material more broadly, the question is quite different. Here a central issue is whether the government has chosen the least restrictive means of preventing the relevant harms to children. In a case involving "dial-a-porn," for example, the Court struck down a ban on "indecent" materials on the ground that children could be protected in other ways.[25] On the Madisonian view, this outcome is questionable, since "dial-a-porn" ranks low on the First Amendment hierarchy. But under existing law, it seems clear that in order to support an extension beyond obscenity, Congress would have to show that less restrictive alternatives would be ineffectual. The question then becomes a factual one: what sorts of technological options exist by which parents or others can provide the relevant protection? To answer this question, it would be necessary to explore the possibility of creating "locks" within the Internet, for use by parents, or perhaps for use by those who write certain sorts of materials. This is the sensible and quite minimalist approach signaled by both *Reno* and *Denver Area*.

Different questions would be raised by the imposition of civil or criminal liability not on the distributors having specific intent to distribute, but on carriers who have no knowledge of the specific materials at issue, and could not obtain such knowledge without considerable difficulty and expense. It might be thought that the carrier should be treated like a publisher, and a publisher can of course be held liable for obscene or libelous materials even if the publisher has no specific knowledge of the offending material. But in light of the relatively low cost of searches in the world of magazine and book publishing, it is reasonable to think that a publisher should be charged with having control over the content of its publications. Perhaps the same cannot be said for the owner of an electronic mail service. Here the proper analogy might instead be the carriage of mail, in which owners of services are not held criminally or civilly liable for obscene or libelous materials. The underlying theory is that it would be unreasonable to expect such owners to inspect all the materials they transport, and the imposition of criminal liability, at least, would have an unacceptably harmful effect upon a desirable service involving the distribution of a great deal of protected speech. If carriers were held liable for distributing unprotected speech, there would inevitably be an adverse effect on the dissemination of protected speech as well. In other words, the problem with carrier liability, in this context, is that it would interfere with protected as well as unprotected speech.

How do these points bear on the First Amendment issue with respect to the Internet? Some of the services that provide access to the Internet should not themselves be treated as speakers; they are providers of speech, but their own speech is not at issue. This point is closely related to the debate in *Turner I* about the speech status of cable carriers. But whether or not a carrier or provider is a speaker, a harmful effect on speech would raise First Amendment issues. We can see this point with an analogy. A state could not say that truck owners are criminally liable for carrying newspapers containing articles critical of the President. Such a measure would be unconstitutional in its purposes and in its effects, even if the truck owners are not speakers. From this we can see that a criminal penalty on carriers of material that is independently protected by the First Amendment should be unconstitutional. Thus a criminal penalty could not be imposed for providing "filthy" speech, at least if "filthy" speech is otherwise protected.

But a penalty imposed on otherwise unprotected materials raises a different question. Suppose that the government imposes criminal liability on carriers or providers of admittedly obscene material on the Internet. The adverse effect on unprotected speech should not by itself be found to offend the Constitution, even if there would be a harmful economic effect, and even unfairness, for the provider of the service. Instead the constitutional question should turn on the extent of the adverse effects on the dissemination of materials that are protected by the Constitution. If, for example, the imposition of criminal liability for the distribution of unprotected speech had serious harmful effects for the distribution of protected speech, the First Amendment issue would be quite severe. But that question cannot be answered in the abstract; it depends on what the relevant record shows with respect to any such adverse effects. We need to know whether carrier liability, for unprotected speech, has a significant adverse effect on protected speech as well. We need to know, in short, whether the proper analogy is to a publisher or instead to a carrier of mail. It is therefore important to know whether a carrier could, at relatively low expense, filter out constitutionally unprotected material, or whether, on the contrary, the imposition of criminal liability for unprotected material would drive legitimate carriers out of business or force them to try to undertake impossible or unrealistically expensive "searches." The answer to this question will depend in large part on the state of technology.

Madisonian Goals

None of the measures discussed thus far has involved governmental efforts to promote Madisonian goals by, for example, increasing the amount of educational or public-affairs broadcasting. In this section I discuss the constitutional status of such efforts.

1. *Requiring competition.* Many actual and imaginable legislative efforts are designed to ensure competition in the new communications markets. There is no constitutional problem with such efforts. The only qualification is that some such efforts might be seen as subterfuge for content regulation, disguised by a claimed need to promote monopoly.

But if government is genuinely attempting to prevent monopolistic practices and to offer a structure in which competition can take place, there is no basis for constitutional complaint. Here First Amendment theorists of widely divergent views might be brought into incompletely theorized agreement.

2. *Subsidizing new media.* It is predictable that government might seek to assist certain technologies that offer great promise for the future. Some of these efforts may be a result of interest-group pressure. But in general, there is no constitutional obstacle to government efforts to subsidize preferred communications sources. Perhaps government believes that some technological innovations are especially likely to do well, or that they could receive particularly valuable benefits from national assistance. At least so long as there is no reason to believe that government is favoring speech of a certain content, efforts of this kind are unobjectionable as a matter of law. They may be objectionable as a matter of policy, since government may make bad judgments reflecting confusion or factional influence; but that is a different issue.

3. *Subsidizing particular programming or particular broadcasters.* In her dissenting opinion in *Turner I,* Justice O'Connor suggested that the appropriate response to government desire for programming of a certain content is not regulation but instead subsidization. This idea fits well with the basic model for campaign finance regulation, set out in Buckley v. Valeo.[26] It also fits with the idea, found in Rust v. Sullivan,[27] that the government is unconstrained in its power to subsidize such speech as it prefers. Hence there should be no constitutional objection to government efforts to fund public broadcasting, to pay for high-quality fare for children, or to support programming that deals with public affairs. The government might even require broadcasters, as a condition (for example) for digital television licenses, to give a certain percentage of their profits to public broadcasting. Perhaps government might subsidize certain uses of the Internet.

To be sure, it is doubtful that *Rust* would be taken to its logical extreme. Could the government fund the Democratic Convention but not the Republican Convention? Could the government announce that it would fund only those public-affairs programs that spoke approvingly of current government policy? If we take the First Amendment to ban viewpoint discrimination, funding of this kind should be held to be improperly motivated. But government subsidies of educational and public-affairs programming need not raise serious risks of viewpoint discrimination. It therefore seems unexceptionable for government, short of viewpoint discrimination, to subsidize those broadcasters whose programming it prefers, even if any such preference embodies content discrimination. So, too, government might promote "conversations" or fora on e-mail that involve issues of public importance, or that attempt to promote educational goals for children or even adults.

4. *Imposing structural regulation designed not to prevent a conventional market failure, but to ensure universal or near-universal consumer access to networks.* The protection of broadcasters in *Turner I* and *II* was specifically designed to ensure continued viewer access to free programming. Notably, the Court permitted government to achieve this goal through regulation rather than through subsidy. Of course subsidy is the simpler and ordinarily more efficient route. If the government wants to make sure that all consumers have access to communications networks, why should it not be required to pay to allow such access, on a kind of analogue to the food stamp program? The ordinary response to a problem of access is not to fix prices but instead to subsidize people who would otherwise be without access. The *Turner* Court apparently believed that it is constitutionally acceptable for the government to ensure that industry (and subscribers), rather than taxpayers, provide the funding for those who would otherwise lack access.

The precise implications of this holding remain to be seen. It is impossible to foresee the range of structural regulations that might be proposed in an effort to ensure that all or almost all citizens have access to free programming or to some communications network, including any parts of the "information superhighway." Some such regulations might in fact be based on other, more invidious motives, such as favoritism toward a particular set of suppliers; as we have seen, this may well be true of the measure in *Turner.* The *Turner* decisions mean that courts should review with some care any governmental claim that regulation is actually based on an effort to promote free access. But the key point here is that if the claim can be made out on the facts, structural regulation should be found acceptable.

5. *Imposing content-based regulation designed to ensure public-affairs*

and educational programming. It can readily be imagined that Congress might seek to promote education via the regulation or subsidy of new media. It might try to ensure attention to public affairs. Congress or the FCC might require broadcasters to provide free air time for candidates, on the theory that such a requirement would promote democratic goals and at the same time diminish some of the problems produced by dependence on private funds. Or suppose, for example, that Congress sets aside a number of channels for public-affairs and educational programming, on the theory that the marketplace provides a disproportion of commercial programming. This notion has been under active consideration in Congress and the FCC. Thus a recent bill would have required all telecommunications carriers to provide access at preferential rates to educational and health care institutions, state and local governments, public broadcast stations, libraries and other public entities, community newspapers, and broadcasters in the smallest markets. The FCC itself has recently required broadcasters to provide at least three hours of educational programming per week.

A minimalist Court should be hospitable to these kinds of regulations. To be sure, *Turner I* and *Turner II* do not stand for the proposition that such efforts are constitutional. By hypothesis, any such regulation would be content-based. It would therefore meet with a high level of judicial skepticism. But the *Turner* decisions do not authoritatively suggest that such efforts are unconstitutional. The Court did not itself say whether it would accept content discrimination designed to promote Madisonian goals. Certainly the opinion suggests that the government's burden would be a significant one. But it does not resolve the question.

Certainly crudely tailored measures give reason to believe that interest-group pressures, rather than a legitimate effort to improve educational and public-affairs programming, are at work. But if the relevant measures actually promote Madisonian goals, they should be upheld. There is of course reason to fear that any such measures have less legitimate purposes and functions, and hence a degree of judicial skepticism is appropriate. But narrow measures, actually promoting those purposes, are constitutionally legitimate. At the very least, the Court should uphold government requirements of educational programming for children or of free time for candidates for public office.

Conclusion

The law of the First Amendment is not, in general, minimalist in character, and happily so. The Court's confrontations, over many decades, with a wide range of free speech issues have produced a high degree of width; most free speech issues are quite clear. There is less depth than width. But the long period of doctrinal development has also produced some degree of depth, especially insofar as the Court, recognizing Madisonian principles, has given broad protection to political speech and disfavored viewpoint discrimination. By contrast, the key cases involving new technologies have indeed been minimalist in character, and this is entirely appropriate. The constitutional issues raised by new communications technologies turn on questions, including changing issues of fact, that cannot be easily resolved in the current period.

In a period of unforeseeable consequences, rapid development, and technological uncertainty, there is much room for tentative, narrow judgments. It is both possible and important to identify a core for free speech minimalism, banning viewpoint discrimination, broadly protecting political speech, and requiring legislation to avoid vagueness and overbreadth. But outside of this core, many of the novel issues raised by emerging technologies are ill suited to judgment by rule. Here the Court is proceeding, as it should, with a high degree of caution.

III

ANTAGONISTS

9

Width? Justice Scalia's Democratic Formalism

Is minimalism inconsistent with the rule of law? Insofar as the minimalist judge seeks narrowness rather than width, minimalism might seem hopelessly ad hoc and particularistic. The result may be to make law unpredictable and at the same time to increase the discretion of public officials, including the discretion of judges. Thus it might seem that judicial rulings should be wide, in the sense of rule-bound, whenever possible. On this view, it is not so important that judicial decisions be deeply theorized. What matters is that judges announce, and abide by, general rules.

This view has considerable appeal. In the last decades, its most prominent supporter has been Justice Antonin Scalia. Scalia is a consistent maximalist, at least in the sense that he seeks width rather than narrowness. The aspiration to rule-bound law is the most distinctive part of his jurisprudence; it unites almost all of his work on the bench, and even helps account for his enthusiasm for "originalism" in constitutional law. Justice Scalia shows enthusiasm for rule-bound judgments in his extrajudicial writing as well. By exploring and developing Justice Scalia's arguments, we can see what might be said for and against width as a legal ideal. My conclusion is that width is a highly contingent virtue. When planning is important, and when judges can devise decent rules, width is all to the good. But when judges lack sufficient information, and when legally relevant facts and values are in flux, narrowness may well be the better route.

Formalism and Democracy

An influential essay[1] collects many of Justice Scalia's maximalist arguments, and here narrowness is the basic target. In this book I have attempted to defend common law methods. By contrast, Justice Scalia seeks to demote, even to exorcise the common law, to complain of its ascendancy in an age committed to the principles of democratic government and the rule of law. Hence his title: "Common-Law Courts in a Civil-Law System." In Scalia's view, the common law is associated with particularism, and it is for this reason simultaneously anachronistic and hubristic. It is anachronistic because it is out of touch with the values and operations of modern government. The charge of hubris is the more serious one. Scalia thinks that common law methods compromise democratic values, by allowing judges an excessive role in policy-making. He also thinks that common law methods, of the kind celebrated here, introduce a high degree of unpredictability, increasing judicial discretion and at the same time depriving others, citizens as well as legislators, of a clear background against which to work.

Justice Scalia intends, then, to defend an important alternative to minimalism: *democratic formalism.* We might even say that Scalia is the clearest and most self-conscious expositor of democratic formalism in the long history of American law. Justice Scalia is a democrat in the sense that much of his jurisprudence is designed to ensure that important judgments are made by those with a superior democratic pedigree, in the sense that they are subject to electoral processes. Above all, he seeks to develop rules of interpretation that will limit the policy-making authority and decisional discretion of the judiciary, the least accountable branch of government.

Justice Scalia is a formalist in the particular sense that he favors clear rules, seeks to treat statutory and constitutional texts as rules, and distrusts the view that legal texts should be understood by reference either to intentions or to canons of construction that live outside of authoritative texts. Democratic formalism finds its interpretive foundation in "textualism." Thus Scalia writes: "Of all the criticisms leveled against textualism, the most mindless is that it is 'formalistic.' The answer to that is, *of course it's formalistic!* The rule of law is *about* form. . . . Long live formalism. It is what makes a government a government of laws and not of men."[2]

As a judicial creed, democratic formalism is intelligible and coherent in part because it argues in favor of interpretive principles and default rules for statutes that will create a clear background for Congress and in the process impose the right incentives on lawmakers. Justice Scalia's preferred default rules are intended to make the law readily predictable and to ensure that Congress will legislate in the constitutionally preferred fashion.

Where does all this leave the common law, or minimalism? For the democrat and for the formalist, both the common law and minimalism raise many doubts. The common law of course owes its content not to electoral processes but to decisions by people who are mostly unelected. And common law judges are free to eschew rules and to act on a case-by-case basis. Indeed, the glory of the common law is often said to consist in its particularism—its careful attention to the facts of the particular case, its provision of an individualized hearing for each litigant. Common law constitutionalism is emphatically incremental rather than rule-bound; consider, for example, the areas of sex discrimination (Chapter 7) and free speech (Chapter 8).Thus Justice Scalia's attack on the common law legacy is rooted in a distrust of minimalism—above all narrowness—and in enthusiasm for rule-bound interpretation that relies, in both statutory and constitutional interpretation, on a single foundation: *the meaning of the relevant legal text as it was understood at the time of enactment.*

Rules and Democracy as Contested Ideals

There are two basic problems with Justice Scalia's brand of maximalism, and thus to his (or any other) call for width. The first problem is that whether rules are desirable depends on the context and on pragmatic considerations. There is no a priori or acontextual argument on behalf of rule-bound law. Of course width has its virtues, but whether those virtues are decisive depends on a set of pragmatic and institutional issues. An abstract catalogue of the virtues does nothing to establish a general case for formalism or width.

The second problem is more general. It is that Justice Scalia's argument on behalf of democratic formalism does not come to terms with three important problems: (1) the internal morality of the democratic ideal; (2) the existence of reasonable, nonformalist views about interpretation, designed also to limit judicial discretion, promote stability, and enhance democratic self-government; and (3) the place of administrative agencies in the structure of modern public law. In short, democratic formalism would not in fact promote democracy, rightly understood. Moreover, there are nonformalist ways of limiting judicial power and judicial discretion, ways that are familiar to the common law tradition as it has come to be understood in the United States. The principal virtue of democratic formalism is that it may be the best way of promoting predictability, but even here there are reasonable alternatives, and predictability cannot trump all other values.

If a goal of a system of interpretation is to constrain judicial discretion, and particularly if we attend to the role of regulatory agencies, it is far from clear that Justice Scalia's approach is superior to the alternatives actually favored by the American tradition of public law. And if a goal of a system of legal interpretation is to promote democratic self-government, it is not at all clear that rule-bound law is better than the approach favored by our tradition, which uses interpretive principles to promote democratic goals, not only in the area of statutory construction but also in administrative and constitutional law.

A great defect of democratic formalism is that it identifies democracy with whatever happens to emerge from majoritarian politics. If we insist (with the Constitution's framers) that there is a difference between a well-functioning system of deliberative democracy and simple majoritarian politics, we may well favor principles of interpretation that promote that very system, probably by allowing administrative agencies some license to adjust text to circumstance, certainly through constitutionally inspired principles of statutory interpretation, and not least by invalidating outcomes that are inconsistent with what we might consider the internal morality of democracy. Some of these principles are minimalist in character, and properly so.

Several more positive arguments emerge from these points. In the interpretation of statutes, courts should treat the text as the foundation for decision, but they should allow administrative agencies to adapt the text to unanticipated circumstances, at least if the adaptation does not violate any considered judgment by Congress. They should also use various principles of interpretation to resolve ambiguities in sensible ways, even if this produces less in the way of width. In constitutional law, courts should indulge a presumption in favor of both democratic outcomes and rules, but the presumption can certainly be overcome. When the internal morality of democracy argues against respect for majorities, the Court need not be deferential. When there is a strong interest in predictability, or when the Court has reason for confidence in a wide ruling, narrowness is a mistake. Thus in the areas of contract and property law, courts attempt to provide guidance through clear rules, and there are constitutional analogues, as in strong presumptions in favor of economic regulation, against "physical invasions" of property rights and against statutes that regulate speech on the basis of point of view. But the case for narrowness is strong when the Court is dealing with an issue that is now receiving sustained democratic attention, when the Court lacks much confidence in its capacity to generate a sensible rule, and when predictability is not especially important.

I am hardly arguing that narrowness is appropriate in all contexts. The problem with Justice Scalia's enthusiasm for width is that it is itself too wide—too general and coarse-grained, insufficiently sensitive to the fact that the argument turns on a set of considerations that are, roughly speaking, pragmatic and institutional in character. It follows that rule-free law is likely to make sense in many of the most contested issues of constitutional law—in, as we have seen, disputes over discrimination on the basis of sexual orientation and over the relation between free speech and new communications technologies. Now let us explore these issues in more detail.

Against the Common Law

Justice Scalia's argument on behalf of democratic formalism comes in three parts. The first part is an attack on the particularism, or minimalism, of the common law. The second part is a discussion of statutory interpretation. The third part deals with constitutional law.

Broken-Field Runners

Scalia thinks that the first year of law school has "an enormous impact upon the mind," and much of that impact comes from the student's immersion in judge-made common law. There is a difference, for Scalia, between law that is common in the sense of "customary" and law that is "common" in the sense that it is the creation of judges. That form of law is created not through practice but the standard emphasis of law schools, hypotheticals and analogical thinking. "What intellectual fun all of this is! It explains why first-year law school is so exhilarating: because it consists of playing common-law judge, which in turn consists of playing king—devising, out of the brilliance of one's own mind, those laws that ought to govern mankind. How exciting!"[3] Thus the student comes to have a distinctive picture of the great judge, with a large influence on American legal culture, as the person "who has the intelligence to discern the best rule of law for the case at hand and then the skill to perform the broken-field running through earlier cases that leaves him free to impose that rule: distinguishing one prior case on the left, straight-arming another one on the right, high-stepping away from another precedent about to tackle him from the rear, until (bravo!) he reaches the goal—good law."

What is wrong with this picture? Justice Scalia thinks that the problem is simple: "a trend in government that has developed in recent centuries, called democracy." Legal realism has taught us what is now obvious, that common law judges make and do not find law. This does not mean that the common law should be eliminated from its own domain; but it does mean that the *attitude* of common law judges is inappropriate for most of the work of federal judges and much of the work of state judges. "We live in an age of legislation, and most new law is statutory law." And the common law method has two basic problems. First, it is insufficiently democratic, since it threatens rule by judges. Second, the common law method is insufficiently formal, because it is too highly particularistic, too unpredictable, too rule-free—too minimalist.

"What a Waste"

Justice Scalia brings these points to bear on the topic of statutory interpretation, one of his passions. Though the topic is a bit afield from my principal concern here, it is well worth exploring, because it creates an especially valuable test on the question of width.

Justice Scalia's basic complaint is that American judges and academics "are unconcerned with the fact that we have no intelligible theory" of statutory construction. His central claim is that what matters is the objective meaning of the text, not the subjective intentions of Congress. Thus interpretation actually turns on "a sort of 'objectified' intent—the intent that a reasonable person would gather from the text of the law, placed alongside the remainder of the corpus juris."[4] Because subjective intent is so murky, Justice Scalia thinks that its use risks substitution of judicial policy preferences for those of the legislature.

His case in chief in this regard is the great case of Church of the Holy Trinity v. United States.[5] There the Court held, contrary to the apparently plain language of the governing statute banning the importation of foreign labor, that the church could pay for the transportation of a rector to the United States. Justice Scalia reads *Holy Trinity* (not at all unreasonably) as a case about the substitution of legislative intent for text. In his view, what the church did violated "the letter of the statute, and was therefore within the statute: end of case." Thus Justice Scalia adopts "textualism," understood as a recipe for width. To interpret the statute in *Holy Trinity* in accordance with its text is to make the law more rule-bound. But he offers two important clarifications. First, he disfavors "strict construction": "I am not a strict constructionist and no one ought to be."[6] Textualists give to the text its ordinary meaning, construing it neither broadly nor narrowly. Nor does Scalia favor "literalism." He emphasizes that meaning is a function of context. What he urges is that courts should refuse to go beyond the range of meaning offered by a reasonable understanding of statutory terms, taken in their context.

Justice Scalia is aware that some cases involve a fairly wide range of textual meanings, and that the text can leave ambiguities. What aids are permissible? It is entirely acceptable to interpret statutory terms with structural aids, resolving ambiguities so as to make statutes both internally consistent and consistent with previously enacted laws. Thus his textualism is supplemented with resort to the structure of the relevant statute and indeed the structure of the law as a whole.

Scalia also defends canons of construction as legitimate and helpful, at least if they are commonsense ways of understanding the meaning of text. This is true of the ancient canons with Latin names, such as the old favorite "expressio unius est exclusio alterius" (expression of the one is exclusion of the other). In urging the use of such canons, Scalia takes a stand against Karl Llewellyn's famous attempt to demolish the canons by showing that for every canon there is an equal canon pointing in the opposite direction.[7] Scalia says, very reasonably, that there really are not opposites on almost every point, and he thinks that the most that Llewellyn has shown is that the canons are not absolute, which is not exactly news.

Justice Scalia is much less enthusiastic about substantive canons or presumptions, as in the idea that courts should construe statutes favorably to Native Americans, leniently on behalf of criminal defendants, narrowly if they are in derogation of the common law, narrowly if they waive sovereign immunity, and so forth. For textualists, substantive canons raise many questions. They lack clear legitimacy (where do courts get the authority to use them?), and they have indeterminate weight, thus increasing the unpredictability and possible arbitrariness of judicial decision. But some substantive presumptions may be reasonable if they attempt to get at meaning or if they have the warrant of antiquity. Thus extraordinary acts, like the congressional elimination of state sovereign immunity or perhaps the waiver of sovereign immunity, require a clear statement, because that is what one would expect were extraordinary acts intended. And the rule of lenity may be justified by its age. But others look like a "sheer judicial power grab."

For a long time Justice Scalia has been critical of judicial use of legislative history, largely on the ground that it makes law less wide—less predictable and easier to manipulate. Here he makes two central points. First, legislative intent is not the proper criterion of the law, and hence legislative history focuses judicial attention on the wrong question, away from meaning and toward subjective understandings of meaning. Second, use of history involves a lot of time and expense, and it is "more likely to produce a false or contrived legislative intent than a genuine one." This is because there is in 99.99 percent of cases no such thing, and the archives are unreliable in any case. "In the only case I recall in which, had I followed legislative history, I would have come out the other way, the rest of my colleagues (who did use legislative history) did not come out the other way either. . . . What a waste."[8]

"A Rock-Solid, Unchanging Constitution"

Constitutional interpretation, for Justice Scalia, is a place not for special principles but for the usual ones just described. He is concerned above all to ensure that law is rule-bound; his basic argument is that the Constitution's meaning is set not by the original intention but by the original meaning of its text. Thus Hamilton and Madison receive attention not because they were framers whose subjective intentions matter, but because they (no more than Jay and Jefferson, who were not framers) can help tell us identify the original meaning. For Scalia, originalism opposes those who think, common law fashion, that the Constitution is "living" and should be understood by reference to "current" meaning. The notion of a "living constitution" is an invitation to the open-field running characteristic of common law thinking, or decision by reference to cases instead of authoritative text. Thus Justice Scalia particularly deplores the fact that constitutional law is made after consulting recent cases rather than original intention. For Scalia, the result is "a common-law way of making law, and not the way of construing a democratically adopted text."[9] The consequence is that the Constitution means whatever (the judges think) it should mean. This is his objection to minimalism in constitutional law.

Against the view that the "living" constitution is necessary to promote flexibility over time, Justice Scalia argues that the living constitution approach actually reduces the capacity for democratic experimentation. Against the view that the "living" constitution is necessary to protect an ample category of rights, Justice Scalia argues that it need not increase the category of rights at all. In many cases—property rights, Second Amendment rights, confrontation clause rights—originalism offers a more rather than less expansive understanding of rights. That understanding may be ill suited to current social desires. But it is emphatically not a truncated understanding of rights.

Justice Scalia's fundamental objections to a common law understanding of the Constitution are natural to critics of minimalism: it lacks legitimacy and it is too discretionary. Freed from the original meaning, judges consult their own judgments of policy and principle and are effectively untethered. "[T]here is no agreement, and no chance of agreement, upon what is to be the guiding principle of the evolution."[10] To be sure, originalists disagree among themselves; history can be ambiguous, and importantly, Justice Scalia notes that there are questions about applying the original meaning to new and unforeseen phenomena, such as sound trucks and television. But these are minor problems compared with those raised when people who, believing in a living constitution, take the Constitution to mean what it should, and hence authorize judges to understand the Constitution to be whatever the majority wants. "This, of course, is the end of the Bill of Rights, whose meaning will be committed to the very body it was meant to protect against: the majority. By trying to make the Constitution do everything that needs doing from age to age, we shall have caused it to do nothing at all."[11] Thus his key argument on behalf of originalism involves the

whole question of width. Narrow judgments are rule-free; they enable
judges to do whatever they wish.

Interpretive Goals: Stability, Democracy, Restraint

A central goal of this approach to interpretation is characteristic of those
who oppose minimalism: to reduce the sheer costs of decision, so that
the burden on courts and litigants is relatively low. A closely related
goal is to make law relatively certain and predictable, so that people
know where they stand and do not have to puzzle much over the content of law. Yet another goal is to control the discretion of those institutions whom we trust least or fear most. Thus a system of interpretation might well be designed to reduce the role of courts in
establishing social policies or governing principles, certainly if it seems
that courts ought not to be entrusted with that kind of business. Justice
Scalia thinks that his version of textualism will effectively control judicial power, while at the same time increasing the policy-making primacy
of the legislature, in part by giving it appropriate incentives. If, for
example, legislative history will not be used, legislators will be under
considerable pressure to increase statutory clarity. These points are
about reducing the burdens of decision and the costs of uncertainty.

With his version of maximalism, Justice Scalia also seeks to promote
democratic self-government and the primacy of the system of lawmaking set out in Article I of the Constitution. The reduction of judicial
discretion via textualism serves both of these fundamental goals.[12] And
in so doing, democratic formalism ensures that statutory and constitutional provisions will not be given "spirits" and "purposes" attributable to the (unenacted) political morality of any particular era. A ban
on "dynamic" interpretation, and a requirement of fidelity to enacted
law, ensures that courts will not bow to political will, or bend statutes
to prevailing political winds except to the extent that they have produced actual enactments.

What I will be arguing here is that such an approach must rely largely
on a set of pragmatic and empirical claims about various governmental
institutions, and on how those institutions are likely to respond to different interpretive strategies. No context-free view about legal interpretation will make much sense. And while judgments about the future
are inevitably speculative, America's own experience, with its distinctive

history, suggests that democratic formalism is likely to be inferior to the alternatives actually favored by the American legal tradition. We might take this to be a neo-Burkean point, intended as a challenge to Justice Scalia's neo-Benthamite attack on the common law. It is highly revealing in this connection that there is a substantial overlap between the interpretive practices of common law and civil law courts, which use similar presumptions and canons, not only linguistic but substantive as well.[13] Thus Justice Scalia's attack on common law practices cannot easily survive an encounter with civil law systems, whose courts are only intermittently textualist, and which are permeated by interpretive practices of the kind he disfavors.

Holy Trinity, Excessive Generality, and Presumptions

Let us approach these points by focusing on *Holy Trinity,* Justice Scalia's bête noire. The *Holy Trinity* case raises a large number of the issues about rule-bound law and the whole topic of statutory interpretation. As we will see, the principal function of that case was to make statutes themselves less wide, and this is Justice Scalia's major complaint.

In 1920, largely in response to an influx of immigrant labor, Congress made it "unlawful for any person, company, partnership, or corporation, in any manner whatsoever, to prepay the transportation, or in any way assist or encourage the importation or migration of any alien or aliens, any foreigner or foreigners, into the United States, . . . under contract or agreement, parol or special, express or implied, made previous to the importation or migration of such alien or aliens, foreigner or foreigners, to perform labor or service of any kind in the United States. . . ." The problem arose when the Church of the Holy Trinity made a contract with E. Walpole Warren, an alien residing in England, to pay for his transportation to the United States, where he was to work as rector and pastor. The United States claimed that the church had acted unlawfully. The Supreme Court disagreed. It said that the text of the act was not controlling.

The Court's opinion was very complex, with multiple strands. It is clear that the Court refused to read the text as a maximally wide rule. But the opinion can be read in three different ways.

1. General language will not be taken to produce an outcome that

would, in context, be taken as absurd by those who enacted it, at least
if there is no affirmative evidence that this result was intended by the
legislature. "[F]requently words of general meaning are used in a statute, words broad enough to include an act in question, and yet a consideration of the whole legislation, or of the circumstances surrounding
its enactment, or of the absurd results which follow from giving such
broad meaning to the words, make it unreasonable to believe that the
legislature intended to include the particular act."[14]

On this view, *Holy Trinity* is a rerun of the famous case of Riggs v.
Palmer,[15] where the New York Court of Appeals held that a statute
governing inheritance would not be interpreted to allow a nephew to
inherit from his uncle's will when the uncle's death resulted from his
murder at the nephew's hands.

2. General language will not be taken to produce an outcome that
was clearly not intended by the enacting legislature, as those intentions
are revealed by context, including legislative history. "[A]nother guide
to the meaning of a statute is found in the evil which it is designed to
remedy; and for this the court properly looks at contemporaneous
events, the situation as it existed, and as it was pressed upon the attention of the legislative body. . . . It appears . . . in the testimony presented before the committees of Congress, that it was this cheap unskilled labor which was making the trouble. . . . We find, therefore, that
the title of the act, the evil which was intended to be remedied, the
circumstances surrounding the appeal to Congress, the reports of the
committee of each house, all concur in affirming that the intent of
Congress was simply to stay the influx of this cheap unskilled labor."[16]

3. General language will not be taken to depart from long-standing
social understandings and practices, at least or especially if the departure
would raise serious constitutional doubts. "[N]o purpose of action
against religion shall be imputed to any legislation, state or national,
because this is a religious people. This is historically true. . . . [S]hall it
be believed that a Congress of the United States intended to make it a
misdemeanor for a church of this country to contract for the services
of a Christian minister residing in another nation?"[17]

On this view, the background tradition of religious liberty thus operates as a "clear statement" principle, one that requires Congress to
speak unambiguously if it wishes to intrude on that tradition. Congress
will not be taken to have barred a church from paying for the trans-

portation of a rector unless there is affirmative evidence that Congress intended to do precisely that. Congress will not be taken to have interfered with religious liberty through inadvertence or loose language.

Justice Scalia appears to think that each of these three principles is wrong, certainly as applied to *Holy Trinity*. Each of these three principles points in the direction of narrowness in the specific and interesting sense that they limit the "holding" of a seemingly clear statute. Each of the principles narrows the reach of an apparently rule-like statute. Let us take them up in turn.

Understood according to principle (1), *Holy Trinity* presents a familiar, even mundane problem, that is, the problem introduced by linguistic generality. In a famous passage, Wittgenstein describes the problem in this way: "Someone says to me: 'Shew the children a game.' I teach them gaming with dice, and the other says 'I didn't mean that sort of game.' Must the exclusion of the game with dice have come before his mind when he gave me the order?"[18]

Wittgenstein's clear implication is that it need not. In daily communication, and without much thinking about it, we understand things contextually and purposively. Sometimes we carve out exceptions from the dictionary definitions of general language; indeed, the process does not appear to be one of carving out exceptions at all. It all happens very quickly and naturally. A friend says, "Don't bother me during the next hour" (but what if the house catches fire?), or a parent says to a child, "Clean up your room completely" (but what if a certain level of messiness is standard in the family?), or a spouse requests, "Pick me up at 2 P.M." (but what if there is a medical emergency?). Ordinary people do not consult the dictionary meaning of the words and act in accordance with what they find there.

It might be tempting to respond that there is a difference between daily communication and a legislative command; perhaps the latter should be presumed not to be sloppy. But this response misses the point, which has nothing to do with sloppiness and everything to do with the cognitive limits of human beings. Because of the inevitable limitations of human foresight, even the most carefully chosen words can become unclear because and not in spite of their generality.[19] Textualists and rule enthusiasts who fail to see this point can be found only in science fiction novels populated by androids and aliens, whose misunderstandings and befuddlement are a direct consequence of their textualism. Now Justice Scalia is not a literalist; he is at pains to distinguish textualism from literalism, and he knows that the meaning of text is a function of context. But once we insist on that point, why is principle (1) so bad? Why isn't it an ordinary application of the idea that the meaning of words depends on context?

Perhaps Justice Scalia might respond that this principle increases the costs of decision for judges; perhaps an approach that takes Congress "at its word" produces more mechanical (simpler, more predictable, wider) jurisprudence. Perhaps Justice Scalia would add that absurdity is in the eye of the beholder, so that principle (1) also introduces risks of error in the form of judicial misjudgments about what counts as absurd. And perhaps Justice Scalia could insist that Congress would respond well to his approach to *Holy Trinity*. Knowledge of judicial refusal to make exceptions for absurdity might increase legislative care with drafting and thus decrease excessive generality before the fact. Or perhaps Congress would respond promptly and effectively to mistakes introduced by excessive generality; Congress would therefore correct the outcome in *Holy Trinity* if it really objected.[20] If all this were true, Justice Scalia's approach would produce few mistakes, and those mistakes that it would produce would find easy correction. This is indeed the best defense of width, in the particular form of understanding texts in accordance with their ordinary meaning and refusing to make exceptions even when the case for exceptions seems especially strong.

If we understand Justice Scalia's argument to be defensible in these terms, the debate over principle (1) is really a debate about the costs of decision and the costs of error;[21] more particularly, it is a special case of the debate over rules and standards (a subset of the debate over minimalism, as we saw in Chapter 2). The *Holy Trinity* Court treated the text of the statute as a kind of standard, inviting inquiry into underlying purposes; Justice Scalia wants to treat it as a kind of rule, fully specifying outcomes in advance. But this dispute cannot be resolved on the basis of abstractions. It is better to ask about which approach will (roughly speaking) minimize the costs of decision and the costs of error. Justice Scalia can be taken to suggest that his approach will reduce aggregate decision costs and the number and seriousness of mistakes; and under imaginable assumptions, he is entirely right. If, for example, courts would much blunder if they investigated the question whether the particular application is absurd, if that investigation would increase unpredictability and uncertainty, if Congress would legislate more clearly if courts acted as Justice Scalia would prefer, and if Congress would respond to the problems introduced by Justice Scalia's approach, by correcting any real absurdity, then there would be little problem with democratic formalism in the context of statutory interpretation.

But are the assumptions correct? This is far from obvious. Perhaps a judicial role of the sort suggested in *Holy Trinity* will not introduce much uncertainty; perhaps cases in which textual generality and excessive ruleness produce absurdity are few in number and easily recognized as such. If so, principle (1) will not much increase decision costs, and it will greatly reduce error (understood as such if the outcome would be by general agreement absurd). And it is very hard for legislatures to anticipate cases of this kind in advance—and also costly and complex for legislatures, with much business to transact, to spend all the resources necessary to fix the errors of excessive generality. Formalism may decrease costs at the judicial level while also increasing costs, perhaps dramatically, at the legislative level. And it seems unrealistic to expect a busy legislature to devote much of its time to correcting the problems introduced by interpreting statutes in a formalistic manner. If all this is true, *Holy Trinity* may well be right as an example of principle (1), certainly if the outcome would generally be agreed to be absurd by members of the community of authors and addressees.

None of this supplies a decisive argument against Justice Scalia's view. What I have said shows only that the underlying considerations involve the likely performance of courts and Congress under different interpretive regimes. If we are talking about the modern state, it makes sense to say that administrative agencies should be permitted to act as the Court did in *Holy Trinity* (a point to which I will return). And a reasonable assessment of the practical issues would suggest that courts should feel free to make exceptions for applications that seem unquestionably absurd; then the question would be whether the application in *Holy Trinity* falls in that category. Certainly it cannot be said that the outcome is implausible or an abuse.

Justice Scalia is correct in objecting to principle (2) if he understands that principle to suggest that clearly expressed legislative history (in, for example, committee reports) should trump clearly expressed text. He is also right to say that the text, and not the history, is the law; no one should doubt that point. And it is sensible for Justice Scalia to insist on a distinction between subjective intent (something actually in the minds of legislators) and "objectified intent," understood as "[t]he intent that a reasonable person would gather from the text of the law, placed alongside the remainder of the corpus juris." But suppose that we do not trouble ourselves with the complexities of psychological inquiry into the subjective intentions of collective decision-making bodies, and suppose that we use legislative history only in cases of interpretive doubt, not because it is "the law" but because it helps identify the meaning of the law. Suppose too that interpretive doubt can be created either by ambiguous terms or by what appears to be excessive generality (consider here gaming with dice; Riggs v. Palmer; *Holy Trinity*). Here legislative history would matter for the same reason that Madison and Hamilton matter. Words are hard to understand without some conception of their purpose, and the distinction between purpose and intention (suitably "objectified") is thin.

Indeed, textualism itself cannot do without some crucial subjective elements; in this way, the claim that textualism makes law rule-bound and wide should be taken with many grains of salt. Recall that meaning is, for Justice Scalia, to be determined by reference to "meaning" as it was commonly understood at the time of enactment. But common understandings are inevitably uncovered by figuring out *what people thought*. Thus the movement from "intentions" to "meaning" is not a movement from something (entirely) subjective to something (entirely) objective. If the question is what relevant people understood a term to mean, legislative history may well be useful. Of course legislative history should not be used when it is uninformative, or when it is so extensive and broad that a judge is using it not to figure out what Congress meant but to support judicial policy preferences. Of course the text has priority, and it is right to insist that what appears in the legislative history may be the view of one side in a debate, or of a private interest group unable to get its way with Congress. But these points do not support a bar on the use of legislative history; they lead in the direction of pragmatism and caution.

As part of his skepticism about minimalism, Justice Scalia suggests that the use of legislative history is akin to "posting edicts high up on the pillars, so that they could not easily be read." The suggestion is certainly relevant, but standing alone it cannot carry much weight. Citizens do not always have easy access to statutory text (ask a nonlawyer neighbor—if you dare—to track down 42 USC 7521j(2)(B)(ii), by, say, tomorrow morning), and those who can find the text can often, without expending a lot more effort, find the history. And where there are ambiguities and doubts, might it not be better to look at legislative history than to consult dictionaries, or one's own views about policy and principle, at least if the ordinary meaning of the term, taken in its context, is what governs? Why mightn't legislative history be useful in showing that the term in question is not sensibly interpreted to cover the problem at hand?

Here too these questions are not decisive. We can imagine a world in which resort to legislative history would be more trouble than it is worth, because courts and legislatures, in that world, would respond well if courts relied only on text and applicable canons of construction. In that imaginable world, legislative history would not be very helpful (because it would be impossibly ambiguous); courts would use legislative history to reach the results that they liked best, which (let us suppose) would be independently very bad; and the use of legislative history would have unfortunate effects on the legislature, by discouraging it from legislating clearly. But we can also imagine a legal culture in which legislative history helps discipline judges, by giving them a sense of context and purpose, without creating serious problems at the legislative stage. There is no way to know whether, in the abstract, use of legislative history is good or bad. As long as courts proceed sensibly, first principles involving political legitimacy cannot resolve that question. Whether it makes sense to use legislative history depends on such issues as the simple costs of using the history, the likelihood that it will increase rather than decrease errors, the availability of other, more reliable sources of meaning, and the consequences for the legislature itself of using legislative history or not using legislative history.

What about principle (3)? Justice Scalia does not discuss it in any detail. But it is easy to defend interpretive principles of this sort. Even enthusiasts for width acknowledge that extraordinary acts are not expected, and thus that courts should not find them unless there is clear indication that they were intended; this idea is part of a defense of principle (3). Courts should also try to fit ambiguous texts with the rest of existing law, and *Holy Trinity* was written very much in this spirit. And there is a third defense of principle (3); it has a great deal to do with the nondelegation doctrine, whose purpose is to ensure that legislatures, rather than bureaucracies or courts, actually make the most important decisions of policy. In short, courts should require Congress—not the executive branch—to decide, with particularity, if it wants to force judges to resolve a serious constitutional problem. Congress, as the basic lawmaking body, is therefore required to make that decision specifically and not by inadvertence. On this view, vague or general language should not be taken to require judicial resolution of a hard constitutional judgment; there is too great a likelihood that if it is so taken, Congress will not itself have thought about the constitutional issue at all. Certainly it is most unlikely that the Congress that enacted the statute at issue in *Holy Trinity* actually decided to apply the ban to churches.

Of course the nondelegation doctrine is effectively dead, in part because courts cannot easily enforce it. But many clear statement principles or substantive canons of interpretation—prominently including the principle requiring Congress to speak clearly if it wants to raise a serious constitutional problem—can be seen as narrower, more modest, more targeted nondelegation doctrines. The basic defense of principle (3) is that it has a democracy-forcing character. It requires the national legislature to make a highly focused decision, reflecting its own decision about constitutionally sensitive issues. Most substantive canons of construction have this purpose. They are designed to ensure that the legislature focuses with particularity on some issue, largely for reasons with roots in the Constitution, American history, or both. Thus ambiguous statutes will be read so as not to preempt state law, or favorably to Native Americans, or so as not to apply extraterritorially, or favorably to criminal defendants, or so as not to intrude on the traditional authority of the President.[22]

We can agree that the statutory text deserves priority over legislative history and that courts should ordinarily rely on a reasonable understanding of the text at the time of enactment. But Scalia provides no convincing argument against principles (1), (2), or (3). A general conclusion follows. Any approach to statutory interpretation depends on judgments, partly pragmatic and empirical in nature, about the capacities of both courts and legislatures, and about the likely effects on both institutions of different interpretive approaches. Those who endorse principles (1) through (3), or imaginable cousins and variations, have to defend those principles against the objection that they increase uncertainty (thus jeopardizing rule of law values) and also the number and magnitude of mistakes. The kind of width produced by democratic formalism must be defended not only on the ground that it increases certainty (a reasonable proposition, though a questionable one if textual ambiguity is pervasive) but also on the ground that it will not lead to errors that are large in number and serious in magnitude. A good deal turns on the likely performance of courts and legislatures, and on legislators' responsiveness to judicial interpretation.

Have Administrative Agencies Become Our Common Law Courts?

There is a notable and surprising gap in the argument offered by Justice Scalia and others on behalf of rule-bound law: the administrative state. The rise of administrative law has greatly transformed the practice of interpretation in public law. Most of the key work of statutory interpretation is now done not by courts at all, but by federal agencies. Justice Scalia himself has written an important and illuminating essay[23] on Chevron v. NRDC,[24] which is unquestionably and by far the most important case about legal interpretation in the last thirty years. Note in this regard that in its relatively short period on the scene, *Chevron,* a kind of counter-Marbury for the administrative state, has been cited more frequently than Marbury v. Madison, Brown v. Board of Education, or Roe v. Wade, and if present trends continue it will before long have been cited more frequently than all those cases put together. Indeed, *Chevron* may qualify, now or soon, as the most cited case in all of American law; it is an indispensable part of an assessment of legal interpretation or of the place of minimalism in legal culture.

Chevron holds that where statutes are ambiguous, courts should accept any reasonable interpretation by the agency charged with their implementation. *Chevron* also appears to accept the suggestion, central to legal realism, that the decision how to read ambiguities in law involves no brooding omnipresence in the sky but an emphatically human judgment about policy or principle. And *Chevron* concludes, in a way endorsed by Justice Scalia and very much bearing on the democracy prong of his argument, that where underlying statutes are ambiguous, Congress should be taken to have decided that agencies are in a better position to make that judgment than courts. Agencies are in that better position because, *Chevron* emphasizes, the President is generally in charge of their policy judgments, and hence agencies have a kind of democratic pedigree, certainly a better one than the courts.

Notably, *Chevron* is a wide principle, in the sense that it extends to the whole universe of agency interpretations of law: where statutes are ambiguous, agencies prevail. But *Chevron* is maximalist only in a complicated sense, for it allows agencies to adjust statutes as they see fit, and in that sense to make law less predictable. A central motivating idea here is that administrative agencies are influenced by shifting public judgments, and their approaches are likely to reflect the President's basic commitments. Thus *Chevron* allows the law to shift over time as a result of agency decisions rather than decisions by courts.

If this is so, debates over statutory interpretation and over minimalism in general must include not only Congress and the courts but also administrative agencies, which are in an especially good position to carry out the updating and particularizing functions of common law judges. As a consistent maximalist, Justice Scalia has argued that plain text always counts against an agency interpretation;[25] in his view, *Chevron* deference is never due to an agency that counteracts text (defined by reference to ordinary understandings). But this view is itself anachronistic. Indeed, we can obtain a good mix of democratic and common law virtues—and get a better handle on the issues posed by judicial minimalism—if and only if we decide that the adaptation of statutory text to particular applications (including the exempting of absurd outcomes), and the use of applicable canons of construction, is an entirely appropriate *administrative* task.

On this view, *Holy Trinity* might be seen very differently in the context of the twenty-first century, whose public law would pose as a central question: what are the views of any agency charged with implementation of this law? To the suggestion that this position means that some statutes (more accurately, their terms in some applications) might be lost or misdirected as a result of new agency rulings, a response might be given in Justice Scalia's own words: "[L]ots of once-heralded programs ought to get lost or misdirected, in vast hallways or elsewhere. Yesterday's herald is today's bore—although we judges, in the seclusion of our chambers, may not be au courant enough to realize it."[26]

As against occasional pleas for judicial "updating" of obsolete statutes, offered most influentially by Judge Guido Calabresi,[27] we might claim that the argument needs to be updated: for the most part, appropriate solutions to the problem of legal obsolescence should come from administrative agencies, immersed in the problems at hand and having both technocratic and democratic virtues as compared with the courts. And as against Justice Scalia, we might urge that administrative agencies should be authorized to reject the "text" in a way that would go well beyond the common law role envisaged by *Holy Trinity*, at least when there is no evidence of a considered legislative judgment against the agency's interpretation. In modern *Holy Trinity* cases, courts would not do the work on their own, but would permit agencies to engage in a degree of statutory adaptation. Courts would grant this permission not at all on the theory that agencies can *violate* the text, but after a finding that despite the generality of the text, there was no considered legislative judgment contrary to the agency's view.[28]

Consider an especially important recent case, upholding the power of the Food and Drug Administration to regulate tobacco products as "drugs" or "devices." The statute defines "drug" to include articles "intended to affect the structure or function of the body of man or other animals," and it defines "device" to include any "article" that is similarly intended, and that "does not achieve its primary intended purposes" through chemical action or through being metabolized. The FDA contended that the current meaning of the Food, Drug, and Cosmetic Act, as enacted in 1938, allows it to regulate tobacco products. At first glance it seems clear that in 1938, the terms "drug" and "device" were not understood to include tobacco products. But the terms are quite broad and seem capable of change over time, with new understandings of underlying facts. Might not an executive agency, subject as it is to political checks and immersed as it is in the technical details, be entitled to interpret those terms to include tobacco products in 1997? The district court upheld the FDA's decision. What is striking is that the court based its judgment not on the ordinary understanding of the statutory terms at the time of enactment, but on the agency's authority to interpret those terms, adaptable as they are to changed understandings of facts, in a way consistent with what (accountable and informed officials could conclude is) their current meaning.

The lower court's decision seems reasonable and correct. To be sure, the original meaning of "drug" and "device" may not, to the relevant community, have included tobacco products. But Congress enacted general terms, not its particular understandings, or intentions, of what those terms meant in light of early judgments of fact and value. And in view of new judgments about relevant facts, and belief-influenced changes in values, it seems appropriate to allow a specialized agency, accountable as it is to political forces, to interpret these (general and ambiguous) terms in the new way that it did in 1997. There can be little doubt that the FDA's decision was a product of both factual judgments and a set of entirely legitimate political influences, and that it emerged after a sustained period of highly visible deliberation on the issues at hand, with involvement from the President himself. Of course Congress can override the interpretation if it chooses.

The tobacco case might seem a bit different from *Holy Trinity*, for in the former case the statutory terms could easily be understood to cover tobacco, and perhaps Congress should be taken to have enacted the principle reflected in those words, rather than Congress's particular understanding of what those words meant. But consider, as a closer analogue to *Holy Trinity*, another modern case, American Mining Congress v. EPA.[29] Congress had not clearly dealt with the problem of how to handle materials held for recycling, and the relevant EPA regulation defined certain materials involved in recycling as "solid waste." In particular, it said that spent materials, sludges, scrap metal, and the like would be treated as solid waste if they were not directly reused but were instead held as part of an industry's ongoing production process. The EPA reasoned that materials that were stored, transported, and held for recycling were associated with the same kinds of environmental harms as materials that were abandoned or disposed of in some final way. The court of appeals struck down the EPA regulation on the ground that the governing statute defined solid waste as "garbage, refuse, sludge . . . and other discarded material"; for the court, material held for recycling was not "discarded." Citing the dictionary, the court thought that the "ordinary plain-English meaning" was decisive.

If the question was an internal dispute on a court of appeals about the best interpretation of a statutory term, perhaps the majority would be right. But the question involved the validity of an EPA regulation, produced after a complex process involving a number of political interests, an extended process of intergovernmental deliberation, and an elaborate inquiry into the underlying issues of substance. Even if a court is reluctant to adapt the meaning of a term like "discarded" to fit with context—even if this is a far weaker case than *Holy Trinity* for contextual adaptation—is it not hubristic for judges, not elected and knowing little about the enormously complex subject at hand, to invoke dictionaries (compiled after all by human beings) to invalidate executive branch decisions that cannot reasonably be said to run afoul of any judgment from Congress? The EPA's decision followed a sustained period of public comment, and undoubtedly the government would be held accountable for any decision about the reach of the Resource Conservation and Recovery Act. If the EPA's decision runs afoul of dictionary definitions but of no actual decision by Congress, should it really be struck down?

An enthusiast for width might reply that the virtues of rule-bound law are crucial, and that those virtues are compromised if agencies are permitted to depart from the original or ordinary meaning of the statutory text. Thus the maximalist arguments against *Holy Trinity* work against use of the *Chevron* principle to allow agencies to depart from the ordinary meaning of the text. But we have seen that those arguments are pragmatic in character, and depend on highly uncertain assumptions. The assumptions seem all the weaker when the institution that is adapting the language is an administrative agency subject, as agencies typically are, to presidential and hence democratic control.

A broader conclusion follows. It is one thing to say that courts should be permitted to ignore original meaning in favor of current meaning; it is quite another thing to say that agencies, with their comparative advantages, should be permitted to do precisely that. These are separate debates, and it is possible to resolve the first question against the courts while at the same time resolving the second question in favor of the agencies.

An Analogy

Allowing appropriate adjustments for the role of administrative agencies, we can better understand statutory interpretation, and the uses of narrowness and width, if we borrow from the law of contract. It is now familiar to see contract law as consisting largely of default rules, specifying how to understand gaps or silences from the parties, and also how to understand provisions that seem vague or ambiguous.[30] The law of contract contains three kinds of default rules. First, some default rules are designed to find out the instructions of the parties. What would they have done, if they had written an explicit provision on the point? Such default rules are *market-mimicking*. Second, some default rules are designed not to implement the parties' will, but to impose on the party who can do so most cheaply the incentive to make a clear provision on the point. Default rules of this kind are *information-eliciting*, intended not to mimic the parties' wishes but to make sure that those wishes are made clear by the parties themselves.

It also seems clear how to choose between market-mimicking and penalty default rules. If the court is clear on what the market-mimicking rule is, it should choose that rule. But if the court is unsure on that question—if the costs of decision and costs of error, for the judge seeking to discern the market-mimicking rule, are very high—the court would do better to impose an information-eliciting default, designed to penalize the party in the best position to make explicit provision on the matter at hand. And courts have a third kind of default rule. Some such rules are based on considerations of public policy that have little or nothing to do with implementing or eliciting the parties' instructions. These considerations might involve, for example, the protection of third parties, or they might be intended to shift the parties' preferences and values in a certain direction. The resulting default rules may well be inalienable, in the sense that the parties are not permitted to change them.

Much of legal interpretation is, or is about, default rules. It may be tempting to suppose that federal courts, lacking common law authority, ought not to use such rules, and that statutory construction should proceed without them. But a moment's reflection should show that statutory default rules, in some form, are not so much desirable as inevitable. As the law of contract helps reveal, words do not and cannot have meaning without background understandings of various sorts. Usually those understandings are so taken for granted, so highly internalized, that they seem invisible, and part of the necessary meaning of words. But they are nonetheless in place; they make communication possible. Without background understandings, we could not understand one another. And often legal interpretation is possible only because of background principles or rules, some of them so taken for granted that they are invisible, some of them contested enough to be visible but not highly controversial, some of them at the heart of spir-

ited debates in public law. (There is a parallel in the substance of minimalism as discussed in Chapter 4.) If, for example, a federal statute
does not say whether state law is preempted, what happens? If a statute
is silent on the existence of private rights of action, do such rights exist?
To answer such questions it is hopeless to say that courts should follow
"the text." A default rule, or principle, or presumption is necessary one
way or the other. The legal system cannot proceed without them. The
question is not whether to have statutory default rules but which statutory default rules to have.

Some default rules are designed to find out the legislature's actual
instructions. Such rules are the analogue, in statutory interpretation,
of market-mimicking default rules. But statutory default rules might
also operate as information-eliciting devices, or as penalties, with the
purpose of encouraging Congress to act in a certain way, by creating
appropriate incentives. Some default rules are wide precisely because of
the goal of imposing good incentives on the national legislature. Courts
might, for example, ask which party is in the best position to correct
any errors in Congress, or ask which approach is likely to ensure that
Congress will legislate clearly. Some of Justice Scalia's jurisprudence is
best understood as a series of information-eliciting default rules. Thus
textualism itself has, as part of its defense, the idea that it will encourage
Congress to state its will clearly. Similarly, the ban on use of legislative
history imposes on Congress an incentive to say what it means in the
constitutionally favored form. And we can understand some statutory
default rules as having purposes not involving congressional instructions; these are the analogue to "public policy" defaults in the law of
contract. Consider the idea that statutes will be construed favorably to
Native Americans, that statutes will be construed so as not to raise
constitutional doubts, that statutes will be construed so as not to preempt state law.

The contract law analogy shows that terms have no meaning without
default rules and that there is an important place for default rules that
serve purposes external to the will of the parties, including the parties
to enacted law. Default rules may be minimalist or maximalist in character; they may allow more or less room for the exercise of discretion
in individual cases. The appropriate degree of width and the appropriate
level of discretion, here as elsewhere, depend on judgments about how
to reduce total costs of decision and total costs of error. Those judg-

ments will depend in turn on an assessment of the capacities of various government institutions—an assessment that would return us to the various issues discussed above.

The Constitution and the Common Law

Now let us turn to the Constitution. My basic claim here is that width is an ambiguous virtue, of special importance where planning is crucial, and also where the Court has reason to be confident about a wide rule. But width is a mistake when the Court lacks sufficient information, when the relevant values have not been adequately clarified, or when the problem is undergoing democratic consideration, at least if planning is not especially insistent. We have encountered a number of areas where this is now so, involving, for example, free speech and the Internet (a problem of inadequate information), homosexuality (a problem of continuing democratic debate), and affirmative action (a problem of inadequate information, unclear values, and continuing debate). But the most fundamental source of wide constitutional rulings is, or purports to be, originalism, and this is the right place to begin.

Originalisms

For most participants in debates over constitutional interpretation, the question is not whether the original understanding is controlling. It is how the original understanding is best understood. Indeed, we cannot know whether the "original understanding" is controlling until we know what this term means. Here the question of the possibility and value of width becomes crucial.

Some people think that the original understanding is best taken as setting out aspirations whose content changes over time; if they are right, originalism by itself leaves a great deal undecided. Others think that the original understanding points to abstract principles[31]—in the context of the ban on cruel and unusual punishment, for example, perhaps the Constitution bans not the framers' particular choices about what punishments are cruel and unusual, but "whatever punishments are in fact cruel and unusual." Here too originalism provides little in the way of rule-bound law; it is the source of incompletely specified abstractions. Some people, most notably Lawrence Lessig, think that however the original understanding is described, its provisions must be "translated" in order to be applied to new problems. Still others think that the Constitution's provisions should be read in very concrete form. This is the camp that rejects minimalism, and that invokes originalism as the foundation for wide rulings, for if history produces concrete judgments, constitutional law can be very wide and rule-pervaded.

Perhaps surprisingly, Justice Scalia claims that he does take the Constitution to embody "abstract principles." But for one who seeks width, what it abstracts "is not a moral principle of 'cruelty' that philosophers can play with in the future, but rather the existing society's assessment of what is cruel." Thus the Eighth Amendment is to be understood not by "what we consider cruel today" but instead by "the moral *perception of the time*."[32] Of course this formulation raises questions of its own. How do we characterize the moral perception of the time? At what level of abstraction? Again in the interest of width, Justice Scalia believes that it must be characterized at a relatively low level of abstraction; his claim that the death penalty cannot possibly violate the Eighth Amendment's "abstract moral principle" appears to be rooted in the fact that the moral principle held by the founding generation did not seem, to the founding generation, to forbid the death penalty. But this raises many further questions, suggesting the considerable difficulties in deciding how an originalist ought to proceed. Does it follow that the equal protection clause permits school segregation? That the national government, not bound by an equal protection clause, can discriminate however it wishes? That the First Amendment does not disturb the common law of libel? That the takings clause does not apply to regulation? Justice Scalia himself does not answer these questions. I emphasize this point only to suggest that there is not one kind of (canonical) originalism but a wide range of (plausible) originalisms. Justice Scalia's brand of originalism is motivated by the desire to ensure width; that is a reasonable aspiration but it is driven less by historical concerns and more by the desire to limit judicial discretion and to make constitutional law as predictable as possible.

Originalism and Stare Decisis

There is a pervasive problem for originalists who seek rule-bound law: how to handle precedents that depart from originalism. In many areas of constitutional law, originalism as understood by its advocates has been repudiated for a fairly long time, and key provisions now mean something other than what, on the suggested versions of originalism, they were originally understood to mean. The question goes to the heart of the relationship between the Constitution and the common law method. Common law lawyers rely heavily on the doctrine of stare decisis; it is a foundation of their method. How should those skeptical of common law constitutionalism deal with the resulting doctrine?

Commenting on Justice Scalia's arguments about constitutional law, Laurence Tribe argues that Justice Scalia is not really an originalist at all. Tribe objects that in several First Amendment cases (involving flag-burning, cross-burning, and animal sacrifice), Justice Scalia has voted to strike down statutes not inconsistent with the original understanding, narrowly understood. But Justice Scalia acknowledges the problem. He answers that his votes are attributable not to a belief that the First Amendment sets out aspirations whose content changes over time, but to the unblinkable fact that for the First Amendment "the Court has adopted long-standing and well-accepted principles (not out of accord with the general practices of our people, whether or not they were constitutionally required as an original matter) that are effectively irreversible."[33] (It is worthwhile to note that there are two points here: judicial understandings and consistency with "general practices of our people," an idea that is designed to promote wide rulings but that raises obvious problems of its own.) The point of originalism is thus not to "roll[ ] back accepted old principles of constitutional law" but to reject "usurpatious new ones."[34] Scalia explains in this fashion his recent votes against "novel constitutional" rights—against excessive damage awards, against being excluded from government contracts because of party affiliation, against single-sex schools.

The difficulty with this claim is that it is very hard to know when an originalist judge, concerned to respect precedent, is applying "accepted old principles" or instead creating "new constitutional rights." Would it not be equally plausible to say that in the nonoriginalist judgments that Justice Scalia joined, the Court created new rights, for example, the right to burn the flag and the cross and the right to sacrifice animals? Would it not be plausible to say that in the judgments from which Justice Scalia dissented, the Court largely applied principles developed in older cases forbidding government from using outmoded sex stereotypes as a basis for segregating schools or from conditioning employment on party affiliation?

To answer these questions, everything depends on the level of generality at which old principles or new rights are described. The precedents in such areas as sex equality are well entrenched, and Justice Scalia offers no basis on which to distinguish between a refusal to create "new rights" and a willingness to follow "old principles." And there is a risk that the originalist judge, refusing to extend the principles reflected in old cases, will ensure incoherence in the law, and thus a form of unfairness, since similarly situated people will not be treated similarly. This might be referred to as the Bowers v. Hardwick problem: "Thus far and no more!" does not produce much coherence in this law. Perhaps this sacrifice is inevitable and worthwhile—if it is the only way to restore judicial legitimacy without renovating existing law—but it creates problems of its own. To decide whether the resulting incoherence, and dissimilar treatment of the similarly situated, are worthwhile, it is necessary to balance the extent of the unfairness against the value of preventing further mistakes and the costs of attempting to do so.

Why (and Which) Originalism?

The original understanding of the Constitution cannot be treated as decisive simply because it *was* the original understanding; a defense of using the original understanding must itself be independent of the original understanding, and thus must be made out in terms of political theory. Judges cannot defend use of the original understanding, let alone any particular species of originalism, solely by reference to history. If history shows that the framers intended their particular understanding to be binding, the question remains: should current judges be bound by the intention?

The question whether the original understanding of old text should bind current generations is not at all simple; we can agree that the Constitution itself should be taken as binding[35] without finding it self-evident that Americans must be bound by past understandings of votes by some segment of the citizenry over two centuries ago. A reference to "democracy" cannot provide the necessary answer. Justice Scalia suggests that his version of originalism will make law more rule-bound and limit the policy-making authority of federal judges, and this is very plausibly true. It would also be extremely important if Justice Scalia were correct in suggesting that judges have only two real alternatives: follow the original understanding as he understands it or basically do whatever they want, through a form of ludicrously narrow, ad hoc law. But this is implausible. Both originalist and nonoriginalist judges come in many different stripes, and the distinctions among them require a good deal of attention. The debate over methods of constitutional interpretation cannot sensibly be resolved by suggesting that anyone who disagrees is inviting judges to rule as they wish. Minimalists have their own devices for limiting judicial discretion.

Generalizing from the discussion in previous chapters, let us imagine some more reasonable alternative positions. We can imagine judges who care a great deal about history but who explore history to identify, not particular understandings of particular problems, but overall goals and purposes. We can imagine judges who think, for example, that the First Amendment, understood in light of its historical roots, is centered above all on the preconditions for democratic self-government, and that this idea calls for particular results contrary to the originalist understanding, for example, limits on use of the law of libel by public officials. We can imagine judges who think that interpretation requires something like an act of translation to accommodate new circumstances, including unforeseen developments not only of fact but also of value.[36] Such judges should try to devise strategies to reduce their own discretion and policy-making authority. They might, for example, care a great deal about precedent, using previous holdings and rationales to constrain their own discretion, at least by limiting the number of possible alternatives from which they can choose. They might also think that courts should be reluctant to invalidate outcomes of electoral processes unless it is very clear that something has gone wrong.

As we have seen, they might emphasize that the case for judicial intrusion is strongest, under an ambiguous constitutional provision, when there is some defect in the process of democratic deliberation that gave rise to the relevant law. Despite Justice Scalia's presentation here, democracy should not be identified with the outcomes of majoritarian politics; it should not be treated as some simple statistical affair. Whatever emerges from a particular political process should not be identified with the ideal itself. We have seen that democracy is equipped with its own internal morality, which constrains what a majority may do, consistently with the commitment to democracy. A majority may not, for example, disenfranchise people, or impose a regime of political inequality, or act solely on the basis of contempt for fellow citizens.

Judges of this kind come in many shapes and sizes; they might well think of themselves as originalists. What matters is that such judges are much influenced by the common law tradition, and even if they are ambivalent about width, it is by no means clear that judges of that kind have less legitimacy, or are worse, than originalist judges of the kind that Justice Scalia favors. A federal judiciary that sometimes proceeds in minimalist fashion and that treats constitutional rights as aspirations (given content by concrete cases, and invoked sparingly to invalidate the outcomes of ordinary politics) might well, because of its very insulation, produce a better system of constitutional democracy. It might do so because it has certain advantages in deliberating on questions of basic justice, or—in my view far more likely—it might do so because and to the extent that it focuses on ensuring the preconditions for a well-functioning democratic regime.

Justice Scalia thinks that even if this is true, a judicial role of this kind is fundamentally illegitimate and without authority, because it is not authorized by the Constitution. But this argument begs the question. The Constitution does not set out the principles governing its own interpretation; certainly the Constitution itself does not contain, or specify, an interpretive principle of originalism. Any judgment about the appropriate content of governing interpretive principles must invoke not the Constitution but political theory of some kind. It is not entirely implausible to claim that the text must be interpreted in light of the original understanding as Justice Scalia conceives it. But this view depends both on contested ideals and on highly contingent and partly empirical claims about which system of interpretation is likely to be or to do best, all things considered.

For America, what system of interpretation would do or be best? The past offers no clear answer, but it is a good place to start. It is highly relevant that an originalist approach of the sort favored by Justice Scalia would have very dramatic consequences. Such an approach may well, for example, mean that Brown v. Board of Education, the cornerstone of modern equal protection doctrine, is wrong; that New York Times v. Sullivan, the cornerstone of modern free speech doctrine, is also wrong; that the government may ban political dissent when it is dangerous; that the establishment clause does not apply to the states; that the federal government can discriminate on the basis of race and sex however it wishes; that much racial discrimination and nearly all sex discrimination by the states is unobjectionable; that compulsory school prayer is constitutionally acceptable; that, in short, most of modern constitutional law, now taken as constitutive of the American constitutional tradition by Americans and non-Americans alike, now taken as symbolic of our nation's commitment to liberty under law, for the last decade in particular an inspiration for constitution-making and constitution-building all over the globe, is illegitimate, fatally undemocratic, a kind of usurpation.

An approach that leads to conclusions of this kind may not be disqualified for that reason; but these possibilities show that slippery slope arguments can work in both directions. It is tempting to think that the choice among interpretive approaches should not depend on outcomes; an important guarantee of neutrality might even be found in indifference to outcomes. But this is a confusion. Once an interpretive strategy has been properly selected, it should not be abandoned simply because it produces a bad outcome in a particular case. (This, no more and no less, is what might be said in support of indifference to consequences.) But any approach to interpretation must be defended partly by reference to its consequences, broadly conceived, and the set of relevant consequences includes emphatically its effects on human liberty and equality. No approach to interpretation can be defended without close reference to the human interests that it affects. If consequences, broadly conceived, do not matter, what does?

My central point is that other approaches to interpretation, whether or in whatever sense originalist, can accommodate our constitutional tradition as it has come to be understood without at the same time authorizing judges to do whatever they want. It is correct to say that common law thinking lies at the heart of American constitutional law, and that the common law sometimes avoids width. But this way of thinking should be seen as part of judicial modesty, not judicial hubris. Certainly it can allow for a degree of flexibility. But it comes with its own constraints on judicial power, brought about through the doctrine of stare decisis, close attention to the details of cases, and a general reluctance to issue rules that much depart from the facts of particular disputes. It is part and parcel of the judiciary's distrust of large theories and its ordinary search for concrete outcomes and cautious principles on which theoretically diverse judges may agree.

Common law thinking is even connected with the Court's general and entirely appropriate reluctance to disturb the outcomes of political processes. To the extent that it partakes of ambitious theories at all, common law thinking, in its current incarnation in American public law, largely attempts to protect the workings of a well-functioning system of democratic deliberation. And common law judges are not insistently opposed to width. They are aware that in some areas of the law, width is extremely important, because predictable law is indispensable, or because judges have good reason for confidence in wide rules.

From the standpoint of promoting democratic ideals, it is hardly clear that Justice Scalia's form of originalism is preferable to the approach to constitutional law defended here. The choice of an approach to interpretation requires a judgment about political theory, and that means that the choice makes it necessary to specify the right content of the democratic ideal. If democracy is not identified with the outcomes of majoritarian politics, and if its internal morality constrains what majorities may do, the American constitutional tradition contains all the ingredients of an appealing approach to interpretation. From the standpoint of constraining judicial discretion, the common law method of constitutional law, properly understood, is at least a plausible competitor to the popular forms of originalism, in light of the many difficult questions that historical inquiry leaves unresolved and the difficulty of matching that form of originalism with a theory of stare decisis. If we are concerned about limiting judicial intrusions into politics, the popular forms of originalism may well be inferior to our tradition in its modern incarnation. That form of originalism may well be better at promoting predictability and stability. But these are hardly decisive virtues, and it is not clear that there is any other dimension along which Justice Scalia's approach is preferable to the serious alternatives.

On Narrowness and Width

Democratic formalism has two foundations: a strong commitment to width, in the form of rule-bound justice, and a desire to ensure that discretion is exercised by democratically elected officials rather than by judges. Hence Justice Scalia's overriding goal is to exorcise the common law from public law. And he is correct to emphasize the common law heritage of the American legal tradition and much of modern public law: judicial treatment of many statutes as standards rather than rules, doctrines of interpretation that operate as standards or factors, and perhaps above all, a system of case-based constitutional law that owes a great deal to the common law heritage. Justice Scalia's goal is to reduce particularity in the hope that it will increase predictability, constrain the abusive exercise of discretion by judges, and increase democratic self-government by imposing good incentives on Congress.

Against this view, I have urged that width is an ambiguous virtue, and that whether its virtues outweigh its vices depends on the context. Where planning is especially important, width is important too. But sometimes courts lack the information to produce a wide rule, and when democratic processes are focusing on a problem, narrowness may well be best. I have urged that courts should make regulatory agencies a central ingredient in their theory of interpretation, on the theory that the common law role of courts is often best carried out by administrative agencies authorized to make sense of statutory text when new applications arise, or when facts and values change. This approach has the virtue of fitting nicely with the needs, values, and actual practices of modern government. Thus I have sketched an alternative approach to statutory interpretation, one that also places a premium on democratic values, and that uses clear statement principles and agency interpretations to supplement and occasionally countermand the text as understood at the time of enactment. In statutory interpretation, this approach would allow regulatory agencies room to adapt text to particular circumstance, and authorize courts, supplementing that agency role, to use canons and presumptions to make sense rather than nonsense out of the statutory law.

In constitutional interpretation, this approach would combine a large dose of judicial modesty, favoring incompletely theorized agreements, with an occasional willingness to invoke the internal morality of democracy to look skeptically at laws that compromise the political process or attempt to impose second-class citizenship on members of disadvantaged social groups. Under current conditions, an approach of this sort would do far better than democratic formalism from the democratic point of view; it would also impose sufficient constraints on judicial power and judicial discretion. Its only comparative defect, a modest one, is that it may suffer along the dimension of promoting

Table 9.1

	Narrowness	Width
Need for planning		X
Lack of information	X	
High future decision costs of rulelessness		X
Risk of unintended consequences	X	
Continuing and healthy democratic debate about appropriate rules	X	
Judicial uncertainty about content of appropriate rules	X	

predictability. In constitutional law, more particular choices between wide and narrow rulings will turn on contextual considerations, most of which can be captured in the way shown in Table 9.1.

Of course these factors cannot be used without knowing the extent of the relevant problems in different contexts. But it is readily apparent that in areas of high controversy, there are usually good reasons for minimalism. Width will often have unintended consequences; courts cannot be confident about the content of wide rules; and democratic debate is likely to be in process. Many of the particular discussions in Part II support this general conclusion.

There is nothing wrong with democratic formalism in the abstract. In an imaginable world, not unrecognizably far from our own, it might be appropriate. But democratic formalism depends for its appeal on implausible claims about the importance of wide rulings in all contexts. Whether narrowness or width is best cannot be decided in the abstract. Equally important, democratic formalism has no good claim to the democratic ideal. American democracy is dedicated not to simple majority rule but to deliberative democracy; minimalist strategies, avoiding width, are often the best way of promoting both democracy and deliberation.

10

Depth? From Theory to Practice

We now turn from the question of width to the question of depth. The two questions have important similarities and differences. Both width and depth impose informational demands on judges, who tend toward both narrowness and shallowness simply because of limitations in their knowledge. But a judgment can be wide without being deep (consider judicial insistence on the letter of a speed-limit law); legal rules typically are wide but command agreement from multiple points of view. Less commonly, a judgment can be deep without being wide; the Supreme Court's decision in United States v. Virginia has this feature.

Moreover, the reasons for and against wide decisions do not exactly track the reasons for and against deep decisions. The case for width is based on rule of law values—maintaining predictability, allowing planning, reducing the risk of arbitrariness associated with ad hoc judgments. The problem with wide decisions is their crudeness; broad rules may not fit diverse circumstances. By contrast, the argument for depth is rooted in a fear of injustice, and the problem with depth is that judges may not be good at ambitious theorizing, and may hence blunder—a special problem when they are invalidating legislation. Even if judges do not blunder, efforts to impose ambitious theories on the nation may not succeed, and judges may do better in their own terms, and from the standpoint of justice, if they proceed incrementally.

In both contexts, a large part of the debate is empirical. Indeed, this is one of my principal claims in this book; high-sounding disagreements about law often rest on tacit empirical assumptions, and much progress can be made by identifying the empirical issues as such. If judges could generate excellent rules, width would be all to the good. If judges do

poorly with theoretical abstractions, and if participants in the democratic process are much better with abstractions, the argument for shallowness would be solid. Of course these empirical questions do not
have simple (or purely empirical) answers, and as Chapter 9 suggests,
the choice is not really between width and narrowness, or depth and
shallowness, but about degrees of both in different contexts. Let us
deal, then, with the question of depth.

Philosophy and Law

Some of the most vigorous challenges to judicial minimalism come
from those who believe that judicial judgments should have theoretical
depth. These challenges tend to be made by the many observers who
have come, in the last generation, to see the Supreme Court as the
"forum of principle" in American government. Some of our most pre-
cious rights appear to be products of not modesty, but deliberative
ambition from the Court. And if judges do not try to think in a principled fashion, and with a high degree of ambition, who will? It seems
reasonable to think that the Supreme Court is in a unique position to
deliberate well on issues of liberty and equality; perhaps this is a central
aspect of its appropriate role.

By contrast, a court that relies on incompletely theorized agreements
may produce unfairness and inconsistency. If judges say that discrimination against African Americans is unacceptable, but that the Constitution tolerates discrimination against homosexuals, isn't it important
to understand why? Without a (relatively ambitious) reason, these judgments may produce grave injustice. The aspiration to theoretical ambition is built on just this concern: without assessing our practices by
subjecting them to higher-order scrutiny, there can be no assurance
that we are behaving fairly. If judges reach an agreement that the First
Amendment gives the highest protection to libelous speech, and also
that the First Amendment gives less protection to commercial speech,
there appears to be a large risk of mistake—so long as the judges do
not give a deeper account of the grounds for these apparently disparate
judgments. People who are similarly situated will be treated differently,
and this is unjust. These points are part of a long tradition of philosophical interest in more ambitious ways of thinking, prepared to ren-

ovate ordinary understandings. With these points in mind, philosophically oriented observers have argued in favor of a greater degree of theoretical depth in law.

Ronald Dworkin, with his interest in the theoretically demanding ideal of "integrity," is a particularly vigorous and lucid enthusiast for theoretical ambition in law.[1] The ideal of integrity requires judges to offer the "best constructive interpretation" of existing legal materials. Dworkin can be taken to pose this question: if judges are not prepared to think deeply, and to reach into theoretical complexities, how can they know if their interpretation is in fact best? Shallowness might seem to be a kind of willful blindness, a kind of ostrich-like behavior, likely to be destructive of some of the highest ideals of American constitutional law.

A Philosophical Brief

The problem can be made more concrete by attending to an unusual brief submitted to the Supreme Court in the assisted suicide cases, a document widely known as "The Philosophers' Brief."[2] The brief bears Dworkin's distinctive mark, and indeed Dworkin is listed as lead counsel, though the brief is also signed by a series of eminent philosophers: Thomas Nagel, Robert Nozick, John Rawls, Thomas Scanlon, and Judith Jarvis Thompson. The Philosophers' Brief offers an ambitious and highly theoretical argument. It says that some "deeply personal decisions pose controversial questions about how and why human life has value. In a free society, individuals must be allowed to make those decisions for themselves, out of their own faith, conscience, and convictions." The brief urges that distinctions between "omissions" (failing to provide continued treatment) and "acts" (providing drugs that will produce death) are "based on a misunderstanding of the pertinent moral principles." Drawing on the abortion cases, the brief says that every person "has a right to make the 'most intimate and personal decisions central to personal dignity and autonomy,'" a right that encompasses "some control over the time and manner of one's death." The brief thus urges the Court to declare a constitutional right to physician-assisted suicide. Dworkin's personal gloss on the brief says that it "defines a very general moral and constitutional principle—that every competent person has the right to make momentous personal decisions which invoke fundamental religious or philosophical convictions about life's value for himself."[3]

Simply as a matter of political morality, the argument in the Philosophers' Brief is certainly reasonable, and it cannot easily be shown to be wrong. But the Supreme Court rejected the argument, and I believe that it was correct to do so. As Chapter 5 suggests, the constitutional questions turned on issues not dealt with in arguments of the sort offered by the philosophers: issues of institutional role, of federalism, and of facts and incentives. To generalize from some of the concrete discussions thus far: the Court should be reluctant to invalidate legislation on the basis of abstract philosophical claims, because the Court is poorly equipped to evaluate those arguments, and because likely consequences, on which philosophical arguments tend to be silent, matter a great deal to law. These points push courts in the direction of minimalism and in particular toward shallowness.

By contrast, some people, including Dworkin himself, appear to think that the Supreme Court should not much hesitate to find a constitutional right of some kind if it is presented with (what judges can be persuaded to find) convincing philosophical arguments for that right, at least if the right "fits" with the rest of the legal fabric. I believe that this view misconceives the role of the Supreme Court in American government, a role that very much grows out of the Court's understanding of its limited capacities and its potential for error. For this reason, it is not enough for advocates of depth to emphasize the importance of attaining justice. Of course no one should disparage that goal. We may agree, with Rawls, that justice is the first virtue of social institutions, while also insisting that courts may not understand what justice requires, or may not be good at producing justice even when they understand it, and that their use of the Constitution is partly a product of their judgments about their own distinctive role as a social institution.

This disagreement with advocates of philosophical ambition in law should not be misunderstood. The argument for incompletely theorized agreements ought not to be rooted in skepticism about whether there is such a thing as moral truth. Skepticism about moral truth is indeed incoherent—hopeless for law or for anything else. Unless we believe in some form of moral truth, how can we believe in any particular approach to constitutional rights? Skeptics have no reason to favor a limited judicial role; skepticism points in no particular direction. Hence there is all the difference in the world between skepticism and a recognition of cognitive or motivational limitations on the part of certain people engaged in distinctive social roles. It follows that as an abstraction or a creed, "anti-theory"—currently popular in some circles inside and outside of law—makes no sense. We may believe that judges are not well equipped to engage in theoretically ambitious tasks, without also believing that political theory is itself problematic or useless. Indeed, the strongest defenses of judicial minimalism must themselves be theoretical in character.

There is a further point. Those who generally believe in shallowness cannot reject the possibility that judges may have to get ambitious in order to think well about some cases; hence conceptual ascents, involving increasingly ambitious arguments, are hardly foreign to law. Conceptual ascents may be desirable; they may even be inevitable. In the area of equality on the basis of race and sex, the Supreme Court has been willing to think fairly deeply, and this is altogether proper in view of the Court's extended exposure to the underlying questions, its general willingness to proceed incrementally, and the obvious problems with relying on democratic processes to solve all of the relevant problems. As I have emphasized, any analogical argument depends on an argument or principle of some kind, and hence those who approve of analogy should be prepared for the possibility that they will have to think quite ambitiously.

With all these concessions, why might anyone be reluctant to join a chorus of praise for theoretical ambition in law? Why might anyone favor a kind of presumption in favor of shallowness? The most basic answer involves the risks and consequences of judicial error, including both moral mistakes and unintended bad consequences. But there are three more particular points. The first involves the needs of ordinary practice. The second relates to the crucial and too frequently overlooked centrality of facts to constitutional adjudication; here we find a large gap in academic work on the Supreme Court. The third involves the limited place of the Court in the constitutional system and the possibility of judicial mistakes; this point lies at the heart of the objection to philosophical ambition in law.

Incompletely Theorized Agreements as Ordinary Practice

As we have seen throughout this book, judges ordinarily work with principles of a low level of theoretical ambition. Conceptual ascents are relatively rare, even for the Supreme Court of the United States. Like all of us, judges have limited time and capacities, and like almost all of us, judges are not trained as philosophers. They live in a heterogeneous society permeated by reasonable disagreements. They know that they may not always be able to disentangle the reasonable positions from the unreasonable ones. They are aware that if they try to resolve large philosophical issues, they may blunder badly, and in a way that has damaging long-term consequences. Both Dred Scott v. Sanford, giving constitutional protection to the institution of slavery, and Lochner v. New York, striking down maximum-hour legislation, are important symbols in this regard. Buckley v. Valeo, invalidating campaign finance legislation, is increasingly coming to be seen in the same light. In these circumstances judges try, to the extent that they can, to bracket large-scale issues of the good and the right, and to decide cases on grounds that seem reasonable to those who have diverse views on those issues, and (perhaps even more important) to those who have little idea what, on those issues, their views are.

This point helps explain the American legal culture's distrust of philosophical abstractions and its comparative fondness for both rules and analogies. Many legal rules can attract support from plural foundations; consider a speed-limit law, or liability for intentional torts, or the rules that make possible a bicameral legislature. Such rules help make possible a form of cooperation that is indispensable to a pluralistic society. Legal rules tend to be incompletely theorized, and this is one reason that diverse people can accept and live by them. A great virtue of analogical thinking is that it often assists in this same endeavor, for people who are uncertain about large-scale issues can often agree that, whatever they think, they agree that X is like Y, for a relatively lower-level reason on which they can converge. To engage in analogical thinking, we need not, much of the time, attempt to think in highly ambitious terms. Thus constitutional law is insistently analogical in character, and often the process of reasoning by analogy makes possible an agreement on some principle that can attract support from diverse theoretical positions.

This idea of course has a resemblance and owes a great deal to John Rawls's influential idea of an overlapping consensus, central to the project of political liberalism.[4] Rawls is concerned to show that people with diverse "comprehensive views"—Kantian, utilitarian, Aristotelian, and more—may converge on certain basic principles; these are the principles that all can share. Liberal constitutionalism can unite behind, indeed can be constituted by, such principles. But there is an important difference between Rawls's project and what I am describing here. As Rawls understands it, the overlapping consensus is itself highly theorized and a matter of relatively ambitious abstractions involving equality and liberty. In an important passage Rawls attempts to show that when people disagree on particulars they can make progress by ascending to a level of greater theoretical ambition.[5] This is true; it helps explain the role of conceptual ascent in both politics and law (and science too). But something different is also true, and this is what I am emphasizing: people can often agree on particulars, including shallow principles, when they disagree about or are uncertain on abstractions. Conceptual or justificatory *descents* may well work best.

The point is particularly important for law within a highly pluralistic culture. It is important because it is a method for promoting a cooperative way of life among heterogeneous people, ensuring stability, reducing strains on time and capacities, and demonstrating mutual respect; it is not very respectful to take on other people's most fundamental commitments if it is not necessary to do so.[6] We might even think that those who stress incompletely theorized agreements believe that ordinary law and politics bear the same relation to political liberalism as political liberalism bears to the great questions in moral metaphysics. Just as Rawls aspires to "leave philosophy as it is," by bracketing the large questions in general philosophy, so participants in law and politics seek, if they can, to leave political philosophy very much as it is, by bracketing the large disputes in political philosophy, such as the dispute between political liberalism and perfectionist liberalism. Hence the ordinary practice is one of avoiding theoretical abstractions.

Why might this matter? To take a large example, the difference bears on the whole idea of substantive due process and thus on the dispute over Roe v. Wade. As we saw in Chapter 5, those who favor incompletely theorized agreements are uncertain about the very idea of a "right to privacy." They seek more cautious grounds; they are reluctant to invoke large-scale abstractions about any such right in order to invalidate the outcomes of political processes. And if the justices had sought incompletely theorized agreements, they would have proceeded very differently. For example, they might have been moved to decide Griswold v. Connecticut—invalidating a ban on the use of contraceptives within marriage and beginning the modern excursion into substantive due process—not on the basis of that highly contentious right, but on some more modest ground. They might, for example, have emphasized the peculiar history and provenance of the ban on the use of contraceptives within marriage, a ban that left most women unaffected and operated only to prevent poor women from getting contraceptives from clinics.[7] Thus the Court might have concluded, in a shallow opinion, that the statute was a largely irrational and discriminatory means of promoting its own asserted goals. A fact-driven decision, bracketing the most controversial questions, would have said little about a right whose scope need not have been much defined in *Griswold* itself. Or—as we have seen—the Court might have decided the case on the narrower and democracy-reinforcing ground that a provision of the criminal law lapses when that provision of law appears to lack any real support from its own citizenry, so much so that it has not, in many decades, been invoked by any prosecutor in any prosecution.

These points help support a critique of Roe v. Wade. As it was written, the decision created unnecessary problems for the Court and the nation. It did so because in its (wholly unnecessary) breadth and in its blindness to matters of fact and institutional role (on which more below), the Court did so much so soon, in a way that has had enduring harmful effects on American life (not least including that part of American life that involves equality on the basis of sex).[8]

I am not arguing that *Roe* should have been decided the other way; but the Court ought not to have invoked ambitious abstractions about privacy or liberty to resolve so many issues so quickly. A court that favored incompletely theorized agreements would have decided *Roe* quite shallowly and narrowly. The Court might have said, for example, that the Texas law was unconstitutionally vague (as Justice Blackmun's initial draft in fact argued). Or it might have said, most minimally, that someone who alleges (as did Roe herself) that she was raped may not be required to bring the child to term. Or—if the Court eventually was forced to think more ambitiously—the Court may have bracketed issues involving the political and moral status of the fetus and argued that if men are not obliged to devote their bodies to the protection of third parties, women may not be so obliged either.[9] This view also requires a degree of theoretical ambition, but perhaps it is less contentious if it succeeds in putting to one side any view about the moral or political status of the fetus.

It does not much matter if any of these particular claims is convincing; I offer them simply for purposes of illustration. I do believe that for the nation the best sequence—akin to that in the area of sex equality in general—would have been a narrow and shallow decision in *Roe,* followed by a process of accommodation in which the federal system might well have devised a range of solutions, followed by a set of decisions deepening the *Roe* right so as to foreclose those approaches that seemed least reasonable. What matters is a more general point: those who stress incompletely theorized agreements on particulars are likely to seek to avoid conceptual ascents if (and only if) they can, especially when courts are asked to invalidate legislation on constitutional grounds. This is the ordinary way that constitutional law works, even on the Supreme Court of the United States.

Facts

What does law actually *do?* What are its actual effects? This is a question on which the content of law must (at least partly) depend, and it is a question that lawyers and judges ask too infrequently, and answer with inadequate tools. What, for example, are the effects of laws, judge-made or otherwise, calling for minimum wages, rent controls, protection of commercial advertising, implied warranties of various sorts, liability for drug manufacturers? Theory alone will not tell us; we need to investigate facts. And much of normative jurisprudence, with its heavy philosophical bent, continues to operate in a factual vacuum.

If normative jurisprudence is intended to produce not only illumination but also answers to legal questions, this is unfortunate, for problems involving libel law, sexual privacy, homosexuality, and the right to die depend in large part on underlying issues of fact. Of course any assessment of facts is theory-laden; we do not know what and how facts count unless we have a (normative) account. Nothing I have said here denies this point. But many legal debates are hopelessly sterile—conceptualistic, terminological, interminable—precisely because the participants do not investigate facts, when it is facts on which they may be able to make some progress. Often constitutional law could do better if it was founded on an understanding of legally relevant facts—and if the factual dimensions of legal disputes could be recognized as such. (Consider, for example, the discussion of the factual components to debates over interpretation, treated in Chapter 9 above.) Equally important, an understanding of the facts may well equip people with different theoretical positions to converge on the same basic judgment.

If, for example, an increase in rent control can be shown to diminish the available housing stock in a way that particularly hurts the poor, perhaps people can reject rent control whatever they think about liberty and equality. If any right to die would mean in practice less rather than more autonomy for patients, the argument for such a right is weakened. Or if constitutional protection of libelous falsehoods greatly increases the number of lies about public officials, perhaps people can agree that the First Amendment is not violated by a right to claim retraction in cases of error. The legitimacy of recent "product libel" laws, designed to deter intentional falsehoods about agricultural products, depends in large part on the effects of such laws. Suppose, for example, that the effect of product libel laws would be to prevent intentional falsehoods, in a way that would prevent consumers from being misinformed and terrified, with adverse effects on the economy, including unemployment. If this were so, the constitutional legitimacy of such laws would seem more secure. Thus an assessment of facts may well aid in the achievement of incompletely theorized agreements. Such agreements may well be shallow when they are a product of an understanding of facts.

For these reasons, an emphasis on the (occasional) need for ambitious theory is not so much wrong—indeed it is not wrong at all—as misdirected. It suggests that a better legal system, or better constitutional law, will come from a legal system that is better at philosophy—as if the real flaw of American law is inadequate philosophy. This, again, is not without truth; better philosophy might well make law better—more fair, more coherent, less confused—in some contexts. But many of the most important gaps in the practice and understanding of law have nothing to do with philosophy at all. Thus any claim on behalf of theoretical ambition should be supplemented and sometimes even replaced by an emphasis on the need for a better sense of underlying facts. Certainly this point applies to the law of tort as tort law is developed by judges; it bears on constitutional law too, emphatically including the claimed right to physician-assisted suicide. Much of the necessary illumination on that issue, for lawyers and nonlawyers alike, comes not from puzzling over the possibility of distinguishing between acts and omissions—a problem that confounds political philosophy, and on which judges are unlikely to make much progress—but instead from thinking about the likely effects of the relevant right, by learning about doctor-patient relations and actual experience in the Netherlands.

This point has concrete consequences for how to do and to think about law. For example, the philosophical abstractions offered in the Philosophers' Brief—about the nature of human liberty—seem to me reasonable; as I have said, it cannot easily be shown that they are wrong. But (even putting basic questions of constitutional method and institutional issues to one side) do they make out a case for a constitutional right, invalidating enacted law in almost all states or calling for its revision on the basis of principles of human autonomy? I do not believe that they do. Even if the theoretical claims are right, much depends on empirical projections, and as we have seen it is altogether possible that the relevant right would decrease autonomy even on the view stated in the Philosophers' Brief.

The same is true of a number of questions that academic lawyers have thought are best resolved through ambitious theorizing. As I have suggested, a great deal might be learned about appropriate libel law by saying little more about the nature of liberty and focusing instead on the sorts of practices that are created by different libel regimes. If newspapers are held liable for negligent falsehoods, would true statements be deterred? By how much? What would be the effects of an automatic right to retraction? In the area of constitutional controls on punitive damages, it would be valuable to learn the source of apparently excessive awards; what leads juries, in fact, to awards millions or billions of dollars by way of punishment?

Or consider affirmative action. Abstractions about equality are of course relevant, and identification of the best account of equality may well turn out to be important to resolution of the affirmative action issue. But perhaps an understanding of the facts would make it less necessary to offer that account; the consequences matter a great deal.

If, for example, a race-blind admissions policy would result in hardly any African-American students at the top law schools, those who generally favor race-blindness may well reconsider. In any case judges should learn a great deal more about the actual consequences of different affirmative action programs. In the key cases, fact-filled briefs would likely provide more illumination than philosophers' briefs. Are such programs actually necessary to ensure a degree of racial diversity in education, or can such diversity be obtained through other means? Without affirmative action programs, would many fewer African Americans be able to attend the most selective medical schools? What are the effects of affirmative action programs on those that they are intended to benefit? Do police and social welfare departments function better with affirmative action programs, or worse, and by what measures?

Of course factual questions are in the first instance for legislators and administrators, not for courts. But an analysis of the constitutional dispute cannot afford to be indifferent to them. Far more progress might be made through an empirically informed constitutional law, and the empirical evidence might well become the foundation for incompletely theorized agreements, ones that do not turn on highly contested arguments about the best conception of equality.

Judicial Capacities and Judicial Role

Who could possibly object to the adoption, by judges or anyone else, of a correct theory about the right or the good? If judges are able to identify the appropriate category of rights, shouldn't they? If, for example, a conception of rights embodies the appealing notion that a heterogeneous society consists of a community of equals, why should not the Court identify that (by hypothesis) very appealing conception? Isn't an antipathy to theory a kind of willful blindness, or a form of philistinism, or a kind of despair about the highest aspirations of a constitutional democracy?

Good judges are not ostriches, and their caution about theory stems from the distinctive place where they stand, which requires an understanding of the particular role of judges in the American political system. Human beings have cognitive limitations, and these limitations, accepted as such by participants in all social practices, are a central part of any account of the responsibilities of those who find themselves in a

particular role. Judges are not (let us repeat the point) trained as philosophers, and judges who make theoretically ambitious arguments may
well make mistakes that are quite costly, especially in constitutional
cases, where their arguments are (at least theoretically!) final. We can
find many instances of ambitious error from judicial philosophers; consider here Dred Scott v. Sanford (protecting the institution of slavery),
Lochner v. New York (forbidding maximum-hour legislation), Buckley
v. Valeo (striking down campaign finance regulation), and Richmond
v. Croson (forbidding an affirmative action program). In all of these
cases, courts invoked theoretically ambitious claims about liberty and
equality to invalidate legislation. In the first two cases, the nation lived
with the consequences for a very long time. In the second two cases,
the nation lives with the consequences still. (Those who think some of
these cases were rightly decided will not have difficulty coming up with
what are, to them, equally egregious blunders.)

But these cases are aberrations, and thankfully so. A large part of the
distinctive morality of adjudication is role-morality, rooted in an understanding of limitations in both knowledge and legitimacy; and it
involves the presumptive avoidance of theoretically ambitious arguments as a ground for invalidating enacted law. Thus courts generally
seek, because of their own understanding of their limited capacities, to
offer low-level rationales on which diverse people may converge. This
is so especially when the consequence of theoretical ambition would be
to invalidate the outcomes of democratic processes. It is here that the
Court properly proceeds most cautiously, again because of its understanding of its limited capacities in thinking about philosophical abstractions.

An analogy may be helpful here. Of course there is a sense in which
philosophy is foundational to law, just as theoretical physics is in some
sense foundational to the construction of airplanes. And at times those
who build airplanes need to know something about theoretical physics.
But in ordinary practice, those confronted with the problems produced
by the construction of airplanes are not assisted by accounts of the
foundations of physics; such accounts may be confusing to people of
limited time and capacities, and attention to the accounts may divert
the builders from successful performance of the tasks at hand. The same
goes for ordinary judges and lawyers. As we have seen, the issues raised
by the asserted right to physician-assisted suicide require intense focus

on particulars and (especially important) close attention to facts. Would such a right, in practice, undermine the autonomy of those approaching death and give excessive power to doctors, in a way that threatens to produce nonvoluntary and involuntary death? Would such a right undermine many particular practices now taken as legitimate (consider the activities of the Food and Drug Administration), and if so how might that fact count against the right? Questions of this kind suggest that the Court should be wary about accepting arguments of the kind offered in the Philosophers' Brief, not because the argument is necessarily wrong, but because judges, in light of their limited role in the constitutional structure, should be cautious about accepting abstract arguments on behalf of rights whose real-world consequences are hard to predict.

I am speaking of a presumption, or perhaps of a mood, and not of a rule. Everything depends on contextual considerations; if judges were in fact superb at identifying the correct category of rights, or if the democratic process were systematically damaged as a mechanism for deliberation about rights, the ultimate conclusion would be different. But nothing is gained by assuming these points. Thus the argument in favor of shallowness depends on particular judgments about institutional capacities, judgments with both evaluative and empirical dimensions.

There are, however, two important qualifications. First, exceptions should be made when theoretical depth has been earned by both thought and experience. A series of incremental steps can culminate in deep judgments, and nothing need be wrong with that. On the contrary, these may be the most stirring moments in a nation's history. Consider Brown v. Board of Education and United States v. Virginia, two cases in which the Court spoke ambitiously and was entirely correct to do so. Sometimes a period of common law development can show that an ambitious argument is too insistent to be ignored. This was the case in *Brown;* it is also the case in the area of discrimination on the basis of sex. It may eventually be the case in the context of discrimination on the basis of sexual orientation. There are close parallels in the law of free speech, where a period of sustained encounter with censorship of political dissent enabled the Court to converge on relatively ambitious bans on restrictions on speech that are vague, unduly broad, or unrooted in a demonstration of likely and imminent harm.

Second, the grounds for judicial humility—for judicial reluctance to disturb the results of democratic processes on the basis of philosophical abstractions—are undercut when it can be shown that political processes are defective from the standpoint of the internal morality of democracy. As we have seen, that internal morality calls for political equality and a high degree of participation and responsiveness. Thus courts should be less reluctant to invoke abstractions as a basis for invalidating enacted law when the relevant law excludes people from political participation, or when it undermines rights to freedom of political speech. I have offered several examples of this point; consider efforts to regulate political dissent on the new communications technologies. Some of the substance of constitutional minimalism is attributable to ideas of this kind; I have argued that the Court should build on these developments.

Of course these conclusions raise many questions, and they are themselves theory-laden. Of course the ordinary work of law is incompletely theorized, and hence courts have not self-consciously adopted theoretical arguments on behalf of either shallowness or the qualifications, even though the law generally seems to follow them. To defend the qualifications, it is necessary to make some claims about institutional capacities. And the view that the judicial role is properly aggressive when democratic obstacles beset ordinary politics will itself have to be theorized a bit, both in defending the general claim and in specifying it by giving content to the notion of democratic obstacles.

These theoretically ambitious arguments should be accepted by courts, as indeed they largely have been, because and to the extent that they can be shown to be clearly true. What must be emphasized is that these arguments suggest—and there really is no contradiction here—that the distinctive morality of adjudication in a pluralistic society calls for a presumption in favor of theoretical modesty, especially when courts are asked to invalidate legislation. There is no (good) abstract argument against abstractions. But there are reasons, both concrete and abstract, both empirical and theoretical, to think that judges in a deliberative democracy do best if they (usually) avoid the most contentious abstractions when they can, especially if they are asked to invalidate enacted law.

Conclusion:
Minimalism and Democracy

In its procedural form, judicial minimalism consists of an effort to limit the width and depth of judicial decisions. Thus understood, minimalism has distinctive virtues, especially in a heterogeneous society in which reasonable people often disagree. When judges lack, and know they lack, relevant information, minimalism is an appropriate response. Sometimes judicial minimalism is a reasonable or even inevitable response to the sheer practical problem of obtaining consensus amid pluralism. Within the Supreme Court, as within other institutions, this problem produces incompletely specified abstractions and incompletely theorized, narrow rulings. And sometimes minimalism is a way for people who disagree to show one another mutual respect.

Minimalism also maintains flexibility for the future, an especially large virtue when facts and values are in flux. Minimalists refuse to freeze existing ideals and conceptions; in this way they retain a good deal of room for future deliberation and choice. This is especially important for judges who are not too sure that they are right. Like a sailor on an unfamiliar sea—or a government attempting to regulate a shifting labor market—a court may take small, reversible steps, allowing itself to accommodate unexpected developments. Certain forms of minimalism can promote democratic goals, not simply by leaving things undecided but also by allowing opinion to coalesce over time and by spurring processes of democratic deliberation. When the Court strikes down a statute as vague, for example, it effectively requires the legislature to make crucial judgments, rather than leaving those judgments to others.

With this idea we can see an especially important strand in constitutional doctrine and a distinctive form of minimalism: decisions that are not simply democracy-foreclosing or democracy-authorizing, but

259

instead democracy-promoting. Such decisions promote both reason-giving and accountability. Democratic goals connect a wide range of seemingly disparate features of constitutional law: the void-for-vagueness and nondelegation doctrines, the requirement that Congress speak with clarity on certain issues, rationality review, the occasional concern with desuetude, and the requirement that certain forms of discrimination be justified by actual rather than by hypothetical purposes.

Minimalist Substance

There are many different forms of both minimalism and maximalism, and the substantive content of any particular form of course comes from substantive ideas, independent of one's judgments about appropriate width and depth. I have made several points here. American law has converged on an impressive set of minimal substantive commitments; these are, at this stage in history, minimalism's substance. The commitments include a right to free political dissent, protection against discrimination on the basis of one's religious beliefs, freedom from torture and police abuse, and freedom from subordination on the basis of race or sex. The fact that the core of these rights is uncontentious should not deflect attention from the fact that they represent an extraordinary social achievement. On the contrary, the fact that the core is uncontentious *is* an extraordinary social achievement.

I have also argued here for a broader core of substantive ideals that a minimalist court should endorse. These ideals grow out of the Constitution's commitments to democratic deliberation and political equality. Hence the free speech principle should operate primarily to provide a large breathing space for political expression and to ensure that Congress legislates with clarity and precision when it seeks to regulate expression. It follows that some efforts to regulate the speech market, in the interest of promoting a well-functioning system of free expression, are constitutionally unobjectionable.

I have argued as well for a particular understanding of the Constitution's equality principle. This principle operates as a ban on the creation of castes and on government expressions of contempt for American citizens. The equality principle should, I suggest, be enforced more aggressively than any constitutional right to privacy. Thus a minimalist court would do well to adopt a particular understanding of both free speech and civic equality, an understanding that can provide a secure basis for exploring new areas of constitutional dispute.

With an eye toward democratic goals, courts might proceed in minimalist fashion with respect to affirmative action, the right to die, discrimination on the basis of sex and sexual orientation, and allegedly harmful speech carried by new communications technologies. In all of these areas, the Court would do well to avoid broad rules and to proceed in a way that complements and does not displace democratic processes. It should do so by combining an awareness of institutional limitations with a sense of the basic point of the underlying constitutional guarantees, through an insistence that the core of the free speech guarantee is a right to uncensored political speech within a context of political equality, and through an understanding that the core of the equal protection guarantee is a prohibition on government efforts to create second-class citizens.

Minimalist Judges

The debate between minimalism and maximalism unsettles some of the categories through which judicial behavior has been understood and evaluated. A maximalist, for example, may be entirely devoted to the principle of judicial restraint; consider the idea that all congressional enactments should be upheld. Indeed, judicial restraint defines certain forms of maximalism. A minimalist may be quite willing to invalidate legislative outcomes, and also to maintain judicial flexibility for the future, as through a series of ad hoc decisions that Congress has gone too far in the particular case. Nor is there any simple connection between one's stand on minimalism and any particular set of substantive convictions. A "liberal" maximalist might want to uphold all affirmative action programs, and to strike down all discrimination based on sexual orientation. A "conservative" minimalist might want to strike down certain affirmative action programs while leaving the general status of affirmative action undecided, and might seek to uphold (for example) the ban on same-sex marriages without saying much else about discrimination on the basis of sexual orientation. Originalism, as a guide to constitutional interpretation, is a form of maximalism; this is one reason that it is simultaneously attractive and repulsive. I have argued here that originalism should be rejected on the ground that it does not promote democracy, rightly understood. It is therefore an unacceptable form of maximalism—judicial hubris masquerading as judicial modesty.

The current Supreme Court is minimalist in character, and we can obtain a far better understanding of its distinctive character, and of continuing debates within the Court itself, if we keep this point in view. The Court's minimalist judges try to keep their judgments as narrow and as incompletely theorized as possible, consistent with the obligation to offer reasons. They are enthusiastic about avoiding constitutional questions. They like to use doctrines of justiciability and their authority over their docket to limit the occasions for judicial intervention into politically contentious areas. The ban on advisory opinions guides much of their work.

Maximalists might challenge a minimalist path along either of two dimensions. Some of minimalism's antagonists, most notably Justice Scalia, are enthusiastic about width, on the ground that rule-bound law has enormous virtues. On this view, particularistic law violates rule of law principles; it may not qualify as law at all. Other antagonists, most notably Ronald Dworkin, are enthusiastic about depth, on the ground that shallow decisions are likely to produce both unfairness and inconsistency. Shallowness may well produce mistakes. Notably, it is possible to imagine decisions that are shallow and broad; consider the *Miranda* rules, creating a virtual code of police behavior without resolving the deepest issues about the meaning of "coercion." It is also possible to imagine decisions that are deep but narrow; the Supreme Court's invalidation of same-sex education at the Virginia Military Institute is a prime example.

These points show that no defense of minimalism should be unqualified. Sometimes minimalism is a blunder; sometimes it creates unfairness. Whether minimalism makes sense cannot be decided in the abstract; everything depends on context, prominently including assessments of comparative institutional competence. The case for minimalism is strongest when courts lack information that would justify confidence in a comprehensive ruling; when the need for planning is not especially insistent; when the decision costs, for later courts, of a minimal approach do not seem high; and when minimalist judgments do not create a serious risk of unequal treatment. Thus minimalism tends to be the appropriate course when the Court is operating in the midst of reasonable pluralism or moral flux, when circumstances are changing rapidly, or when the Court is uncertain that a broad rule would make sense in future cases. If a court has reason for confidence about the theoretical foundations of some area of law, it has earned the right to depth; I have suggested that this is now true for the area of sex equality. When there is a great need for predictability, and good reason for confidence that an adequate rule can be devised, width is entirely appropriate and perhaps indispensable; consider property and contract law.

In some areas, broad rules make a good deal of sense, and in some cases diverse judges can and should converge on theoretically ambitious abstractions involving liberty or equality. These are the most glorious moments in any nation's legal culture. I have been stressing another point. When a democracy is in a state of ethical or political uncertainty, courts may not have the best or the final answers. Judicial answers may be wrong. They may be counterproductive even if they are right. On occasion courts do best by proceeding in a way that is catalytic rather than preclusive, and that is closely attuned to the fact that courts are participants in an elaborate system of democratic deliberation. Minimalism is not always the best way to proceed. But it has distinctive uses in constitutional law, where judges, well aware of their own limitations, know that sometimes the best decision is to leave things undecided.

Notes

Acknowledgments

Index

Notes

1. Leaving Things Undecided

1. United States v. Virginia, 116 S. Ct. 2264 (1996).
2. Richmond v. Croson, 488 U.S. 469 (1989).
3. Romer v. Evans, 116 S. Ct. 1620 (1996).
4. On economizing on moral disagreement, see Amy Gutmann and Dennis Thompson, *Democracy and Disagreement* 84–85 (Cambridge: Harvard University Press, 1996): "Citizens should seek the rationale that minimizes rejection of the position they oppose. . . . This form of magnanimity tells citizens to avoid unnecessary conflict in characterizing the moral grounds or drawing out the policy implications of their position."
5. There is an obvious connection between what I am saying here and what is said in Alexander Bickel, *The Least Dangerous Branch* (New Haven: Yale University Press, 1962). Here are some points of commonality: appreciation of passive virtues, endorsement of the doctrine of desuetude for the "privacy" cases, and an insistence on the need for the Court to think strategically and pragmatically about whether the nation is ready for the principles that the Court favors. But there are important differences as well. My argument here finds its foundations in the aspiration to deliberative democracy, with an insistence that the principal vehicle is the legislature, not the judiciary; the judiciary is to play a catalytic and supplementary role. For Bickel, the Court was the basic repository of principle in American government; because of its insulation, it was the central deliberative institution. By contrast, a central point here is that the Court's conception of the (constitutionally relevant) principle may well be wrong; I think Bickel erred in seeing the Court as having a systematically better understanding of "principle" than other branches.

    In addition, Bickel's belief in "prudence" was based on a generalized fear of political backlash, and not on social scientific evidence. We now know that it may be counterproductive for courts to insist on social reform even if the Court is right. See Gerald Rosenberg, *The Hollow Hope* (Chicago: University of Chicago Press, 1991). In his conception of the division of labor between courts and legislatures (principle/policy) and in his absence of attention to empirical issues, Bickel is in his own way under the influence of the Warren Court. In brief, my treatment is more skeptical of judges and less so of majoritarian institutions. It is also in a sense more prudential and strategic (for better or for worse): Bickel was focused on the decline of jurisdiction, with the apparent thought that once assumed, jurisdiction should result in the most principled and candid of opinions. I am suggesting that opinions should be self-consciously narrow and shallow, at least some of the time.

There is also an evident resemblance between what is said here and what is suggested in both Robert Burt, *The Constitution in Conflict* (Cambridge: Harvard University Press, 1994), and Guido Calabresi, "Foreword: Antidiscrimination and Constitutional Accountability" (What the Bork-Brennan Debate Ignores), 105 Harv. L. Rev. 80 (1991). I am indebted to both of these excellent discussions.

6. 60 U.S. 393 (1857). See Christopher Eisgruber, "Dred Again: Originalism's Forgotten Past," 10 Const. Commentary 37 (1993).
7. See James Bradley Thayer, "The Origin and Scope of the American Doctrine of Constitutional Law," 7 Harv. L. Rev 129 (1893).
8. See Ronald Dworkin, *Law's Empire* (Cambridge: Harvard University Press, 1985); Ronald Dworkin, *Freedom's Law* (Cambridge: Harvard University Press, 1996). There are many complexities in Dworkin's position and I do not claim that this thumbnail sketch is adequate to them. An interesting contrast is provided by Bruce A. Ackerman, *We the People*, vol. 1: *Foundations* (Cambridge: Harvard University Press, 1992). Ackerman urges courts to "synthesize" constitutional moments; thus the meaning of the equality principle in the late twentieth century comes from an understanding of the relationship between the Civil War and the New Deal. Doubtless ideas of this sort help account for some aspects of Supreme Court decisions, and the theoretical underpinnings of large-scale social developments do have an impact on constitutional law. But thus far Ackerman has not discussed the theory-building weaknesses of the judiciary, and an understanding of those weaknesses must play a role in the evaluation of the idea that courts are to synthesize constitutional moments. At least most of the time, constitutional law is narrower, shallower, more minimal, based on analogies.
9. See Griswold v. Connecticut, 381 U.S. 479 (1965); Roe v. Wade, 410 U.S. 113 (1973).
10. See Buckley v. Valeo, 424 U.S. 1 (1976); Virginia Board of Pharmacy v. Virginia Citizens Consumer Council, 425 U.S. 748 (1976).
11. Richard A. Epstein, *Takings* (Cambridge: Harvard University Press, 1985).
12. United States v. Carolene Products, 304 U.S. 144, 152 n. 4 (1938). There the Court said that the presumption in favor of democratic processes would be overcome if a right central to democratic processes were itself at stake, or if "discrete and insular minorities," not able to protect themselves in the political process, were at risk.
13. 17 U.S. 316 (1819).

14. Baker v. Carr, 369 U.S. 186 (1962); Reynolds v. Sims, 377 U.S. 533 (1964); Shaw v. Hunt, 116 S. Ct. 1894 (1996).

15. See J. H. Ely, *Democracy and Distrust* (Cambridge: Harvard University Press, 1981). The same theme can be found in Jürgen Habermas, *Between Facts and Norms* (Cambridge: MIT Press, 1996).

16. See 44 Liquormart v. Rhode Island, 116 S. Ct. 1495, 1520 (Thomas, J., concurring) (1996); Richmond v. Croson, 488 U.S. 469, 520–528 (1989) (Scalia, J., concurring in the judgment).

17. Note Justice Rehnquist's votes against the constitutionality of affirmative action in, for example, Metro Broadcasting, Inc. v. FCC, 497 U.S. 547, 602 (1990); Richmond v. Croson, 488 U.S. 469, 476 (1989).

18. There are intrapersonal parallels, quite outside the context of law. Sometimes people try to make narrow and shallow decisions in personal matters and to leave the broader and more deeply theoretical questions for another day. For discussion, see Edna Ullmann-Margalit, "Opting," in the 1985 *Yearbook* of the Wissenschaftskolleg zu Berlin. Sometimes people try to leave things undecided because they seek to avoid the responsibility for making the decision or because they know that any decision, even the right decision, will cause injury to themselves or others. A great deal of work remains to be done on this important topic.

19. A more detailed discussion is Cass R. Sunstein, *Legal Reasoning and Political Conflict* (New York: Oxford University Press, 1996).

20. IDASA's Parliamentary Information and Monitoring Service, Parliamentary Whip 4 (South Africa, May 17, 1996).

21. Illuminatingly discussed in Frederick Schauer, "Giving Reasons," 47 Stan. L. Rev. 633 (1995).

22. Romer v. Evans, 116 S. Ct. 1620 (1996); United States v. Lopez, 115 S. Ct. 1624 (1995); Denver Area Educational Telecommunications Consortium v. FCC, 116 S. Ct. 2364 (1996); Brandenburg v. Ohio, 393 U.S. 444 (1969); Roe v. Wade, 410 U.S. 113 (1973); Reynolds v. Sims, 377 U.S. 533 (1964); Dred Scott v. Sanford, 60 U.S. 393 (1857); Brown v. Board of Education, 349 U.S. 294 (1955); United States v. Virginia, 116 S. Ct. 2264 (1996); 44 Liquormart v. Rhode Island, 116 S. Ct. 1495 (1996).

23. See Dworkin, *Law's Empire.*

24. 395 U.S. 44 (1969).

25. United States v. Darby, 312 U.S. 100 (1941); Erie Railroad Co. v. Tompkins, 304 U.S. 64 (1938).

26. 404 U.S. 71 (1971).

2. Democracy-Promoting Minimalism

1. John Dewey, *How We Think and Selected Essays* 1910–1911, at 93, in 6 *The Middle Works of John Dewey* (1985).

2. See Lemon v. Kurtzman, 403 U.S. 602 (1971). Those who reject the contro-

versial Lemon "test" can endorse the ban on legislation supported solely on religious grounds.

3. Papachristou v. City of Jacksonville, 405 U.S. 156 (1972).

4. See Schechter Poultry v. United States, 295 U.S. 495 (1935).

5. Kent v. Dulles, 357 U.S. 116 (1958).

6. See John Rawls, *Political Liberalism* 231–240 (New York: Columbia University Press, 1993).

7. Miranda v. Arizona, 384 U.S. 436 (1966); Loving v. Virginia, 388 U.S. 1 (1967); Roe v. Wade, 410 U.S. 113 (1973); New York Times v. Sullivan, 376 U.S. 254 (1964); Rostker v. Goldberg, 453 U.S. 57 (1981); Korematsu v. United States, 323 U.S. 214 (1944); Romer v. Evans, 116 S. Ct. 1620 (1996); United States v. Lopez, 115 S. Ct. 1624 (1995); Kent v. Dulles, 357 U.S. 116 (1958); Hampton v. Mow Sun Wong, 426 U.S. 88 (1976); Cleburne v. Cleburne Living Center, 473 U.S. 432 (1985); United States v. Virginia, 116 S. Ct. 2264 (1996); Ferguson v. Scrupa, 372 U.S. 726 (1963); Denver Area Educational Telecommunications Consortium v. FCC, 116 S. Ct. 2374 (1996).

8. Consider, for example, Justice Black's vote against a right of privacy in Griswold v. Connecticut, 381 U.S. 479 (1965), his view that the Fourteenth Amendment incorporates the Bill of Rights in Adamson v. California, 332 U.S. 46 (1947), his opposition to any form of substantive due process in Ferguson v. Scrupa, 372 U.S. 726 (1963), his insistence on a wide free speech right in many places, for example, New York Times v. Sullivan, 376 U.S. 254 (1964).

9. 115 S. Ct. 1624 (1995).

10. 357 U.S. 116 (1958).

11. 381 U.S. 479 (1965).

12. Id. at 505–507.

13. Regents of the University of California v. Bakke, 438 U.S. 265 (1978).

14. 426 U.S. 88 (1976).

15. 60 U.S. 393 (1857).

16. Bernard Schwartz, *A History of the United States Supreme Court* (New York: Oxford University Press, 1993).

17. Cf. Ruth Bader Ginsburg, "Some Thoughts on Autonomy and Equality in Relation to Roe v. Wade," 63 North Carolina L. Rev. 375 (1985).

18. Brown v. Board of Education, 349 U.S. 294, 301 (1955).

19. See Gerald Rosenberg, *The Hollow Hope* (Chicago: University of Chicago Press, 1991).

20. See Alexander Bickel, *The Least Dangerous Branch* (New Haven: Yale University Press, 1962).

21. See, e.g., Louis Kaplow, "Rules vs. Standards: An Economic Analysis," 42 Duke L.J. 557 (1992); Kathleen Sullivan, "Foreword: The Justices of Rules and the Justices of Standards," 106 Harv L. Rev. 22 (1992); Isaac Ehrlich and Richard Posner, "An Economic Analysis of Legal Rulemaking," 3 J. Legal Stud. 257 (1974).

22. See Kaplow, "Rules vs. Standards." Some qualifications emerge from Stephen

Bundy and Einer Elhague, "Knowledge about Legal Sanctions," 92 Mich. L. Rev. 261, 271 n. 25 (1993).
23. This is discussed in more detail in Cass R. Sunstein, *Legal Reasoning and Political Conflict* ch. 4 (New York: Oxford University Press, 1996).
24. 508 U.S. 223 (1993).
25. Bailey v. United States, 516 U.S. 137 (1995).
26. See Alvin Goldman, "Ethics and Cognitive Science," 103 Ethics 337, 341 (1993): "The exemplar theory suggests . . . that what moral learning consists in may not be (primarily) the learning of rules but the acquisition of pertinent exemplars or examples. This would accord with the observable fact that people, especially children, have an easier time assimilating the import of parables, myths, and fables than abstract principles."

The point is related to the availability heuristic, discussed in Daniel Kahneman and Amos Tversky, *Judgment under Uncertainty: Heuristics and Biases* (Cambridge: Cambridge University Press, 1982). People tend to think that events are more probable if examples of those events are "available" in the sense that they come readily to mind. It is predictable that judgments about probability, based on the availability heuristic, will often be mistaken. A case can operate as a "prototype" that orients inquiry into subsequent cases. There is a large question in law about which (of the countless possibly relevant cases) cases operate as relevant prototypes and why.
27. See Itzhak Gilboa and David Schmeidler, "Case-Based Decision Theory," 110 Q. J. Econ. 605 (1995).

3. Decisions and Mistakes

1. See the discussion of heuristics and other techniques in John Conlisk, "Why Bounded Rationality?" 34 J. Econ. Lit. 669, 682–683 (1996). A discussion of responsive strategies is Cass R. Sunstein and Edna Ullmann-Margalit, "Second-Order Decisions," manuscript, April 1998.
2. See William Landes and Richard A. Posner, "The Economics of Anticipatory Adjudication," 23 J. Legal Stud. 683 (1994).
3. John Rawls, *Political Liberalism* (New York: Columbia University Press, 1993), is the classic treatment.
4. See id.
5. See id.
6. See the fascinating treatment in Dietrich Dorner, *The Logic of Failure* (New York: Free Press, 1996). See also James Scott, *Seeing Like a State* (New Haven: Yale University Press, 1998).
7. See the reference to "small steps" in Scott, *Seeing Like a State*.
8. See Joseph Raz, *The Authority of Law* (Oxford: Oxford University Press, 1986), defending analogical reasoning as a response to problems associated with one-shot interventions into complex systems.
9. See Denver Area Educational Telecommunications Consortium v. FCC, 116

S. Ct. 2374 (1996). Of course there are many different conceptions of democracy, and the word itself cannot justify deference to majorities.

10. FCC v. Pacifica Foundation, 438 U.S. 726 (1978).

11. Strictly speaking this point is false. Some regulatory system is necessary to create property rights. Without a regulatory system of some kind, operators would have no right to exclude anyone. As stated Justice Breyer's point is off the mark, and for this reason Justice Thomas's opinion is especially confused; operators have no natural or prelegal right to exclude anyone from cable programming. Any right of exclusion is a creation of law. Cf. in this regard Justice Breyer's clear-headed response to the court of appeals' holding that there was no "state action," with the suggestion that the congressional enactment at issue was very much state action. On the other hand, Justice Breyer's reference to this factor can be supported not by implausible claims about property rights preexisting law, but by a suggestion that ordinarily owners, including owners of speech, have rights of exclusion; that this ordinary course serves important free speech interests, at least under competitive rather than monopolistic conditions; and it is therefore a relevant consideration.

4. Minimalism's Substance

1. See, e.g., John Rawls, *Political Liberalism* (New York: Columbia University Press, 1993); Sissela Bok, *Common Values* (Columbia: University of Missouri Press, 1995); Michael Walzer, *Thick and Thin* (Notre Dame: University of Notre Dame Press, 1995).

2. I deal with this issue in detail in Cass R. Sunstein, *Legal Reasoning and Political Conflict* (New York: Oxford University Press, 1996).

3. For various treatments, see Amy Gutmann and Dennis Thompson, *Democracy and Disagreement* (Cambridge: Harvard University Press, 1996); Jürgen Habermas, *Between Facts and Norms* (Cambridge: MIT Press, 1996); William Bessette, *The Mild Voice of Reason* (Chicago: University of Chicago Press, 1994).

5. No Right to Die?

1. 80 F.3d 716 (2d Cir. 1995).

2. 79 F.3d 790 (9th Cir. 1995) (en banc).

3. Washington v. Glucksberg, 117 S. Ct. 1781 (1997).

4. There is an extensive philosophical literature on the right to die. A particularly illuminating discussion is Dan Brock, *Life and Death* 202–230 (Oxford: Oxford University Press, 1993) (arguing for autonomy rights and challenging the distinction between withdrawal of treatment and active euthanasia). See also John Keown, "Euthanasia in the Netherlands: Sliding Down the Slippery Slope?" in *Euthanasia Examined* 261, 261–262 (John Keown ed., 1995) (collecting vari-

ous positions about whether voluntary euthanasia will lead to involuntary euthanasia). As will become apparent, the philosophical issue is far from coextensive with the constitutional issue, and there is a limit to how much progress can be made through philosophical discussion alone; many of the key questions are empirical, involving the real-world effects of the relevant right and the status quo.

5. 497 U.S. 261 (1990). The Court said: "The principle that a competent person has a constitutionally protected liberty interest in refusing unwanted medical treatment may be inferred from our prior cases. . . . Although we think that the logic of the cases . . . would embrace such a liberty interest [in resisting the forced administration of life-sustaining medical treatment], the dramatic consequences involved in refusal of such treatment would inform the inquiry as to whether the deprivation of that interest is constitutionally permissible. But for purposes of this case, we assume that the United States Constitution would grant a competent person a constitutionally protected right to refuse lifesaving hydration and nutrition" (id. at 278–279). Justice O'Connor was much clearer on the point. See id. at 289 (O'Connor, J., concurring) ("The liberty guaranteed by the Due Process Clause must protect, if it protects anything, an individual's deeply personal decision to reject medical treatment, including the artificial delivery of food and water.").

6. It has been suggested that modern pain-management techniques make this an unlikely event. For example, Brock, *Life and Death,* at 170, writes: "There are not great numbers of patients undergoing severe suffering that can only be relieved by directly killing them. Modern methods of pain management enable physicians and nurses to control the pain of virtually all such patients without the use of lethal poisons, though often at the cost of so sedating the patient that interaction and communication with others is limited or no longer possible."

7. See the discussion in Christine Jolls, Cass R. Sunstein, and Richard Thaler, "A Behavioral Approach to Law and Economics," 50 Stan. L. Rev. 1171 (1998).

8. See David P. Phillips, "The Influence of Suggestion on Suicide: Substantive and Theoretical Implications of the Werther Effect," 39 Am. Soc. Rev. 340 (1974).

9. Abortion is an interesting analogy along this dimension. Even without Roe v. Wade, and even in places in which abortion is unlawful, abortions occur, sometimes in large numbers. But this is not much of an argument against *Roe,* since the relevant abortions tend to be extremely dangerous. The term "back-alley butchers" reflects the point. In the case of physician-assisted suicide, there is a weaker parallel in the informal processes I am describing. No one should deny, however, that the ban on physician-assisted suicide can produce some ugly informal outcomes. See Compassion in Dying v. Washington, 79 F.3d 790, 834 n. 35 (9th Cir. 1996) ("When he realized that my family was going to be away for a day, he wrote us a beautiful letter, went down to his basement, and shot himself with his 12 gauge shot gun. He was 84. . . . My son-in-law then

had the unfortunate and unpleasant task of cleaning my father's splattered brains off the basement wall.")

10. 117 S. Ct. at 2303.

11. Griswold v. Connecticut, 381 U.S. 479 (1965); Eisenstadt v. Baird, 405 U.S. 438 (1972); Carey v. Population Servs. 431 U.S. 113 (1973); Roe v. Wade, 410 U.S. 113 (1973); Bowers v. Hardwick, 478 U.S. 186 (1986); Skinner v. Oklahoma, 316 U.S. 535 (1942); Cruzan v. Director, 497 U.S. 261 (1990); Washington v. Harper, 494 U.S. 210 (1990); Michael H. v. Gerald D., 491 U.S. 110 (1989); Moore v. City of East Cleveland, 431 U.S. 494 (1977); Village of Belle Terre v. Boraas, 416 U.S. 1 (1974); Loving v. Virginia, 388 U.S. 1 (1967); Zablocki v. Redhail, 434 U.S. 374 (1978); Califano v. Jobst, 434 U.S. 47 (1977).

12. See Michael H. v. Gerald D., 491 U.S. 110, 127–128 n. 6 (1989) (plurality opinion of Scalia, J.); Bowers v. Hardwick, 478 U.S. 186 (1986) (White, J.); Moore v. City of East Cleveland, 431 U.S. 494 (1977) (plurality opinion of Powell, J.); Griswold v. Connecticut, 381 U.S. 479 (1965) (Harlan, J., concurring).

13. Of course the whole idea of "substantive due process" is quite doubtful as a matter of text and history. But we might see that idea as doing the work of the privileges and immunities clause, which could plausibly have been used for an enterprise of this kind. See Charles Fairman, "Does the Fourteenth Amendment Incorporate the Bill of Rights?" 2 Stan. L. Rev. 5 (1949).

14. This point is intended as a description, not as a full defense of the cases and especially not as a full defense of Roe v. Wade. Note also that it is possible to think that any physical invasion is legitimate either because the invasion is the product of the woman's voluntary actions or because protection of the fetus counts as sufficient justification. These points bear on the question whether government may intrude on the right as I have understood it; I cannot discuss them here.

15. 115 S. Ct. 2097, 2117 (1995) (quoting Fullilove v. Klutznick, 448 U.S. 448, 519 (1980)).

16. See Keown, "Euthanasia in the Netherlands" at 261–262.

17. See, e.g., Herbert Hendin, *Seduced by Death* (New York: W. W. Norton, 1996); Keown, "Euthanasia in the Netherlands" at 271–272.

18. Keown, "Euthanasia in the Netherlands" at 289.

19. Richard Posner, *Aging and Old Age* 242–243 (Chicago: University of Chicago Press, 1995); Richard Epstein, *Mortal Peril* (Reading, Mass.: Addison-Wesley, 1997).

20. See Ruth Bader Ginsburg, "Some Thoughts on Autonomy and Equality in Relation to Roe v. Wade," 63 North Carolina L. Rev. 375 (1985).

21. Planned Parenthood v. Casey, 505 U.S. 833 (1992).

22. Alexander Bickel, *The Least Dangerous Branch* 148–156 (New Haven: Yale University Press, 1962) (discussing desuetude).

23. See id.; see also R. Posner, *Sex and Reason* 326–328 (Cambridge: Harvard

University Press, 1992) (discussing role of Catholic Church in preventing statutory change).

24. I am referring here to the general view of constitutional interpretation set out in John Hart Ely, *Democracy and Distrust* (Cambridge: Harvard University Press, 1981).

It might be thought there is such a defect in light of the fact that religious groups can block change for religious reasons, and perhaps this accounts for current practice in some states. The short answer is that this is not the sort of defect that would justify a more aggressive judicial role. Religious groups of course are entitled to participate in democratic processes, and even if there are constraints on the kinds of arguments that they are entitled to make, the arguments typically invoked against physician-assisted suicide do not run afoul of those constraints. The case is different from Griswold v. Connecticut, where a well-organized religious minority, invoking a purely religious argument, was able to block a repeal that was very generally favored of a law that was never directly enforced through the criminal law.

25. See Gerald N. Rosenberg, *The Hollow Hope* 175–201 (Chicago: University of Chicago Press, 1991) (discussing limits of courts in producing social reform and complex effects of Roe v. Wade).

26. Cf. id. at 182–184 (discussing growing popular support for repeal of abortion laws). But see David Garrow, *Liberty and Sexuality* (New York: Macmillan, 1994) (contending that states would not have moved in direction set by *Roe*). Whether or not *Roe* is a good example, the point certainly holds in general.

27. 405 U.S. 438 (1972).

28. 80 F.3d 716 (2d Cir. 1996).

29. See 80 F.3d 716, 731 (Calabresi, J., concurring).

30. 116 S. Ct. 2264, 2277–79 (1996); see also Califano v. Goldfarb, 430 U.S. 199, 223 n. 9 (1977) ("Perhaps an actual, considered legislative choice would be sufficient to allow this statute to be upheld, but that is a question I would reserve until such a choice has been made."); Thompson v. Oklahoma, 487 U.S. 815, 857–858 (1988) (O'Connor, J., concurring) (voting to strike down law imposing death penalty with no minimum age provision on grounds that statute did not reflect actual and recent legislative judgments in light of subsequent statute allowing minors to be dealt with as adults in some cases).

31. NLRB v. Catholic Bishops, 440 U.S. 490, 507 (1979) (construing statute so as to avoid constitutional doubts); Kent v. Dulles, 357 U.S. 116, 129 (1958) (same); Industrial Union Dep't v. American Petroleum Inst., 448 U.S. 607 (1980).

32. See, e.g., Papachristou v. City of Jacksonville, 405 U.S. 156 (1972) (striking down vagrancy law for vagueness). The same basic idea underlies the development of death penalty doctrine. In Furman v. Georgia, 408 U.S. 238 (1972), the Court did not hold that all death penalties were unconstitutional, but only that the death penalty had to be assessed under clear standards. Once the public reaffirmed its commitment to capital punishment after this form of "constitu-

tional remand," the Court retreated. Gregg v. Georgia, 428 U.S. 153, 179–181 (1976).
33. See Garrow, *Liberty and Sexuality.*
34. 426 U.S. 88 (1976).

6. Affirmative Action Casuistry

1. An outstanding discussion of "preference falsification" is Timur Kuran, *Private Truths, Public Lies* (Cambridge: Harvard University Press, 1995).
2. See Robert E. Goodin, "Laundering Preferences," in *Foundations of Social Choice Theory* 75 (Jon Elster and Aanund Hylland eds.) (Cambridge: Cambridge University Press, 1986).
3. François, Duc de La Rouchefoucauld, *Reflections; Or Sentences and Moral Maxims,* Maxim 218 (1678), quoted in John Bartlett, *Familiar Quotations* 65 (Justin Kaplan ed., 16th ed. 1992).
4. See Jon Elster, "Strategic Uses of Argument," in *Barriers to Conflict Resolution* 237–250 (Kenneth J. Arrow et al. eds.) (New York: W. W. Norton 1995).
5. See Gerald Rosenberg, *The Hollow Hope* 339 (Chicago: University of Chicago Press, 1991) (noting that "reliance on the Court seriously weakened the political efficacy of pro-choice forces").
6. See, e.g., Motor Vehicle Mfrs. Ass'n v. State Farm Mut. Auto. Ins. Co., U.S. 29, 57 (1983) (remanding to the National Highway Traffic Safety Administration for further consideration of decision to rescind the passive restraint requirement); Industrial Union Dep't v. Am. Petroleum Inst., 448 U.S. 671 (1980) (remanding to Occupational Safety and Health Administration to reconsider the permissible exposure limit established for benzene).
7. 438 U.S. 265 (1978).
8. 448 U.S. 448 (1980) (upholding a federal law requiring that 10 percent of federal funds granted for local public works be used by minority-owned businesses).
9. Wygant v. Jackson Bd. of Educ., 476 U.S. 267, 277–278 (1986) (requiring an official finding of past discrimination by the government department involved before racial classifications can be used to remedy discrimination); *Fullilove,* 448 U.S. at 490; *Bakke,* 438 U.S. at 315–318 (Powell, J.); United States v. Paradise, 480 U.S. 149 (1987) (considering whether a race-conscious promotion system is narrowly tailored); Sheet Metal Workers v. EEOC, 478 U.S. 421 (1986) (approving affirmative action program for a union with a history of continued and egregious racial discrimination).
10. The legitimacy of affirmative action in the statutory context is more clear. United Steelworkers of Am. v. Weber, 443 U.S. 193, 208 (1979), held that Title VII does not ban voluntary race-conscious actions by an employer. I believe that the best argument for this result is consistent with the democracy-reinforcing concerns traced in this chapter. In 1964, Congress made no considered judgment that affirmative action programs were unlawful. When it

spoke in terms of race neutrality, it was thinking not of remedial programs, but of discrimination based on malice. See Johnson v. Transp. Agency, 480 U.S. 616 (holding that Title VII forbids discrimination against whites at least if it is not part of an affirmative action program). In the absence of a considered judgment by Congress, the Court should not ban voluntary programs of this kind.

11. 488 U.S. 469 (1989).
12. 115 S. Ct. 2097 (1995).
13. See Eric Schnapper, "Affirmative Action and the Legislative History of the Fourteenth Amendment," 71 Va. L. Rev. 753 (1985) (discussing the legislative history of these programs with emphasis on the 1866 Freedmen's Bureau Act).
14. See Andrew Kull, *The Color-Blind Constitution* 79 (Cambridge: Harvard University Press, 1992).
15. Alex Haley, *The Playboy Interviews* 115 (Murray Fisher ed., 1993).
16. Martin Luther King, Jr., *Why We Can't Wait* 146 (New York: Harper and Row, 1964).
17. Id. at 147.
18. See Cass R. Sunstein, "The Anticaste Principle," 92 Mich. L. Rev. 2429 (1994).
19. See Exec. Order No. 11,246, 3 C.F.R. 339 (1964–65), reprinted in 42 U.S.C. s 2000e (West 1994).
20. See Washington v. Seattle School Dist. No. 1., 458 U.S. 457 (1982); Hunter v. Erickson, 393 U.S. 385 (1969). See Sunstein, "Public Values, Private Interests, and the Equal Protection Clause," 1982 Supreme Court Review 183, for general discussion. In this paragraph I quote *Seattle*, 458 U.S. at 459, 461, 462.

7. Sex and Sexual Orientation

1. 116 S. Ct. 1620 (1996).
2. 404 U.S. 71 (1971).
3. 116 S. Ct. 2264 (1996).
4. 478 U.S. 186 (1986).
5. 116 S. Ct. at 1624–28.
6. Id. at 1627–29.
7. John Rawls, *Political Liberalism* 430–431 (New York: Columbia University Press, 1993).
8. Zobel v. Alaska, 457 U.S. 55 (1982); Hooper v. Bernalillo County Assessor, 472 U.S. 612 (1985); Metropolitan Life Insurance v. Ward, 470 U.S. 869 (1985).
9. U.S. Department of Ag. v. Moreno, 413 U.S. 528 (1973).
10. City of Cleburne v. Cleburne Living Center, Inc., 473 U.S. 432 (1985).
11. Note that Amendment 2 involved status as well as conduct, a point emphasized by the Court. It would be hard to imagine a similar measure directed against polygamists, adulterers, or fornicators, which points to an important distinction

between such people and homosexuals. The former are punished through law or norms because of what they do; homosexuals are subject to a deeper kind of social antagonism, connected not only with their acts but also with their identity. It is this feature that links discrimination on the basis of sexual orientation with discrimination on the basis of race and sex.

12. See Avishai Margalit and Gabriel Motzkin, "The Uniqueness of the Holocaust," 25 Phil. & Pub. Aff. 65 (1996).

13. 83 U.S. 130 (1873).

14. It is notable that the *Hardwick* Court explicitly created a distinction between heterosexuals and homosexuals. The plaintiffs attacked the sodomy law in a way that was neutral with respect to sexual orientation. It was the Supreme Court that made the distinction, by upholding the law as applied to homosexuals (while, in good minimalist fashion, leaving undecided its status as applied to heterosexuals). Thus it may be thought very odd to say that the equal protection clause draws discrimination on the basis of sexual orientation into doubt, when the Court, in *Hardwick,* discriminated on just that basis. The best answer to this suggestion is that there was no equal protection claim in *Hardwick.* The Court gave the minimal answer necessary to decide the due process attack. When an equal protection challenge is raised, it is not terribly odd if the Court's distinction turns out to raise problems.

15. The thoroughgoing minimalist would want the Court to dismiss the case as moot. And while I have not defended thoroughgoing minimalism here, I do think that would have been best, all things considered.

16. See Avishai Margalit, *The Decent Society* (Cambridge: Harvard University Press, 1996).

17. See id. Of course there are many complexities in the term "humiliation." To be usable for purposes of political theory, the term depends on a substantive account of some sort, not just on people's feelings, as Margalit makes clear.

18. I draw here on a well-known discussion by Alexander Bickel, who also invoked Lincoln's thought in urging a cautious judicial role, with particular reference to the passive virtues. See Alexander Bickel, *The Least Dangerous Branch* (New Haven: Yale University Press, 1962).

19. Abraham Lincoln, speech at Peoria, Illinois (Oct. 16, 1854), in 2 *The Collected Works of Abraham Lincoln* 256 (Roy P. Basler ed., 1953).

20. 116 S. Ct. at 2277–79.

21. Id. at 2285–86.

22. Richard Posner, *The Problematics of Legal Theory* (forthcoming 1999).

23. Frontiero v. Richardson, 411 U.S. 677 (1973).

24. Craig v. Boren, 429 U.S. 190 (1976).

25. Michael M. v. Sonoma County Superior Court, 450 U.S. 464 (1981); Rostker v. Goldberg, 453 U.S. 57 (1981).

26. JEB v. Alabama ex rel. TB, 114 S. C. 1419 (1994); Mississippi University for Women v. Hogan, 458 U.S. 718 (1982).

27. See id.; Califano v. Goldfarb, 430 U.S. 313 (1977).

8. The First Amendment and New Technologies

1. See Yosal Rogat, "The Judge as Spectator," 31 U. Chi. L. Rev. 213 (1964).
2. See Richard A. Epstein, *Takings* (Cambridge: Harvard University Press, 1985).
3. See Turner Broadcasting System, Inc. v. FCC, 512 U.S. 622 (1994), reh'g denied 115 S. Ct. 30 (1994) (Turner I); Turner Broadcasting System, Inc. v. FCC, 117 U.S. 1174 (1997); Denver Area Educational Telecommunications Consortium, Inc. v. FCC, 116 S. Ct. 2374, 2390 (1996); Reno v. ACLU, 117 U.S. 2329 (1997). A valuable discussion, to which I owe a great deal here, is Lawrence Lessig, "The Path of Cyberlaw, " 104 Yale L.J. 1757 (1995).
4. Abrams v. United States, 250 U.S. 616, 624 (1919) (Holmes, J., dissenting).
5. 418 U.S. 241 (1974).
6. Syracuse Peace Council v. Television Station WTVH, 2 F.C.C.R. 5043, 5054–55 (1987).
7. Whitney v. California, 274 U.S. 357, 375 (1927) (Brandeis, J., concurring).
8. Alexander Meiklejohn, *Free Speech and Its Relation to Self-Government* (New York: Harper, 1948).
9. 376 U.S. 254 (1964).
10. Red Lion Broadcasting Co. v. FCC, 395 U.S. 367 (1969).
11. Bernard Nossiter, "The FCC's Big Giveaway Show," The Nation 402 (Oct. 26, 1985).
12. See Cass R. Sunstein, *Democracy and the Problem of Free Speech* (New York: Free Press, 1993).
13. See Turner Broadcasting System, Inc. v. FCC, 512 U.S. 622 (1994), reh'g denied 115 S. Ct. 30 (1994); Turner Broadcasting System, Inc. v. FCC, 117 U.S. 1174 (1997).
14. Denver Area Educational Telecommunications Consortium, Inc. v. FCC, 116 S. Ct. 2374, 2390 (1996).
15. FCC v. Pacifica Foundation, 438 U.S. 726 (1978).
16. 117 U.S. 2329 (1997).
17. See generally Robert Frank and Philip Cook, *The Winner-Take-All Society* 207–209, 228 (1995), for an illuminating discussion, from the economic point of view, of how marketplace pressures can produce an outcome that people generally do not like, and how regulatory provisions can increase freedom by removing those pressures.
18. 395 U.S. 444, 449 (1969) (holding that the First and Fourteenth Amendments condemn a statute that purports to punish mere advocacy and to forbid assembly with others merely to advocate the described type of action).
19. Geoffrey R. Stone et al., *Constitutional Law* 1025 (Boston: Little Brown, 2d ed. 1991). See also Masses Publishing Co. v. Patten, 244 F. 535 (SD N.Y. 1917), rev'd, 246 F. 24 (2d Cir. 1917).
20. Masses Publishing, 244 F. at 539.
21. See Abrams v. United States, 250 U.S. 616 (1919) (Holmes and Brandeis dissenting); Whitney v. California, 274 U.S. 357 (1927) (Brandeis and Holmes

concurring). But see Brandenburg v. Ohio, 395 U.S. 444 (1969) (overruling *Whitney*).

22. 341 U.S. 494 (1951).
23. Watts v. United States, 394 U.S. 705, 706 (1969).
24. See United States v. Progressive, Inc., 467 F. Supp. 990 (WD Wis. 1979), dismissed by 610 F.2d 819 (7th Cir. 1979) (unpublished order).
25. *Sable Communications,* 492 U.S. at 128–131.
26. 424 U.S. 1 (1976).
27. 500 U.S. 173 (1991).

9. Width? Justice Scalia's Democratic Formalism

1. See Antonin Scalia, *A Matter of Interpretation* (Princeton: Princeton University Press, 1996).
2. Id. at 25.
3. Id. at 7.
4. Id. at 17.
5. 143 U.S. 457 (1892).
6. Id. at 23.
7. Karl N. Llewellyn, "Remarks on the Theory of Appellate Decision," 3 Vand. L. Rev. 395 (1950).
8. Id. at 37.
9. Scalia, *A Matter of Interpretation* at 40.
10. Id. at 45.
11. Id. at 47.
12. Note in this regard that after victory in World War II, Britain and America responded to Nazism in part by ensuring that laws that had been enacted in the Hitler period, and had not been voided, were to be interpreted in accordance "with the plain meaning of the text and without regard to objectives or meanings ascribed in preambles or other pronouncements." Ingo Muller, *Hitler's Justice* xvi (Oxford: Oxford University Press, 1994). Note also Muller's demonstration that the principal technique used by Hitler's judges was emphatically antiformalist, a form of purposive, dynamic statutory construction intended to link statutory meaning with prevailing ideals. See, e.g., id. at 92, 104–105, 117.
13. See *Interpreting Statutes: A Comparative Study,* Neil MacCormick and Robert Summers, eds. (Oxford: Oxford University Press, 1991).
14. 143 U.S. at 459.
15. 115 N.Y. 506, 22 N.E. 188 (1889).
16. 143 U.S. at 463–465.
17. Id. at 465, 471.
18. Ludwig Wittgenstein, *Philosophical Investigations* 33 (G. E. M. Anscombe trans., New York: Macmillan, 1960).

19. See H. L. A. Hart, *The Concept of Law* 124–136 (Oxford: Oxford University Press, 2d ed. 1994), and in particular the following passage: "[W]e are men, not gods. It is a feature of the human predicament (and so of the legislative one) that we labour under two connected handicaps whenever we seek to regulate, unambiguously and in advance, some sphere of conduct by means of general standards to be used without further official direction on particular occasions. The first handicap is our relative ignorance of fact; the second is our relative indeterminacy of aim. If the world in which we live were characterized only by a finite number of features, and these together with all the modes in which they combine were known to us, then provision could be made in advance for every possibility . . . Plainly this world is not our world; human legislators can have no such knowledge of all the possible combinations of circumstances which the future may bring. This inability to anticipate brings with it a relative indeterminacy of aim." Id. at 128.

20. Relevant evidence can be found in William Eskridge, "Overruling Supreme Court Statutory Interpretation Decisions," 101 Yale L.J. 331 (1991).

21. See Conroy v. Ansikoff, 113 S. Ct. 1562 (1993) (Scalia, J.). There are of course qualitative differences among the various kinds of errors, and judgments must be made about which errors are worst, both qualitatively and quantitatively. There is also a question about what counts as an error at all. Perhaps Justice Scalia would contend that his approach—textualism—produces no errors. But this begs the question, by defining errors as those that emerge from other approaches. To be sure, it is not clear that errors can be defined as such apart from some account of interpretation. I am attempting to build on the common intuition that an interpreter blunders if he takes a word to produce an outcome that would generally be taken as absurd by the relevant community. As I suggest in text, the notion that a term does not apply in such a context can be seen as part of the idea, endorsed by Justice Scalia, that meaning is usually a product of the ordinary understanding of those in the community of addressees.

22. See the extensive catalogue of background norms and principles in William Eskridge, *Dynamic Statutory Intrepretation* Appendix 3, at pp. 323–33 (Cambridge: Harvard University Press, 1994).

23. Antonin Scalia, "Judicial Deference to Agency Interpretations of Law," 1989 Duke L.J. 511.

24. 467 U.S. 837, 842–845 (1984).

25. See Scalia, "Judicial Deference to Agency Interpretations of Law" at 517.

26. Antonin Scalia, "The Doctrine of Standing as an Essential Element of the Separation of Powers," 27 Suffolk L. Rev. 881, 897 (1983).

27. See Guido Calabresi, *The Common Law in an Age of Statutes* (Cambridge: Harvard University Press, 1989).

28. On this view, the cases interpreting the Delaney clause (banning the use of carcinogens as food additives, even if the relevant risk was trivial or de minimis) literally were thus wrongly decided. Public Citizen v. Young, 831 F.2d 1108 (D.C. Cir. 1987); Les v. Reilly, 968 F.2d 985, 989 (9th Cir. 1992).

29. 824 F.2d 1177 (D.C. Cir. 1987).
30. See Ian Ayres and Robert Gertner, "Filling Gaps in Incomplete Contracts," 99 Yale L.J. 87 (1989).
31. Compare Dworkin, who says that he is a "semantic originalist," interested in what the Constitution "says," and who claims that what it "says" is a matter of abstract principles. But what it "says" is a function of the best account of interpretation, and it doesn't contain abstract principles unless we have decided, according to our (pre- or extra-semantic) account, that it should do so. Thus Dworkin's approach, insofar as it is about judicial review, needs to be rooted in arguments about institutional capacities.
32. Scalia, *A Matter of Interpretation* at 145.
33. Id. at 138.
34. Id. at 139.
35. This judgment also rests on considerations with pragmatic dimensions: to say that the Constitution is not binding would create a form of chaos, and in any case the Constitution is a pretty good one.
36. See Lawrence Lessig, "Fidelity and Translation," 47 Stan. L. Rev. 395 (1995).

10. Depth? From Theory to Practice

1. See Ronald Dworkin, *Law's Empire* (Cambridge: Harvard University Press, 1985).
2. See New York Review of Books, vol. 44, no. 5, p. 41 (1997).
3. Id.
4. See John Rawls, *Political Liberalism* (New York: Columbia University Press, 1993).
5. John Rawls, "Reply to Habermas," 92 J. Phil. 132, 134 (1995).
6. See Amy Gutmann and Dennis Thompson, *Democracy and Disagreement* (Cambridge: Harvard University Press, 1996), for the important idea of economizing on moral disagreement.
7. See Richard Posner, *Sex and Reason* 326–328 (Cambridge: Harvard University Press, 1991).
8. See Gerald Rosenberg, *The Hollow Hope* (Chicago: University of Chicago Press, 1991). Rosenberg argues—to summarize a complex discussion—that Roe v. Wade helped demobilize the women's movement, create the Moral Majority, and ruin the prospects for the Equal Rights Amendment—ironic consequences for a decision meant in part to promote sex equality.
9. See Cass R. Sunstein, *The Partial Constitution* ch. 9 (Cambridge: Harvard University Press, 1993).

Acknowledgments

It is a pleasure to thank the many people who helped me with this book. My first debt is to my editor, Michael Aronson, who had the original idea. In keeping the book together, Marlene Vellinga skillfully performed a variety of tasks. For a number of months I have served on the President's Advisory Committee on the Public Interest Obligations of Digital Broadcasters, and this service has helped throughout and especially with Chapter 7; I am very grateful to my fellow members. For helpful discussion and comments on parts of the manuscript, I am grateful to many people: I single out for particular thanks Bruce Ackerman, Richard Craswell, Jack Goldsmith, Amy Gutmann, Stephen Holmes, Daniel Kahan, Louis Kaplow, Charles Larmore, Lawrence Lessig, and Geoffrey Stone. Don Herzog deserves separate thanks for detailed comments and for suggesting the distinction between narrow and shallow decisions in comments several years ago.

Special thanks are due to my daughter, Ellen Ruddick-Sunstein, and also to three wonderful friends. Richard Posner read every chapter and many drafts; his comments (usually delivered within forty-eight hours, sometimes less) and his own related work have been a great help. David Strauss also read every chapter, and I have learned a lot from his high standards, his comments, our six hundred or so discussions of these topics, and his own forthcoming book on constitutional common law. Martha Nussbaum, another reader of every chapter, is no minimalist in law or in life, or in the kindness and good sense that she has shown to this book and its author.

This book contains a great deal of new material, but I have also drawn on a number of previously published essays, portions of which appear in substantially revised form here. I am grateful to the following journals for permission to borrow from the following: "Leaving Things Undecided," 110 Harv. L. Rev. 4 (1996); "The Right to Die," 106 Yale L.J. 1123 (1997); "Justice Scalia's Democratic Formalism," 107 Yale L.J. 529 (1997); "Public Deliberation, Affirmative Action, and the Supreme Court," 84 Cal. L. Rev. 1139 (1996); and "From Theory to Practice," 29 Ariz. State L.J. 389 (1997).

Chicago, Illinois
May 1998

Index